Penguin Books

THE LETTERS

RACHEL HENNING

Rachel Henning was born in England in 1826. She was the eldest of five surviving children who, when Rachel was fourteen, lost their father, and, when she was nineteen, their mother. In 1854 Rachel went to Australia to join her brother, Biddulph, and sister Annie. But homesick for English countryside and appalled by the heat of Australian summers she returned to England in 1856. After nearly five years in England she returned to Australia where she settled permanently. Rachel Henning died in 1914 at the age of eighty-eight.

These letters, which were written between 1853 and 1882, give a vivid and fascinating insight into life in Colonial Australia as seen through the eyes of a previously sheltered young English woman.

Penguin Australian Women's Library

Series Editor: Dale Spender

The Penguin Australian Women's Library will make available to readers a wealth of information through the work of women writers of our past. It will include the classic to the freshly re-discovered, individual reprints to new anthologies, as well as up-to-date critical re-appraisals of their work and lives as writers.

THE LETTERS OF RACHEL HENNING

Introduced by Dale Spender

Edited by David Adams
Pen drawings by Norman Lindsay

PENGUIN BOOKS

Penguin Books Australia Ltd
487 Maroondah Highway, PO Box 257
Ringwood, Victoria, 3134, Australia
Penguin Books Ltd
Harmondsworth, Middlesex, England
Viking Penguin, A Division of Penguin Books USA Inc.
375 Hudson Street, New York, New York 10014, USA
Penguin Books Canada Limited
10 Alcorn Avenue, Toronto, Ontario, Canada M4V 1E4
Penguin Books (N.Z.) Ltd
182-190 Wairau Road, Auckland 10, New Zealand

First published by the Bulletin, 1951-2
First published in Sirius Books by Angus & Robertson Ltd 1963
Published in Penguin Books 1969
Reprinted 1977, 1979, 1985
Reprinted in this edition by Penguin Books Australia, 1988
7 9 10 8 6

Printed and bound in Australia by The Book Printer, Maryborough, Victoria

National Library of Australia
Cataloguing-in-Publication data:

Henning, Rachel, 1826-1914.
The letters of Rachel Henning.

ISBN 0 14 012047 5

1. Henning, Rachel, 1826-1914 – Correspondence. 2. Frontier
and pioneer life – Australia. 3. New South Wales – Social
life and customs – 1851-1891. 4. Queensland – Social life
and customs – 1824-1900. I. Adams, David, 1908-

994.03'1

CONTENTS

ACKNOWLEDGEMENT

Publication of the letters of Rachel Henning was the result, in the first place, of the efforts of Mrs Gerald F. Dampney (who was Hilda Biddulph Henning), of Newport Beach, N.S.W.; she is the daughter of Biddulph Henning and a niece of Rachel.

Mrs Dampney sorted out the letters from a mass of family correspondence that had been preserved, in some instances, for nearly a century, and hers was the task of reading the letters in the original and having them transcribed into typescript. Rachel Henning's family contemporaries had sufficient appreciation of what she had written to collect the letters from different recipients and to bring them together in Australia, where they lay undisturbed for many years in an old leather valise, apparently a relic of Biddulph's North Queensland days.

It was by special arrangement with Mrs Dampney that the letters of Rachel Henning were published by the *Bulletin* and first appeared in the Sirius Books edition.

PREFACE

The letters of Rachel Henning, written between 1853 and 1882, were first published in the *Bulletin* in 1951 and early 1952, about thirty-seven years after their writer's death. Though originally intended for family eyes only, they represent a fascinating fragment of Australian history, and are unique in our published historical and literary records. They have a charm and provocativeness that are all their own, and tell of Australia nearly a century ago as no one else has so far told us.

The outstanding characteristic of the letters is the chatty, day-by-day, observant and often downright description of events in Australia's past from the pen of a previously sheltered young Englishwoman (daughter of a clergyman and granddaughter, on her mother's side, of another clergyman) who left the culture and comfort of England to follow the fortunes of her younger brother in a raw, gold-chasing and land-seeking new community. There is a gossipy intimacy about the letters that recaptures the atmosphere of the times. The daily life of the young Hennings in Australia, as told by Rachel, is absorbing and refreshing to readers of this age, and vastly entertaining so far as it reveals Rachel's own character to us.

Consciously and unconsciously, in her letters, Rachel tells of herself. Though loath to reveal her feelings to any but her intimates she is clearly torn, at the beginning, between her love for "the green lanes and fields of England", with its country walks and flowers, and her fondness for her younger brother Biddulph. But Biddulph is at once at home in Australia, and sets out enthusiastically to seek his fortune. The newness of Australia of that time, with its alluring horizons, seems to spur him on. He moves purposefully from place to place, making mistakes and learning from them. Rachel, on the other hand, out of her social and intellectual element in New South Wales, becomes dreadfully homesick. She feels that she is of little use to Biddulph, and the drought and heat of Australian summers appal her. She gets into "a great fidget as to what I can possibly do with myself"; and so returns to England.

But the tie with her brother and two sisters in Australia is too strong, and after nearly five years in England she comes back to Sydney resolved to "make a do of it". As she says, "I believe the only way is to live on in the present from day to day, and do what is to be done, and enjoy what is to be enjoyed, and there is really plenty of both here." When she and her sister Annie join Biddulph in his Queensland pastoral activities she begins to enjoy and appreciate Australia to the full, though she never loses that individuality, that reserve and that class-consciousness of her age which are a feature of her very first letters. But in Queensland she has at last stepped out of the pages of *Pride and Prejudice* into the Australian out-of-doors, which she has taken to her heart. And she is in company with the pioneers.

From that moment the story of the Hennings merges irrevocably, notwithstanding reluctant acceptance of "colonialism", into that of Australia.

Rachel Biddulph Henning was born in England in 1826. She was the eldest of five surviving children (a brother and sister had died from scarlet fever) who, when Rachel was fourteen, lost their father, and, when she was nineteen, their mother. She then became, in effect, head of this youthful family, and the responsibilities she thus accepted appear to have influenced the whole of her later life. Her sister Henrietta ("Etta" in the letters) was born in 1827, Annie in 1830, Amy in 1832, and her brother Biddulph (his first name was Edmund, but he was always known as Biddulph) in 1834. Their father was the Reverend Charles Wansbrough Henning, M.A. (Cambridge), and formerly chaplain to H.R.H. the Duke of Cambridge. He was the son of Edmund Henning, of Poxwell House, Dorset. Her mother, who was Rachel Lydia Biddulph, married Charles Henning in 1825.

Charles Henning died at Exeter in 1840. His widow and family lived on there for some years, and then moved to Taunton, to be near Mrs Henning's sister, Mrs Pinchard. Here Biddulph Henning went to school with his cousins the Pinchards and the Biddulphs. When Mrs Henning died in 1845 Rachel, then only nineteen, took charge of the household. On the death of an uncle, the Reverend Henry Biddulph, M.A., the family moved from Taunton and went to Backwell, a village in Sommerset, where Uncle Henry had left his house to the young Hennings.

Biddulph Henning soon afterwards went as a boarder to King Edward's Grammar School, Bromsgrove, near Birmingham, where his cousins Tregenna Biddulph and Biddulph Pinchard were also pupils. After Biddulph Henning finished school the family left Backwell and moved to Wilmslow, about thirteen miles from Manchester. Biddulph joined his cousin Edmund Buxton in a Manchester firm of East India merchants. While at Wilmslow, Etta married the Reverend Thomas White Boyce. Biddulph's health had been affected by the epidemic of scarlet fever which had caused the death of a brother and sister, and it was because of his delicate health as a youth that he was persuaded to go to Australia.

The letters of Rachel Henning, as presented in this book, begin in

1853, when Biddulph and Annie set sail, on 11th August, for Australia in the *Great Britain*, an auxiliary steam clipper regarded as a crack passenger ship of its time, renowned for its ability to reach Melbourne sixty days out from Liverpool, travelling round the Cape.

In Australia only a few tentative miles of railways had been laid, though in England Rachel had come to enjoy railway travel. Victoria had only lately become a colony separate from New South Wales, and Queensland was still governed from Sydney. Governor Sir Charles Fitzroy had recently moved his establishment from Parramatta to Sydney. It was to Parramatta that the first railway ran in 1855.

The population of Australia, following the gold-rushes of a year or two earlier, had grown considerably. But there was yet no cable communication between Australia and England, and it often took six months to get an answer to a letter sent from either country. Uniform Australian twopenny postage had come in in 1849, the year of the exodus to the Californian goldfields.

In Britain Charles Dickens had not long published *David Copperfield*, while mid-Victorian England was still rather startled by the novels, a few years earlier, of Charlotte and Emily Bronte, and young women were amazed that females should publish such books. Queen Victoria's eldest son and second child, later to reign as Edward VII, great-grandfather of our present Queen, was just twelve years old.

DAVID ADAMS

INTRODUCTION

Rachel Henning is one of the most significant contributors to the Australian literary tradition and it is most fitting that she should have an esteemed place in the Australian Women's Library. A pioneer in every sense of the word, she was born in England in 1826 and later travelled to Australia, and to the outback; she was one of the courageous young women who challenged convention and the proper role of a lady, and she gave a new dimension to story-telling when she took the art of letter writing to new heights.

Her literary journey began when, in 1853, on the grounds of health, Rachel Henning's brother Biddulph, along with her sister Annie, set sail for Australia. The day after the two departed, Rachel started to write her entertaining — and comforting — letters, in the attempt to maintain the links with her loved ones. But at that stage the letters were not enough to compensate for the personal loss and even before Biddulph and Annie had landed in the new land, Rachel determined to follow them. Of course this meant separation from her married sister, Etta, and from everything she had come to think of as 'home'.

For two years she experienced some of the difficulties and delights of colonial life, but like so many 'migrants', Rachel Henning found herself torn by conflicting cultural and family ties. When she and sister Amy, along with Etta, had remained in England, she had so missed Biddulph and Annie (and the possibility of adventure) that she could find little contentment in her settled existence. But when she took the momentous step and, with Amy, set out in search of a starkly different life in a strange new land, she learned on reaching her destination that it provided no simple solution.

In Australia, it was not only Etta for whom she pined; Rachel Henning was homesick for the green fields of England and for the ordered and regulated life that she had left behind. Much of her ambivalence about where she should live and what sort of existence she would find rewarding is worked out in her letters home, during this period. Her decision finally made, she returned to England in 1856 — but not to a sense of satisfaction.

After the freedom and triumph of rural survival in New South Wales, for Rachel Henning the constraints of the drawing-room and polite

English society in a clergyman's household with her married sister enjoyed little excitement and less significance. Apart from her role as maiden aunt, it was difficult for Rachel Henning to see any meaning in her life. She longed for some of the action and independence that she had experienced on her Australian 'visit'; even more, she longed to be useful, to be needed and valued and to lead a purposeful existence.

Back to Australia she sailed in 1861, but this time she went as a mature woman who knew what she would find and who had *chosen* to make the new world her home. Again she joined Biddulph and Annie (Amy had married), this time at the colonial outpost of Exmoor in the Bowen Basin in Queensland. And although she was never to be entirely free of the feeling of separation from much of what she held dear, Rachel Henning never regretted and never wavered in her commitment to her new country.

This is one reason that her letters form such a marvellous record of period and place. It is not just that she provides a first-hand and fascinating record of pioneering and property life, but that she also portrays some of the inner turmoil and conflict that this dramatic change implied. Such feelings were — and often still are — common to settlers in a new land; they are characteristic of women's literary traditions in Australia.

No matter where Rachel Henning resided, she had an eager audience awaiting her letters on the other side of the world. While in England she had tried to keep Annie and Biddulph (and later Amy) informed on the familiar people and places of their past, in Australia, however, her task was quite the reverse; confronted with a continent and circumstances that Etta could not know and would find hard to visualise, Rachel wrote to her sister trying to describe and explain some of the unfamiliar characters and customs so that they would become real.

During the nineteenth century when the post took so long from Australia to England, there was plenty of time in between letters for suspense to build up on what was happening to loved ones in the far flung reaches of the Empire. Had the baby been born? Were they all well? Had the fire or the flood done much damage? Had the new farm been bought or the new house built? Oh for the next episode in this gripping saga! When letters arrived from England it was generally the occasion for the family to gather round and to hear the latest in the tales of adventure. It was just like a regular serial, except that the heroine was personally known to the readers and that the stories that were told were often stranger and more thrilling than fiction.

Rachel Henning was aware of the part that her letters played in family life and sought not only to enlighten, but to entertain. There's no doubt that she could 'spin a good yarn'* and this is why her letters make such a vital contribution to the literary heritage. As a serial account of one woman's life, the letters read very much like an impressive novel, the only difference being that it is a true story which unfolds. With their high spirited and likeable narrator who is prepared to reveal some of her struggles along with her strengths, and who traces her own development from dissatisfaction to mature contentment, the letters of Rachel Henning provide one of the most remarkable and rivetting Australian chronicles of the nineteenth century.

She wanted to let her English family know what life was like in her adopted land, but she also wanted to let them know what *she* was like, what influences were working on her to bring about change. Because the woman who lived on the property in Queensland, who roughed it 'out-back', who faced physical danger and all manner of threats was not the same prim and proper spinster who had lived in England. So she wrote to make clear her emerging identity as well as to give some idea of the eventful life that she was leading.

It wasn't all good news of course. But in keeping with the customs of the day, Rachel Henning tried not to unduly worry her family. Usually it was only after certain disasters had been averted and dangers had passed that details of dreadful possibilities were conveyed. And if the drought had broken, the patient recovered or peace had been made, why then it could become material for a striking short story!

So when Rachel Henning sat down to write her letters, it was often with the sense that she was creating her tales. As she wrote the long letters which helped bring close her English family and origins she not only kept alive precious links, she carved out her own creative space as she practised and perfected her own literary art.

Women have been writing letters since women learnt to write and there is a rich though not readily appreciated tradition of letter-writing which warrants attention in its own right. Even when women were not supposed to write anything else, they were still allowed to be letter-writers partly because — as Virginia Woolf has suggested — letter-writing could be a help rather than a hindrance to the head of the family, and a means of maintaining family ties. 'Letters did not count,' comments Virginia Woolf in *A Room of One's Own*, 'A woman might write letters while she was sitting by father's sick-bed. She could write them by the fire whilst the men talked without disturbing them.' The letter-writing of women was not a challenge — while it stayed as letter-writing.

But of course once women started to write letters, they also started

*A spinster originally meant a person who tended the spinning wheel; it is appropriate that spinsters should be 'spinners of good yarns'.

to use them for purposes other than those which were intended. As early as 1664 Margaret Cavendish, the Duchess of Newcastle wrote her *Sociable Letters* which were not to inform her family of her well-being or her whereabouts, but which were specifically for publication; a series of epistles on the meaning of life and the desirable forms of behaviour, these *Letters* were the foundation stones of the short story, and the essay. More than a century later 'the letter' once again showed its versatility as a form when the youthful Fanny Burney had published *Evelina; The History of a Young Lady's Entry into the World* (1778); one of the first and best epistolary novels, these 'letters' also trace a young woman's journey to maturity — and with no effort spared to show some of the pitfalls that can tempt the unwary on the way. A lively and amusing tale of manners and morals in the eighteenth century, *Evelina* is one of the classic contributions to the literary heritage.

While she wrote her novel in secret and had it published without the knowledge of her father, Fanny Burney still intended her epistles to have a far wider audience than did Rachel Henning. It wasn't until 1951–2 that the Australian letters were published — in the *Bulletin* — but this certainly doesn't mean that Rachel Henning had no notion of audience. On the contrary, it was because she knew her family audience so well, because she knew how to amuse, reassure, how to tantilise and intrigue them, that her letters were so sparkling and refreshing. The genuine care and concern she has for her audience gives her letters an added dimension.

Like Fanny Burney, Rachel Henning was aware that her epistles could well be read out loud to an assembled family, and like Fanny Burney, she was conscious of the importance of rhythm and tone as well as the content. And, like her British sister, Fanny Burney, Rachel Henning deserves praise and prominence in Australia for her own literary achievement.

Rachel Henning's letters span a period of thirty years and although not published until thirty seven years after her death, they delighted and impressed readers and critics. The edition printed here has been admirably edited by David Adams and illustrated by Norman Lindsay who gives rein to his own individualistic talent. In her own time Rachel Henning overcame the barriers created by distance to provide a shrewd, amusing and illuminating account of her life for her audience back home; today she breaks down the barriers created by time as her letters continue to speak vibrantly to contemporary audiences. She stands among the first and foremost in the Australian Women's Library.

Dale Spender
August 1988

SOME PEOPLE IN THE LETTERS

Rachel Henning, the writer of the letters. Born 29th April 1826, arrived in Australia in 1854, returned to England in 1856, and settled permanently in Australia in 1861. She married Deighton Taylor on 3rd March 1866.

Henrietta ("Etta") Henning. Born 18th October 1827, married the Reverend T. W. Boyce on 14th August 1851, and remained in England.

Annie Henning. Born 3rd March 1830, arrived in Australia in 1853 with Biddulph. On 24th January 1866 she was married to George Hedgeland.

Amelia ("Amy") Henning. Born 24th March 1832, arrived in Australia with Rachel in October 1854, and in September 1855 married Thomas Sloman, a banker, of Bathurst, N.S.W.

Edmund Biddulph Henning, always called Biddulph in his sister's letters. Born 30th January 1834, arrived in Australia in 1853. He leased a farm from the Reverend Mr Sparling at Appin, N.S.W. Later he bought 180 acres of Crown land near Rixon's Pass, Bulli Mountain, at twenty-five shillings an acre, and built a house there in 1855. He sold this in 1857 to Henry Osborne and in November 1858 bought Marlborough station, 64,000 acres, near Rockhampton, for £900. In 1862 he moved north to Exmoor, on the Bowen River, near Port Denison, his sisters Rachel and Annie accompanying him. He married Emily Tucker, eldest daughter of William Tucker, on 26th November 1872.

The foregoing were the children of the Reverend Charles Wansbrough Henning, M.A. (son of Edmund Henning, of Poxwell House, Dorset), and of Rachel Lydia Henning nee Biddulph. The parents were both born in 1797, and married in 1825. Charles died in 1840, his wife in 1845.

Lindon Biddulph and Tregenna Biddulph were cousins to Rachel Henning on her mother's side, and belonged to the well-known titled family of the name. Tregenna married in England in 1857 and then settled in the Shoalhaven district of New South Wales.

The Tuckers, friends of the Hennings and Biddulphs. William Tucker was founder of the Australian firm of Tucker and Co. Captain James Tucker was his brother.

Other people are described by Rachel as the letters progress.

I

ENGLAND AND AUSTRALIA

My Dearest Annie,

I was so rejoiced to see your handwriting again and to get the two letters from you and Biddulph. How kind it was of you to write twice to me before the ship sailed, in the midst of all the confusion there must have been on board!

What a wretched day that Thursday was! After I had watched the steam-tug you went by, out of sight, I came back to the pier, for I could not rest anywhere else while I knew the ship was still in the river, and I saw the last steamer, with Mr Bright and his friends and the mail, go off; but they refused to let me go.

After that I went up in the town, shopping. But came down to the magnetic pier again in the afternoon, but the *Great Britain* had then gone down the river; so, finding it was all over, I betook myself to our lodgings, where perhaps it was as well that I had my hands full of work till quite late at night.

I do not know why I am writing you this long account of that miserable day. Before this reaches you, it will be one of the many black days we have to look back upon in our lives. It is already a past thing, and I suppose we shall not always have such a vivid remembrance of it as I have now.

You left behind you your two teaspoons after all. I am so sorry I forgot them. Everything you or Biddulph have had or used seems valuable now; certainly the way to be valued and missed is to go to Australia. I think I shall try it next year, and see if it will arouse my friends to a due sense of my merits, but I am sure nobody could miss me as I do you and darling Biddulph. Even here I am reminded of you by something every hour of the day.

COLCHESTER, SEPTEMBER 27TH

I sleep in the room looking out on the garden, the same that we had when we were here together six years ago. Dear Annie, you cannot think how everything here puts me in mind of you and of the time when we were here together. All the walks here and the garden, and above all our room, where you used to read to me sometimes when we had taken refuge there from the numerous troublesome children (it is better supplied with drawers now than it was then, for I have a whole chest to myself instead of the *one* drawer we had between us, and the room is not a refuge now, for some of the girls are always there; however, I like them far better than we did then).

There is more in parting than we thought when we used to talk so quietly about it. I only then thought of the actual loss of your company (you will say I valued it little enough when we were together!), and I forgot the terrible feeling of regret with which one looks back to almost every incident of our lives, regret that it is all past and sorrow at the countless things I was wrong in; things seem so pleasant when we look back upon them.

September 29th. Michaelmas Day, and the girls have been pestering Aunt to order a goose for dinner, and she replies "My dears, the housekeeping is beyond all reason already," which I do not doubt, as no one ever looks after the servants, and from Priscilla's account they ate butter enough last week to supply most families for a month. No doubt you will be favoured with geese on board ship, though I do not know where the sage and onions are to come from.

We are just now sorely set with a second cousin of the Carrs, whom Uncle[1] has inconsiderately asked here for a few days. He is rather a nice-looking young man, and has just left Oxford, but

[1] The Reverend Samuel Carr, Vicar of St Peter's, Colchester. Priscilla and Carry, Rachel's cousins, were his daughters.

2

he is either shy, or stupid, or both, and most difficult to amuse. (I don't try.) He only came yesterday, and Uncle is just come up to announce that he stays till Saturday. Carry is very fond of flirting, but it is no use, because he will not be flirted with.

"He will not be flirted with."

I need not tell you anything about Colchester life, because you have been here so lately. My principal employments are writing letters to a considerable extent, doing wool-work and reading Scott's *Life*. The wool-work consists of another square for aunt's unhappy ottoman, which is not finished yet, and it was in progress when we were here six years ago! I found there was only one square wanted to complete it, as some lady had sent one so atrociously worked, it could not be put in, so as I have not anything particular to do, I thought I would finish it for them. I got a very handsome single-flower pattern at Spadings—a great tiger-lily with its buds and leaves. It is to be grounded with white and will, I think, look very well.

3

They are reading *Chilton* aloud, and though we read it at Backwell,[2] I have forgotten the story, so it is very pleasant to work the square and be read to. I think our four squares are among the prettiest in the lot, and yours and mine the prettiest of these. I suppose you saw the piece they have put together; it looks very well.

I suppose you hardly remember our reading Scott's *Life* at Dawlish—how Miss West used to read it in the evenings and dear Papa used to go to sleep. I remembered it as being very interesting, and it is so, one of the very few biographies which are readable. Some of it is like a romance, it is so amusing. We get very nice books from the Castle Library, but Uncle is very particular about what they read. Carry got the *Life of Salvator Rosa*, but was not allowed to finish it.

We got a novel called *Ruth*, by the author[3] of *Mary Barton*, but we took the precaution of keeping it out of Uncle's way.

They have a new piano here, a very pretty rosewood Piccolo. I think Priscilla plays nicely and they both sing well. There is a Miss Meadows here who sings beautifully; she is the daughter of a clergyman, whose father was Brakarn, the great singer, but he changed his name to Meadows because he did not like the stage associations of "Brakarn". She is a very fat, vulgar-looking girl, but good-natured enough.

I am helping Priscilla arrange her dried flowers, which are in a great mess. She does not know much about them. She brought down some which she brought from Cromer and left upstairs to dry, and they were all mildewed, and one of them, a sort of stonecrop, so damp that it was actually growing little branches, shooting out at the joints of the stem.

I hope the *Great Britain* will not be much behind her time, else I am afraid your supply of clothes will run short. I am glad you took one warm dress with you, as Biddulph says it will be so cold during one part of the voyage. Also his pilot suit will come into requisition if you go as far south as the Shetland Isles are north. I hope all your things will reach their journey's end in safety, without any visitations of salt water. If they do, you will not want any new clothes for a long time.

When I was at Adlington, Mr Buxton[4] gave me one of those

2 Backwell, a village in Somerset, where the Hennings were bequeathed a home by their Uncle Henry Biddulph.

3 Mrs Gaskell.

4 The Buxtons, of Adlington (near Macclesfield, in Cheshire) were cousins of the Hennings. Sir Thomas Fowell Buxton, born 1837, was Governor of South Australia from 1895 to 1899.

printed muslins, the same that you had. I had only blue and pink to choose between, and I chose the blue. I shall not make it up till next year: it is too late for muslins now. I hope you will like your new bonnets, etc., when you unpack them. Do you remember that busy week in Liverpool?

I hope to hear that you are with the James Tuckers. I am sure you will be more comfortable in Sydney than anywhere up the country till Biddulph has a farm of his own. If so, if you and Biddulph both settle in Australia, I shall certainly come out unless you had rather I stayed at home.

Believe me, my own dear Annie, your most affectionate sister,

RACHEL HENNING

DANEHILL,
SUSSEX,
JANUARY 30TH 1854

My Dearest Annie and Biddulph,

I am getting very weary of the long time which has passed since you left England without our even hearing a word from you. We were very thankful to hear of the safe arrival of the *Great Britain* at Melbourne, for I was beginning to make myself miserable and to fancy all sorts of things, it seemed so long since she had been heard of. Brown, junior, wrote to Etta the moment he saw the news in the shipping intelligence, which was very kind of him, for otherwise we should not have known it till today.

You seem to have made a splendid passage and to have been only one day behind the time fixed upon for the passage to Melbourne. The news came by the *Hurricane,* and we have been looking out ever since for letters from you, which we think she may also have brought, as you could probably have written from Melbourne.

Etta and I have been talking of you this morning, and I have done little else but think of you for days past, partly perhaps because we have been getting so very anxious to hear from you and also because I want so to see you again. I have quite made up my mind to go to Australia. Sometimes I think of going with Amy and the Tuckers, and sometimes that it will be better to wait for another year. However, what we hear from you will greatly decide this.

Vincent Macey has come back, and by Lucy's account brings a poor idea of the prospects in Australia and says it is a great chance if you can get a living. However, he had no money to begin with. His health is quite restored.

5

There is an account in the London news today of a terrible wreck of an Australian passenger ship[5] off Dublin Bay, only one day after she had sailed from Liverpool. She was a very large ship and had too small a crew to manage her and struck on a reef of rocks. The greater part of the passengers were drowned. We were very thankful to hear the same day that the *Great Britain* had arrived safe at Melbourne, for such an accident brings more vividly before one the dangers of the sea.

It is nearly dark, and your birthday, Biddulph, is coming to an end as far as England is concerned. I suppose it is only just dawning in Australia. I must put away my writing till tomorrow.

February 1st. No letters from you! We are rather disappointed but we must now wait patiently for the regular mail; perhaps the *Hurricane* did not bring letters, for I am sure you would have written if you could.

Mr Boyce has just set off to Uckfield in company with Mr Hughes, Colonel Davis and Mr Pluckerrett, in Mr Hughes's carriage; they are all going to appeal against taxes, and will probably drive the commissioners out of their senses.

I like Danehill[6] more and more. The country is so beautiful, and I have plenty of time to do just as I like, and this quiet sort of life is most pleasant.

February 2nd. Aunt Pinchard writes to me: "The girls have some very pretty new dresses. Rose, however, began taking some music lessons of Miss Wingrove today. She accompanies John Lester's flute and wants a little help.

"Bella gave an immense ball last night, the last she is to give; none of our party were present, all gave it up at my request, which I consider very good of them.

"On Friday, we have a party here. I feel everything is for the last time that we shall all be together as one unbroken family. Tregenna and Rose will certainly be gone before another Christmas, if not Rachel. I suppose Kate will live with us till she is married. If Mr Arnold[7] were not a poet and a professed squire of dames, I should have no doubt of his intentions regarding Kate. He is now reading for a 'first'.

"I intend Rose to have a very elegant trousseau, but not many things, as she will have her Indian outfit to get afterwards. John would load her with presents if I did not interfere. He has magnificent ideas.

5 The *Tayleur*, 20th January 1854, with 380 drowned.
6 The home of Rachel's sister and brother-in-law, the Reverend T. W. Boyce, where Rachel at this time was staying.
7 Later Sir Edwin Arnold, author of *The Light of Asia*.

"Tregenna hopes to be ordained in June and marry soon after, but I don't think he can be."

All this is from a letter I received from Aunt last week. In one dated January 29th she says, after mentioning the arrival of the *Great Britain* at Melbourne, of which she also had heard:

"Rachel's love affair [not Rachel Henning's] is the most fierce, and throws all others into the shade. I suppose it is their youth; they have neither eyes nor ears for anyone else. They sometimes walk twice a day, and Shields slips into the drawing-room immediately after dinner and spends the evening with us. We all increasingly like him. There is an honest simplicity in his character; his face also improves, he is very handsome, in short, and has a splendid bass voice, a great addition to our musical quire. His mother is coming to see us at Easter, and then we shall talk about their future plans.

"John and Rose have fixed the early part of August for their wedding, which will give them a few good months of travel on the Continent. Rose wishes so much to spend another Christmas here. We are already beginning to think of the wedding, which will be on a magnificent scale if John had his way. I really am not equal to the occasion.

"I shall see that Rose is very elegantly and very youthfully drest. We are to have eight bridesmaids, your royal self among the number if you will come, and eight bridesmen, all in white (the 'maids', not the 'men'), and Mr Parr and Mr Barne to marry them.

"There is a dreadful fear hanging over us, lest in consequence of the war and the part Persia is taking all officers should be ordered back to India. John hears from his friends that it is expected. Being on sick certificate, it would not necessarily affect him, but he has a conscientious feeling that he ought to go, and the whole matter would then have to come off in a fortnight. It is too bewildering to think of!

"Rose's habit and hat came home today, a wide-awake and feather, and they take their first ride on Monday. I know pride will have a fall."

There, Annie, I hope I have told you enough "Mount"[8] news, but Aunt contrives to put things down in such a much more entertaining way than I can, that I prefer copying her words to distilling them into mine.

I think she ought to ask Etta and Amy to Rose's wedding also,

8 "The Mount", Taunton, was the home of Biddulph Pinchard, a cousin of the Hennings.

but very likely she will, as it was the bridesmaids she was speaking of when she only mentioned me, but Amy will very likely be on her way to Sydney, for Mr Tucker's health is so failing that I think they will very likely go out earlier than they intended doing.

I am not sure that I shall not also be on my way, for I have quite made up my mind to come out unless indeed I should hear anything from you that would make it downright foolish to do so. But if you both settle out there, as I fully expect you will, I shall come out also, either this year or next. If I do not, perhaps we shall never meet again, and that is not for one moment to be thought of. I have felt that more and more every day since you went. I don't think I should dislike Australia after all; and I would rather be anywhere with you than in the most beautiful place without you.

I am very happy here indeed. The country is lovely. Mr Boyce generally sits in his study now, having had a new grate put in there, large enough to roast a sheep by, rather to Etta's dismay, who mourns over the consumption of coal, which is 50s. a ton in London this winter. But, though I like Danehill very much, I do not like the idea of always living at one end of the world and you at the other.

I am reading Gibbon by way of history, and have been very busy arranging the flowers and mosses I got last summer. They all put me so in mind of you both, for we were generally together when we got them. I have finished my square for Aunt Carr's ottoman, and it looks very well. I am going to send it to her soon, and then I hope the unlucky ottoman will be made up. It has been in hand these seven years.

I am going to do one of Mr Boyce's slippers, and Etta the other. We got a very pretty pattern from Mrs Hughes. She is most good-natured and lends me all her music, which it is not everyone would do. Few people like lending new music.

It is getting dark and I am afraid the postman will come every minute.

God bless you, my dearest sister and brother.

Ever your affectionate

RACHEL HENNING

DANEHILL,
FEBRUARY 27TH 1854

My Dearest Annie and Biddulph,

I do not think you can have the least idea of the delight it was to us to get your parcel with such quantities of letters. It did not arrive till late Saturday afternoon, for Vince Wood did not arrive on Friday as we expected, and the revilings bestowed on him in consequence would have overwhelmed him if he had only heard them.

I was practising when Etta came into the drawing-room with the parcel in her hand. I have never exactly discovered how it came, but there it was! We cut the string in a moment with my old knife, though Mr Boyce suggested we had better untie the knot! And then we saw the delightful collection of letters and the journal! It was just post-time, and I hope you will properly appreciate my self-denial in rushing into the other room, before I had opened a single letter, and stamping and sending off those directed to others.

Then we sat down to read and finished the letters before tea, and after we read the journal aloud. I cannot think why Annie made any excuses for it. It was a capital journal and most interesting to us. It was very good and kind of her to keep it, for I am sure it must be a very difficult thing to do on board ship among so many people.

The wooden pear arrived in high preservation. What a curious thing it is. I suppose it is not intended to be eaten. Thank you, dear Annie, for the beautiful collar you sent me. Indeed I shall not put it away after my "old fashion". You must forget and forgive the crochet collar which, I am afraid, I did treat so, but this one is really beautiful. You have arranged and sewn on the Honiton so tastefully, and it is not the least larger than some collars I am wearing now. So I shall be sure to wear it thankfully. I am sorry for one thing, though. I am quite convinced that you must have put all the Honiton on it and not kept any for yourself.

February 28th. All letters from here must be dull to yours; everything you can tell about yourselves and your new country is so interesting. Thank you, dear Biddulph, for your long letter to me. We were very much amused by it. I should have been very uneasy about you if I had had the least idea the *Great Britain* contemplated an exploration of the South Pole, for the sudden change from great heat to great cold was enough to make anyone ill, and especially you.

However, Annie says you are well, and we were most thankful to hear it. I rejoiced to think that you had a "pilot suit" to keep out the cold, but Annie was not the least prepared for it, and I cannot think how she got on. I am sure she must have had

9

chilblains and all sorts of cold discomforts. However, you seem to have enjoyed the voyage in spite of everything, and some of it must have been very amusing—crossing the Line, for instance. I am glad Biddulph escaped a drenching; he must be quite a sailor to climb to the masthead.

We seem now to know all your friends on board, thanks to the letters and Annie's journal. I should like to see Mr Gray.[9] How kind and pleasant he seems to have been. Mr Boyce wrote to him yesterday to thank him for sending the parcel and to ask him when he would sail again, as we are going to send you a budget of letters, etc. It is too good an opportunity to let slip. If the *Great Britain* makes such a good passage again, I dare say you will get them nearly as soon as this.

Melbourne must be rather a nasty place from your description of it, and the prices of everything seem enormous—fancy £3. 10s. for three unfurnished rooms—I only wish we could transport Backwell House out there—our fortune would be made.

I am very glad you have such comfortable lodgings, and so cheap, too. You would not have got them for less in England. It must be very pleasant for you to be together in the mornings and to have a sort of house of your own, but I forget that it is three months ago that you wrote, and that you are probably settled elsewhere by this time. I hope Biddulph's advertisement is answered, and that he is deep in the mysteries of cows and sheep.

March 1st. It is a lovely day, fine and bright and warm as summer. We are sitting in the dining-room with the window open and (don't be too much surprised) the blind drawn up! And the rays of the sun falling full upon Etta's mahogany table and upon a great plate full of primroses, dressed with moss, which I brought home from some of my walks. Mr Boyce is walking about outside, superintending Baker's operations, which I hope may be rather hastened thereby, for the field, as we call the lower part of the garden below the banks, has not been cleared yet, but lies in its primitive state of brambles and stumps and pools of water. I think that by the end of next summer it may be in order.

Mr Boyce has felt himself so much encouraged by the fine weather that he has just written off for the paperers to come and finish papering the house. I hoped they would not be here till April, when I should be gone to Exeter, for as Etta's room and the dressing-room have to be done, I must move into the little

[9] Commander of the *Great Britain*.

10

room with bag and baggage, dried plants and all; besides which I am convinced that Etta will take the opportunity of turning the house out of window to clean it, and of all minor afflictions, house-cleaning is the worst. Think of all the carpets up and the floors flooded and tables with their legs in the air and chairs piled up in towers and Etta reigning queen of the confusion, for she is in her glory when cleaning is going on. Mr Boyce says he is sure she was born with a duster in her hand.

We have been walking about a great deal lately, or rather, I should say, I have, for I generally take long solitary rambles, while Mr Boyce and Etta make a solemn march down to the turnpike on Sheffield green and back again; the former not "feeling equal" to long walks.

I am very fond of exploring the innumerable paths in Sheffield Woods, but I do not believe anybody knows them all, or ever will. I am not the only person, it seems, who is fond of exercise in the neighbourhood, for Cherriman went to see her little boy the other day, and on her return she informed us that she had asked someone to accompany her home "because a woman walks on the Sheffield road"; and on further inquiry as to what objection there could be to any respectable female using that mode of progression, it turned out that several veracious witnesses had seen an Apparition disappear among the bushes by Ormiston's cottage, nearly opposite Colonel Cavis's gate.

You must remember the place. We heard this story at night, and the next morning at breakfast Etta and I were laughing about it and wondering whether Cherriman really believed it, when I saw Mr Boyce looking very much the reverse of pleased, but I thought that perhaps his breakfast had not agreed with him.

However, he got up and rang the bell for prayers, a thing which by no means happens every day, and after reading the chapter he began an extemporary commentary on it. He talked about ignorant superstition, and said very gravely "I understand there's been an Apparition seen." Human nature could endure no more. Etta, I and Cherriman all laughed, and Etta out loud! Mr Boyce was, of course, extremely angry, broke off and went and shut himself into his study, leaving us all divided between laughter and consternation; and Elizabeth, a sort of human cormorant, who helps Cherriman, with her mouth wider open than usual.

I am very glad you kept clear of the "Gambling Club", Biddulph, not that I should ever have suspected you of playing high, but yet the excitement of it must be very fascinating on board ship, where there is so little to do. I shall be very anxious to hear your account of Wollongong in your next letter.

I think Lindon's establishment must be a queer one from all accounts, and I hope you will not belong to it. The stars are, no doubt, very beautiful and desirable objects in themselves, but it is too much of a good thing to be able to make astronomical observations through the roof of your bedroom.

I am very glad Biddulph is going to farm. I am sure you will like it far better than business. When I come out I expect I shall find you in a bush farm, galloping after cattle with a long whip and quite expert in branding unruly ones. I am certainly going to Australia, but whether this year or next, I don't know.

It will be Annie's birthday the day after tomorrow. With my kindest love I wish her many happy returns of it. I had no room to write about it in my yesterday's letter. Do you remember Annie's last birthday? We walked along the cliffs to that sunny field by Turret Castle and found the first primroses.

What do you think of our being at war again, for I suppose it is inevitable. I hope the Russians will get well beaten, and I think it pretty certain with such enemies as France and England. I saw an article in the paper about the defences of Australia, which appear to amount to little. If they call out a force of volunteers, do not join them; you are far too good to be shot at.

Good-bye, my dearest Annie and Biddulph. You will soon hear again I expect, as of course, we shall write in the parcel and the *Great Britain* sails this month. How I wish you were here to take a walk with me in the woods this lovely afternoon! You don't know how I long to see you again. Well, perhaps I shall before long.

Till then, believe me, your own affectionate sister,

RACHEL HENNING

P.S., *March 31st.* I liked the account Biddulph gave of the country in his last letter very much. I think Wollongong must be beautiful and that a farm in that neighbourhood would be anything but unpleasant. I believe I shall come out with Amy after all, or if I did not this year I certainly should next year, but very likely it will be this. It would be very pleasant to be together again and I should delight in a warm climate.

We are in great confusion this week, as the house is being papered and we are fairly blockaded, the enemy being in possession of the passages, staircase and all the rooms except the drawing-room, in which "missis lives", as Elizabeth remarked, and two bedrooms. We usually get out of the drawing-room window and in again by the front door to go upstairs. Etta's room is the only one done; it has a handsome crimson paper, but the pattern is too large, so that it makes the room look low. The two other bedrooms and the drawing-room were papered last autumn.

We are having a most lovely spring to make amends for the sharp winter. The woods are full of wood anemones, wood sorrel and primroses, and all our Wilmslow flowers are out in the garden: hyacinths, polyanthuses and hepaticas. Mr Boyce spends lots of money upon shrubs, and new loads of them constantly arrive, but the field is not made yet, nor do I think it ever will be.

RACHEL HENNING

EXETER,
DEVON,
APRIL 22ND 1854

My Dearest Annie and Biddulph,

What a long, long post it is; it takes six months or more to get an answer to any letter.

How curious a hot Christmas Day must seem! You fared better for your Christmas dinner than we did, for we were minus turkey, apricots and mulberries. Etta and I sat by the fire, as close to it as we could, for it was a bitterly cold day, and talked about former Christmas-times when you were with us, and drank your health in some sherry which Mr Boyce produced for the purpose.

I will send you out the London news for this week by the *Great Britain*. You will have heard that war[10] has at last been declared. We have sent a tremendously powerful fleet to the Baltic under Napier. I hope the war will be short and sharp and that the Tsar will lose what he deserves, viz., some of his ill-gotten territories.

There are all sorts of opinions afloat, of course. Some say that Russia is too strong for us, but I don't believe a word of that. *Punch* says this week that the greatest comfort is that we are not fighting for the Bourbons, and we beat even in that bad cause, so I am sure we shall win this time, now that we are in the right.

The people in general, with the exception of the hopelessly insane of the Peace Party, are quite enthusiastic for the war. I suppose you saw in the papers an account of the deputation

10 The Crimean War.

of donkeys who went to Russia with the full expectation of doing what all the statesmen of Europe had failed in, namely, bringing the Tsar to reason. He received them very civilly and sent them away as wise, or rather as foolish, as they came.

I heard something the other day about a bill being brought in to prevent, in future, the English name being made a laughing-stock of throughout Europe by the idiotic exertions of the Peace Society. It is time something should be done.

The 26th is fixed upon as a day of national humiliation for the war. I hear the income tax is to be doubled, which will be unpleasant, but they must have money. The worst is for those who have relations in the fleet or Army.

April 23rd. We have been on several excursions since we came here. We went to Starcross last week by train and then walked across the Warren to Dawlish. I had not seen Dawlish since the time when we all spent a winter there fifteen years ago. Amy and I walked up to Barton Terrace to see our old house there, and, I rather think, excited the suspicion of the inhabitants by standing and looking in at the windows, for an old lady came and asked us if she could direct us anywhere. I believe she thought we were looking for an eligible place to break in at. The railroad was not made, either, when I last saw Dawlish. It does not spoil it so much as I expected: the tunnels are rather picturesque.

You ask when our friends' curiosity will be satisfied. I think they ought to be quite content if you write a public letter now and then, not every mail. I am going to send round the interesting one we got from you by the *Harbinger*. It is now gone to Aunt Pinchard, then the Carrs and Buxtons and Sophy Henning will have it. Also Mary Ball and Mrs Barlow; the latter has not seen an Australian letter for a long time, and she is always greatly interested in hearing about "poor dear Annie", as she has always called you since you left England.

I hope, Biddulph, you have found something to suit you long ere this. It seems rather an undertaking for both of you to take a farm, even if a small one, especially as neither of you are fit for hard work.

You need not be afraid I shall think you extravagant, dear Annie, I am sure you will never be that. Of course you must have money to begin anything, but I am vexed that Biddulph should have to give £117 for £99 in cash. Of course, in a time of war, the Funds must be low. If you take this farm, I cannot think how you will manage for furniture. You know there is a package of bedding at Mr Buxton's office, though not much. I suppose you will send for it and for your books, etc., if you really take the house and farm.

April 24th. I was quite surprised at your account of the climate of Sydney. I thought that whatever else was objectionable, that was beautiful, but it must be far worse than England, and the country round Sydney must be frightful, but perhaps it is better in other parts. You say that it was beautiful round Wollongong, Biddulph, but there can be nothing anywhere like the green lanes and fields of England.

The Government gardens must be very pretty, but it is a great loss to have no country walks. I should think Biddulph fully appreciated the oysters; he used to be so fond of them. How I should like to spend a day under the trees with you both! You do not know how I long to see you again, sometimes.

You seem to have plenty of friends in Sydney and to be always out, but it must seem very strange to go out after tea. Perhaps the custom has been introduced in consideration of the high price of provisions. It is rather provoking that none of your evening dresses are of any use, Annie. I wish you had taken out others instead, but I dare say you will send for some things when we go out.

April 26th. This is the fast-day appointed in consequence of the war, but we are not all going to make ourselves ill by fasting all day, as we did on that memorable occasion at Taunton. Mr Hugh Hedgeland, who is rather fond of eating, observed rather crossly, when someone asked him if he was going to fast, that abstaining from food was no use and that it was fasting in spirit that was meant—so that is exactly how we are going to fast, and bodily we are going to eat cold beef and bread-and-butter pudding.

We took a long walk yesterday to Pinhoe, a pretty little church about three miles from here. Emily met with her usual misfortunes in the shoe line. The day we went to Dawlish she wore tight boots and could hardly walk at all, and yesterday she wore such old ones that they split all across and she had to walk with her toes on the stones all the way home, but luckily they are not the worse for it.

I got a great many wildflowers, and we have quite a nice bunch of them in the middle of the table

Tomorrow, if it is fine, we are going to Waddlesdown, in a fly part of the way, and then to walk on to Newton St Agnes

15

and home by the train. Both old Mr Hedgeland and his son are going with us; in fact, the fly is chiefly for the benefit of the former.

Mr Tucker, of an evening, sits up somewhere in a corner with his back to the light looking the picture of misery, or else he walks up and down the room. I am always so sorry for him, although we cannot help laughing at him. Last evening I saw him take off his boots, warm his feet at the fire and then put them on again, to the no small astonishment of the Miss Hedgelands. I hardly know what Emily will do when we are gone and she is alone with him; it will be so dreadfully dismal for her. I do hope William Tucker will come and fetch him out to Sydney, for he  will never go out unless he does; he cannot make up his mind to the exertion.

And now, good-bye, Annie and Biddulph, and believe me, your ever affectionate sister,

RACHEL HENNING

[*In August 1854 Rachel, her sister Amy and cousin Tregenna Biddulph left England in the* Calcutta *for Australia. Her first letter at sea is addressed to her sister Henrietta ("Etta") Boyce, who remained in England.*]

ABOARD THE "CALCUTTA",
FINISHED AUGUST 14TH 1854

My Dearest Etta,

I begin to write to you today, as we hope to reach St Vincent's on Sunday or Monday and shall be able to send home letters from there.

16

Amy, Tregenna and I watched you from the deck of the steamer on that rainy morning till we were so far from the shore that we could not see you any longer, and then returned to the corner of the cabin where you left us, and whence we did not move again till we arrived alongside the *Calcutta*.

We three betook ourselves to the saloon, where we sat and talked about you on your way homeward, and got rid of the time as well as we could till we were called to dinner.

Amy and I had been looking about and speculating upon the passengers, and had pitched upon a pretty-looking girl of about eighteen, dressed in mourning, as the only one we should like for a cabin companion, and when we went down to look at our berths after dinner, there she was.

She is very pleasant and good-tempered, and, I think, a lady, so we are very well off in that respect. She is going to Melbourne with her uncle and brother, the former a queer old gentleman who patronizes us and objects to shaving; the latter, a good-tempered boy of fourteen. Both these are in Tregenna's cabin, together with a man of the name of Trench, who looks like a West India planter and whom Tregenna pronounces "jolly".

We found our berths more comfortable than we expected. Miss Maunder has the one under the porthole, and Amy the upper one on the opposite side, and I have the lower one. We put away all our things after dinner and found plenty of room for them. The two boxes which Mr Arnold conveyed on board were safe in the empty berth, and as soon as the ship was fairly off, I nailed up the moreen bags and put up some brass-headed nails, besides, and no one said anything to me. Our cabin is directly over the screw, so that I dare say they did not hear.

It poured the whole day on Friday, so that we could not go on deck and see the last of old England. The last I did see was the Needles from the stern windows. We have had very fine weather since, with the wind directly in our favour, and hitherto we have come very fast. Yesterday the wind freshened so that they took up the screw and the ship went on under canvas. I thought it a much pleasanter motion, but we rolled about a good deal more, and there were several alarming smashes of crockery, and some of the passengers having, contrary to orders, opened their portholes, the lower deck was streaming with water, so the first officer had all the handles taken off the portholes, and now they cannot be opened at all.

Some of the passengers have been dreadfully ill, and Mr Arnold would have lost his bet, for I was seasick all Saturday afternoon, which I spent in my berth. I got better in the evening

17

and came up to tea and went on deck, and have been perfectly well ever since; although yesterday and today the ship has rolled and pitched a great deal. I thought myself very well off to get off with half a day of it as, if people are ill at all, they generally are so for a week.

It did me a great deal of good. Tregenna and Amy have felt nothing of it. I believe Amy would be better for it, for she has a constant headache and always complains of being "dreadfully tired", and spends half her time lying on the sofa, with her hands over her eyes. I read to her sometimes, but she does not care about it, nor is she fond of being on deck. She finds the voyage very dull, as might be expected, and I believe that what she feels now is her old complaint of want of excitement rather than any bodily malady, and I have no doubt she will get better as we go on.

The voyage is exactly what I expected: very tiresome, but bearable, like the other wearinesses of life. I do not venture to think how we shall live out three months of it, but I suppose day after day will pass away imperceptibly.

We breakfast at 9 a.m. and then stay in the saloon and write journals, etc., or go on deck and sit and read. They give us no end of a breakfast, hot meat and potatoes and fish, etc. We lunch at 12 p.m. and dine at 4 p.m. This is the great event of the day with most of the people, and they certainly feed the menagerie very well, giving us soup and fish, all sorts of meat and poultry, pudding and dessert. After dinner we generally read till tea-time, which is at 7 p.m., and after tea we stay on deck till it is dark. This is the only pleasant part of the day. The sea was most beautiful last night in the light of a full moon, but they put out the lights at 10 p.m., so we are obliged to go down at a quarter past nine, unless we like going to bed in the dark.

We already see the difference of climate and of time. The evenings are much shorter than at home and it is getting very hot. I do not feel the heat much, but I am afraid Amy does rather.

I have not said anything to you about the passengers because we do not know anything of them. There are very few of whom I can remember the names, though Tregenna sometimes tries to enlighten me about his friends. He has found a set, some of them Oxford men, with whom he smokes and drinks beer, but in general all the passengers keep to themselves, which I think much the pleasantest way. I do not think there are fifty first-class, but I do not know the exact number. There are very few ladies

18

among them at all, and hardly any in the real sense of the word.

The captain is the only one of the officers of the ship whom I know, as I sit by him at dinner. He is quite a gentleman, but I have hardly exchanged ten words with him. This is his first voyage as captain; he came home last time as first officer of the *Argo*.

One of our passengers is a dumpy little German lady (?) who plays very well, but has most remarkable manners. She was screaming with laughter just now at some compliments which we paid to her music, and then she asked Amy if she could play, and on her answer, whatever it was, she took her round the waist and gave her something between a shake and a hug, to

"She has not been married very long."

Amy's extreme astonishment. I shall take special care to avoid a similar salute, though I have never yet spoken to her.

Mr and Mrs Donaldson[11] are in their own eyes the great people on board, he being actually a member of the Australian Parliament (I did not know they had one). He is very stout, very bumptious and a great eater. She is handsome and affected and has not been married very long. She has been dreadfully seasick, and today, for the first time, appeared at breakfast.

There are also a Mr and Mrs Westgarth. He has written a book about Australia, which is handed about on board, but I do not feel inclined to read it. She looks like a lady, but I have never heard her speak. Then there is a dismal-looking Mrs Macdonald, who is going to Melbourne to look for her husband, that worthy not having been heard of for two years; a very hopeful expedition, I should think. She also is awfully ill even now, and retires in the middle of every meal.

We rather like a Mrs Hake, who is handsome and speaks like a lady. But her husband, Tregenna says, is a linen-draper in Sydney, of whom we shall probably purchase future gowns.

I have been writing this in little bits at a time and hardly know what I have told you.

Of course we do not know any of the fore-saloon passengers, but one of them has attracted considerable attention. She is a German girl, who is going out, quite alone, to open concert rooms in Melbourne. She dresses and wears her hair in the most extraordinary style, and last Sunday she walked for nearly an hour by herself up and down the lower deck, just in front of the quarter-deck, while the officers and passengers were leaning over the rails looking at her and betting as to whether she was painted or not. She certainly has a most beautiful complexion if she is not. She has a piano on board, which she was foolish enough to have unpacked and taken into the fore-saloon. They say she does not play very well.

Some of the second-class passengers are very troublesome. The first day one of them with his wife took their seats at the captain's table, and refused to show their tickets, alleging that they were first-class passengers. However, the purser enforced the appearance of the ticket and the steward expelled them.

Saturday, August 12th. I have not written yesterday, as I have had a sort of feverish attack from a cold, but I am well again today.

11 Stuart Donaldson, who became Premier and Chief Secretary of New South Wales in 1856, married Amelia Cowper in England in February 1854. In September 1851 he had fought a duel with Sir Thomas Mitchell, Surveyor-General of New South Wales.

Yesterday year, Annie and Biddulph sailed. What a little while ago it seems, and yet, though we have only been on board a week, it seems about a year. If we ever survive to reach Australia, I am sure we shall stay there for life, for I do not think I could undertake another voyage even to get home again. It is most wearisome. The noise is wearisome, the people are wearisome and life is wearisome. It is too hot to work, and I am getting quite tired of novels, and there is nothing else on board.

I do not even think that a voyage is so good for people's health as it is said to be. Amy has never been well since she came on board, and I, besides the attack of fever, which was not pleasant, am continually getting sore throats owing to sitting in draughts. The saloon is a sort of Temple of Aeolus, and yet if the windows are closed we could not live. Most of the people live on deck, but we generally betake ourselves to the saloon. We like the sofas, and the glare of the sea makes Amy's eyes bad.

We have a band on board, but they do not play particularly well. Some of their instruments are out of tune. They play at dinner-time and most of the evening and wash the dishes of the establishment at intervals.

The waiters must have a life of it, for they are continually at work. First, the children's breakfast, then ours; then luncheon, then the children's dinner, then ours; then the children's tea, then ours. One waiter is so like Lindon that we generally call him so. Another, who is likewise the bedroom steward, Tregenna took the precaution of feeing when he first came on board, and he accordingly stands behind our chairs at dinner and waits on us most assiduously. We like the stewardess. She is very kind and attentive, and tells us long stories at night, which we do not believe, but which are just as amusing as if we did.

There are eight or ten children on board, but they do not bother us much, as they live chiefly on deck. One baby screams dreadfully at night.

August 14th, Monday. I must finish my letter today, as they expect to reach St Vincent's at five this afternoon. We shall not be able to write to you again till we get to Melbourne, as the mail steamers are not allowed to send letters on board a ship even if they meet one. They must not stop. I have written a journal up to the day I began these letters and shall go on again now, but it will never be worth sending home, for there is nothing to tell. Nothing ever happens except an extra amount of rolling about, or a downfall of crockery.

We stay two days at St Vincent's and I suppose we shall go on shore to see it, but they say it is a bare rock with only a few houses and a heap of coal, and not a tree on it. The real trial of the voyage will begin after we leave it. I wish they would stop at the Cape.

St Vincent's is in sight now, and they close the mail-bag this evening, so if we visit it, which I rather doubt—the sea is running so high for a boat—we must give you an account of it in the journal. We have had a most prosperous voyage hitherto, and I believe that the same Providence which has watched over us hitherto will keep us to the end. I dare say we shall both like the voyage better when we are got more used to the confinement of the ship and have forgotten England a little more.

How pretty Danehill must be looking now; those green woods quite haunt me! I wonder how the flowers are getting on in your garden and how the ducks are and if you often walk to Sheffield wood.[12]

Good-bye, my dearest Etta. Kind love to 'Mr Boyce and with very, very much love to yourself. Believe me,

Your ever affectionate sister,

RACHEL HENNING

12 Sheffield Park wood, Sussex.

[On reaching Australia Rachel finds that her brother Biddulph has rented a farm at Appin, ten miles south of Campbelltown, N.S.W. But he is keen on getting another property.]

ELLADALE COTTAGE,
APPIN,
MARCH 29TH 1855

My Dear Mr Boyce,

We have been hoping that we should get letters from England in time to answer them by the *Pacific*, but although the *Lightening* has arrived and brought some for the Biddulphs, there are none for us. I suppose Etta wrote by the *Red Packet*, and that ship is not yet come in.

Thank you for your note to me. I received it at Sydney, where I spent the two first months of this year. I told Etta all about my pleasant visit there when I last wrote.

I returned to Appin on the 5th of this month and found Amy alone, as Annie had gone to Shoalhaven about a week before. I only mean alone as far as her sister's company was concerned, for Biddulph and Tregenna were here, of course.

I cannot say that I was glad to get back again, though I dare say I ought to have been; but I found that matters had slightly improved during my absence. The servant I had sent up from Sydney turned out to be a very good one, so that there was no longer any necessity for our doing hard work.

There had been some rain, so that the fields looked greener and the cattle less like skeletons than formerly, and Amy was established as housekeeper and had contrived to become a very good cook. I was only too glad to leave her in full possession of the former dignity, and entertaining strong doubts of my own capacity in the latter respect, I thought it as well not to interfere beyond the occasional stoning of raisins and beating of eggs. Her eyes are not very strong still, and she says that she is very glad to employ herself part of the day in work that will not try them, and I am very glad to be saved the measuring out of flour and dispensing of salt beef.

I draw, or mend the stockings of the establishment in the mornings, and after dinner generally read to Amy while she works or nets. We wander about in the bush for an hour before tea by way of a walk, or I go down to Appin to fetch the letters. Amy goes part of the way with me and then returns when this is the case, as a four-mile walk is rather too much for her. In the evening we play cribbage and backgammon, or work and read and go to bed at nine. And so the days pass quickly enough, if not very pleasantly.

I dislike this bush life extremely and find it sometimes difficult to amuse myself, though at home the days used to seem too short for what I had to do.

I seem to have left out Biddulph altogether in my account of our daily life, but he and Tregenna left us for Shoalhaven very soon after I came back to Appin, and he only returned home last night. He goes off again on Thursday, as he is now thinking about buying land at Shoalhaven instead of on the top of the Bulli Mountain. It would have the advantage of being accessible, which would hardly be the case on the top of the mountain, and the land there is equally rich. In other respects all parts of Australia are alike, I suppose. They are so to me at least.

I am glad he is going to leave Appin, however, for I am sure he will never make any money on this farm. Do you remember our saying that there must certainly be something the matter with it, when he wrote word of how low the rent was, that there must be a want of water or that nothing would grow? There are both these drawbacks here.

The soil is wretchedly poor, and this is said to be the very driest part of Australia. Frequently, when there have been torrents of rain at Wollongong and Sydney, on each side of us, we have not had a drop here. There are no springs on the farm, only a waterhole, and that was dry for nearly six weeks in the summer, and then we had to fetch water from the river[13] three miles off. It is a pity Biddulph ever took this farm; still, he has gained some experience here, and, as his expenditure was chiefly in cattle and furniture, he has not lost much.

Annie is still at Shoalhaven, and she is going to pay a visit to Sydney on her way back, so I do not much expect her here till June. The truth is that when once we are liberated from Appin we are in no great hurry to return to it again.

Lindon has a very comfortable house at Shoalhaven and seems to be making a great deal of money by surveying, and if he will only stick to it, I have no doubt that he will do well. He is very anxious that Biddulph should settle near him, and perhaps it would be pleasanter for Annie and Amy to be near them than away on the mountain-top. He came up with Biddulph last night and stays here till Thursday to take him back to Shoalhaven with him. I think he is afraid he will return to the "Mountain" plan if he loses sight of him.

Biddulph, however, will not be persuaded into anything unless

13 King's Falls, George's River.

he thinks it will be best. I can hardly fancy that the thoughtful, steady man of business, which he really is now, can be the same with the almost childish schoolboy we considered him in England; and yet he has lost none of his gentleness or simplicity of character.

Mr Sparling,[14] the clergyman, of Appin, wants him very much to be churchwarden this year, but he says he is too young and has enough to do to mind his own business without the business of the parish: and for the same reason he refused to be put on the Patriotic Fund Committee at Campbell Town.

He is at present gone out with Jack to fell a bee-tree, dressed-up in a blue gold-digger's shirt over his clothes, a thin silk handkerchief tied over his hat, and my gardening gauntlets on his hands. I hope he will get some honey and not many stings. Jack is helping him, likewise got up in a silk handkerchief. Lindon is sat on a log in the toolshed smoking and Amy is making a plum pudding for dinner.

We bought Lindon's cows when he went to Shoalhaven, and we have now plenty of milk and butter to use and some of the latter to sell. We send it to one of the shops where we get two shillings a pound for it. We have begun to dig our potatoes, but they are very small and many of them diseased owing to the dry weather. We have also a few pumpkins in the garden, but our stock of vegetables is not large.

We can get nothing to grow in this dry soil, and the fowls scratch up the little there is. We have a quantity of poultry. I have just been standing with Amy at the back door to take a review of them. Biddulph put up two to fatten yesterday and we have already killed and eaten some. They were not very plump, though in better case than those famous ones you helped us to dispose of at Backwell.

The *Lightening* seems to have brought no satisfactory news about the war. Will Sebastopol ever be taken? There is a long article in the Sydney *Herald* copied from *The Times* which speaks strongly of the want of generals in the English Army, and, though in a lesser degree, the French.

I should think there must be some such reason for their comparative inactivity. It can be from no fault in the troops, for we have seen what they can do at Alma and Inkerman. How I should like to have a good chat with you about it all!

Nobody here cares much for the war, and indeed it is so long before we get the news that it loses half its interest, when we remember that perhaps by the time it reaches Australia affairs

14 From whom Biddulph rented his Appin farm.

may be wearing quite a different aspect at home. Perhaps now, for instance, Sebastopol may be taken, the Tsar frightened into a peace, and the French and English quarrelling over their conquests, or they may have been driven out of the Crimea and a Russian fleet be sailing up the Channel, though I hope this last is a very unlikely event.

But it is very tantalizing to know nothing of what is going on. The Australians have subscribed very well to the Patriotic Fund, though a few find it convenient to belong to the Peace Party when asked for their subscriptions.

There is an old Dr Cox, who sometimes comes here to see Biddulph, who puts me out of patience with the nonsense he talks about peace. He is a Quaker, and considers such texts as "If thine enemy smite thee on one cheek", etc., as applicable to our relations with Russia. It is no use to argue with him, as Tregenna said—for even he was roused—for he only goes off into a long string of heterogeneous and misapplied quotations. I told him I was thankful the English Government did not think like him, and went off to feed the fowls; Amy and Biddulph also took opportunities of stealing away, leaving Tregenna, who was too lazy to move, to endure the full brunt of a "yarn" which lasted the whole morning.

• • • • •

I must finish my letter today, as the mail for the *Pacific* closes tomorrow. Biddulph and Lindon have set out on their return to Shoalhaven, and a very wet ride they will have as it is pouring with rain.

Miss Anna Gurney wrote to forward me two letters of introduction from Sir William Hooker to two botanical friends of his in Sydney. I got Mrs Burton to ask him if there was any "Flora of Australia" yet published, and he says not, but sends these letters instead to two gentlemen who have studied the plants of the country. It is extremely kind of him to take the trouble, but I do not think they will ever be delivered, as I hope I shall not be long enough here to make any collection, and I do not care enough about the Australian flowers to take much trouble with them.

I often wonder what can be the difference. I suppose it is the want of any pleasant associations connected with them. I often see very pretty flowers in the bush and just gather them to take a look at them, and then throw them away again without any further interest, while at Home every wildflower seemed like a friend to me.

The Danehill woods must be getting full of wood anemones,

26

primroses and wood sorrel now. How beautiful they must be, and how I should like to see them!

We have not been riding lately, as there is nothing to ride upon. My horse got so thin in the dry weather that he was sent off to recruit in a place called Gerar, where "feed"—as they always call grass here—was plentiful, and I have not been able to get him back yet. Biddulph has changed "the wild mare", a beast that nobody can ride, for a very tall animal which, he says, he can break into a side-saddle. I rather doubt it, though, for it is as much as he can do to hold her in. She did not look very promising when he departed for Shoalhaven upon her yesterday, as she capered sideways all down the bush path, till they were out of sight. An eighty-mile journey, however, with the roads in their present wet state, must take some of the superfluous spirit out of her.

I like this autumn weather, for it feels like England. Yesterday was still and cold with that dull grey sky we so often have at home in the fall of the year, and today it is pouring with rain, like a genuine English November day.

Amy rejoices in the cool weather, and I was tired of the perpetual glare of sunshine. Fine days here bring me no pleasure as they do in England: they are too hot and too numerous, and besides, you cannot enjoy them by taking nice walks—there are no walks to take.

I suppose you have been drawing a great deal lately. Your pictures of Backwell and Danehill are hung up in our sitting-room and make us long for home whenever we look at them. I have never yet unpacked my picture-case, as it is so nicely done up in tin that I thought it was a pity to open it in my present uncertainty about staying here. My books are also still in the great case which I brought from Danehill. All except a few which I wanted. Biddulph made two new bookcases while I was in Sydney, but even now there is not room for all Amy's with his and Annie's.

We are longing for letters from home. I used to be very glad to get letters from Australia, but it was nothing to the desire we feel here for home news; and yet I can hardly call it a pleasure to receive it, for an English letter makes me feel miserable for at least a day, and Tregenna says the same; he is nearly as homesick as I am. But I have said too much about this; it is like King Charles's head, and will get into everything I write.

Kindest love to Etta and yourself. Believe me, your affectionate sister,

RACHEL HENNING

27

My Dear Mr Boyce,

I hardly know how to write of your kindness in being so sorry for the miseries of our first experience of bush life, and in promptly desiring a remedy for them by inviting us all to return and take up our abode with you. I accept with thanks and gratitude.

I speak only for myself, as you see, for Amy's destiny is decided in a different way,[15] as you will have heard before you receive this; and Annie, as Etta anticipated, decides to remain. I dare say she has written to you by this mail and told you her own views and feelings on the subject. She is the most generous and disinterested character I ever saw, for she not only stays, but says she would not go home if she could at present, and that this life suits her and that she really likes it.

I can only hope that she speaks truly and not from kindness in saying that she likes the bush. I have no doubt of her liking Sydney, as she had a great number of friends there, and it certainly is a pleasant place to visit.

But in spite of what she says, I think it must be a sacrifice to stay here when she might go to England. It is a great comfort, however, in leaving her to think that things are very different and very much improved to what they were when we first came. We have a good stout Irish servant, who I hope will stay. She makes good yeast bread and we have plenty of milk; and pigs and poultry frequently relieve guard with the salt beef. Lucy also does all the washing and ironing, so there is no hard work on our hands.

Biddulph is writing to you, so he will tell you about the land he means to buy on the Bulli Mountain. I think he is sure to make it answer in time, but of course the first clearing will be expensive.

Annie is so much liked in Sydney and everywhere else that I consider my stay in England as of very uncertain duration; still, if only for one or two years, it will be worth the expense. If you were to be imprisoned for life you would give much for only two years of liberty.

How I wish we all were coming back together! Biddulph and all! My first pleasure at the thought of return has been terribly damped since the idea of leaving them all. Annie and Biddulph

[15] Amy had become engaged to be married to Thomas Sloman, a banker, of Bathurst.

especially, and sometimes I think I can never go. However, things have lately turned out so much better than I ever hoped that I think of giving up despondency for the future, and hoping and believing that we shall all meet again. Even Biddulph says that he hopes to go home in a few years.

Appin did not agree with Amy, and she was never well here; and yet she has been so delicate this winter, even in this climate, that I do not believe she could have lived in England. Everyone speaks most highly of Mr Sloman, to whom Amy is engaged. I have not seen him yet. He wrote a nice letter to Biddulph. It seems so curious to see Biddulph addressed as standing *in loco parentis* to Amy, and he wrote a most business-like letter in return; signifying his gracious approval, etc. The only objection is in Mr Sloman being settled so far from Sydney, which will separate Amy from all her friends.

I do not know the distance between Sydney and Bathurst, but Biddulph has just read me an advertisement from the *Herald* stating that a spring-wagon has been opportunely established between the two places, which starts from Sydney on Monday morning and arrives at Bathurst at twelve on Saturday night. It takes twelve passengers, and the wagon is fitted up with every accommodation (I suppose not fourpost beds) for those sleeping in it—if they can. If this hopeful conveyance is to be the only means of communicating between Amy and her despondent friends, the sooner Mr Sloman carries out his intention of settling in Sydney the better for all parties.

We are glad to get the *Illustrated News* every month. The pictures of the frozen Thames and snowy streets seem so strange out here, where we all run out in the morning if a thin cake of ice is reported on the puddle outside the kitchen door, and gaze upon the rarity with admiring eyes.

It is becoming quite a task to read the reports of the progress, or rather want of progress, of the war. If there was ever a just war this is one; the people, with the exception of a few *Bright*[16] spirits, seemed heart and soul in the matter at the beginning, and we have the best troops in the world, and yet we seem to have done nothing except lose our army and our prestige in Europe, and, perhaps, by this time have patched up some dishonourable peace. I do not like to read about it now, nor to talk about it.

Believe me, your affectionate sister,

RACHEL HENNING

16 The reference is to John Bright, who, with Richard Cobden and others, was opposed to the war.

My Dearest Etta,

How I should like to see you once more; to find myself in England again and of all parts of England, at Danehill. It is what I have been longing for, though I never hoped it, ever since I came here, and yet with the contrariety of human nature, now that through the kindness of Mr Boyce, the way is smoothed for my return, I every now and then hesitate about it and think that I can never leave Annie and Biddulph.

I rather wanted to go before Amy's wedding, not that I am in such a hurry to leave them, but because, in the bustle and excitement of preparing for that event, I do not think I should be much missed. While afterwards it might make more difference when there are but two at home. But I heard today from Mrs Macdonald, who came out with us from England in the *Calcutta* and whose name you must have often seen in Amy's letters to you, and she tells me that she cannot possibly go till October, and as we both wish to go together perhaps I shall wait for her.

But I shall know more certainly by the time the next mail goes, when I have talked to Annie about it. Dear Etta, it is such a pleasure to think of seeing you again soon. I seem never to have valued your company half enough when I was with you. There are many things in which I think I shall be wiser if I come back, but do not reckon upon it with certainty.

Annie may follow Amy's example and marry, and then I suppose I am fixed here for life. It is no use to look far forward, but I have little doubt that this will be the end. I may be at home for one, two or three years; then Annie will marry, and I must keep house for Biddulph. He at present declares his intention, notwithstanding Mr Boyce's exhortation, of not taking to himself a wife for the next ten years, and I am much mistaken if he is left in quiet possession of Annie for all that time. He is at present sitting opposite to me, cutting up lemons for marmalade.

They are "sweet lemons", and make better marmalade, I think, than oranges do. Dr Cox gave us eighteen dozen which Biddulph brought home from Wollongong in a sack, to the amazement of his horse. We have already boiled up eight dozen and mean to do about six dozen more, as the fruit cost nothing and sugar is cheap, and, as our supply of butter is precarious, it is very useful. The difficulty is to find receptacles for it all, as jars are hardly to be had. We have already filled all manner of pickle and mustard bottles, and for the next lot we shall be reduced to coffee tins.

Biddulph has also been doing a little in the butchering line today, as we have been cutting up a little pig which a benevolent neighbour slew on Saturday for us. We roasted a piece of him (not the neighbour) for dinner, and I stuffed it with sage and onions to my own, and Biddulph's, admiration. The pig was killed in honour of Annie and Amy's return, but that happy event has been put off so many times that it is possible we may have to eat all the pork ourselves.

Annie has been absent twenty, and Amy ten, weeks. If my coming has done no other good, it has enabled the former to have a nice holiday, and she has thoroughly enjoyed her stay in Sydney. They have been very gay there, having been to the theatre very often, and to two public balls, besides "friendly" parties. We expect them back tonight, or rather tomorrow morning, but it looks so threatening that I doubt if they will come.

July 17th. Annie and Amy arrived this morning to breakfast; both are looking very well, but of course they are rather tired by their journey. Biddulph could only stay and talk to them for a little while, and then he set off to Illawarra to look at the land he intends to buy.

Of course you have heard from them full particulars about Amy's wedding, etc. I do not like the idea of not being present, and yet it will be better for Annie. They are busy unpacking now, but they have left most of their smart clothes at Sydney till they go down there again, as it is no use to convey them backwards and forwards.

I have to go to Appin with the English letters, which must be posted today. Good-bye, my dearest Etta.

Ever your affectionate sister,

RACHEL HENNING

[*Following Amy's marriage to Thomas Sloman on 6th September 1855, she went to Bathurst, which was to become her home. In the following letter Rachel writes to her from Appin. About this time Biddulph bought land on Bulli Mountain. He described it as being "as beautifully situated as it can possibly be. It stands very high, about 1000 ft above the level of the sea, and you look down over the mountain and see the whole district of Illawarra lying at your feet with the broad sea in front. You can see every vessel that goes to or returns from Sydney, as they keep very near the shore. Although only a short distance from Appin, it is like*

31

*going into a new country; the trees and vegetation are entirely
different. Vines and all sorts of clematis climb to the treetops
and hang down in festoons to the ground. Below the tall trees
are all sorts of smaller trees; cabbage-trees, palm- and fern-trees.
The bush at Appin is quite open, and you can ride through it in
any direction; but at Bulli Mountain there is an impenetrable
wall of green; you can't, in many places, get a yard off the road,
the vines and creepers are so matted together, and grow so rankly.*

*"I bought 180 acres at about twenty-five shillings an acre.
There was some of the finest timber in Illawarra on my land,
both hardwood and brush timber. I engaged men to clear part
of the land, but the expense was very heavy. The agreement
was that they felled all trees not over six feet diameter, but it
left several to the acre over, up to nine feet.*

*"I put up a small place at first in 1855, which was afterwards
used as a kitchen, men's room, etc., and later built a nice cottage
with one large sitting-room with French lights and four bedrooms, with a veranda in front with a splendid view of the
district and ocean. The timber was cut on the ground and the
cottage was put up by a runaway ship's carpenter. It was floored
and lined with sassafras, and doors costing £1 and windows 30s.
made of cedar. The cedar from a small tree I found on my
land. The sitting-room had a stone chimney, which was built
for me by a man who had been convicted by my grandfather,
John Henning, of Poxwell, Dorset. He did not tell me the nature
of his offence. I think the whole building only cost me £60."]*

ELLADALE COTTAGE,
APPIN,

SEPTEMBER 21ST 1855

My Dearest Amy,

I hope that by this time you are safely arrived at your new
home. You must have had a pleasant journey, as here the
weather has been beautiful. I am longing to hear all about it.
How you like the place and people. Annie promised to write
me a long letter as soon as she arrived, so tell her not to forget.

There is little to tell you about Appin, as usual. Biddulph
was very busy on Monday, as Nicholls killed a calf (it was not
a fatted one) to supply the men on the mountain with meat,
and he had to fetch wood and water besides writing English
letters.

After the usual scrimmage we got him off at about eleven

o'clock on Tuesday, with two packhorses laden with provisions, and Nicholls's mare. Fanny is completely laid up for the present, as I knew would be the case, for she is not fit for a packhorse. He took Josh Nicholls with him, and, of course, intended to reach the mountain that evening, but all the bridges had been washed away in the rains, and he had to encamp for the night with the surveyor's men who are making the road. He unloaded the horses, but did not hobble them properly, and Jack and the little mare quietly walked home before morning, leaving Nicholls's mare, which had been more securely tied, to carry the whole load the rest of the way. Luckily it was only a mile or two, and Josh brought her back last Wednesday evening looking none the worse for her exertions.

Biddulph sent word he should be back on Saturday evening, so I hope he will. I see no prospect of the kitchen being built yet, as they are building a hut for stores instead; if it is up by November it will be a wonder.

Lucy, the servant, went down and washed at the waterhole yesterday, to save bringing up water. She is much elated by one of the men having sent her a message by Josh, and I am thankful to say she has given up tears for the present. She does everything, and I have no trouble except the infliction occasionally of a string of Irish anecdotes.

I sent Mrs Sparling the wedding cake by Biddulph, as I thought otherwise I might have to take it myself. I have seen nothing of her, and whether her curiosity about the wedding will be sufficient to make her ascend that spirited steed of hers and come up here remains to be proved.

I have just been writing to Mrs Macdonald. She wrote to me to inquire about your plans, as she had received no answer to her letters to you, and she wanted to see you before you went to Bathurst. I told her how short a time you were in Sydney after you were married and that you could not manage to see her. I also gave her an account of the wedding, and informed her that I was not going home at present.

I never half thanked you for my share of the smart things for the wedding. I wish you had got more for yourself and less for us.

Remember me very kindly to Mr Sloman, and with kindest love to Annie and yourself. Believe me,

Your very affectionate sister,

RACHEL HENNING

My Dearest Etta,

It is most vexing that I have not been able to send off your parcel before, as most of the things are suited for winter and now it will not reach you till the spring; but I could not help it. I was detained at Appin so long then when I got to Sydney the case had to be made, and finally Mr Hirst, who undertakes the sending-off part, advised its going direct from here by the *Wimera* instead of being shipped to Melbourne and thence on by one of the mail-packets.

There is something from each of us for you, my dearest Etta. I have marked them from whom they come, and though they will arrive late, I hope they will still be of use next winter.

Amy sends you a cloth mantle. Also a scarf for the neck. You must not think this latter old-fashioned, it *is* an old fashion revived again, but everybody wears them here and I think them pretty. There is also a brown ribbon which she brought from England with her. She told me to put it in as it may do for a common bonnet. She also sends her own and Mr Sloman's likenesses. Hers is pretty good, though rather fierce-looking. Mr Sloman should not have stuck a rose in his buttonhole.

Annie sends a winter dress, also a collar and ribbon. I chose the two latter as well as Amy's scarf, so I must be considered responsible for them. I hope you will like them. I hope also you will like the silk dress. It is rather dark, but it was meant for winter, and you do not get such a choice of things here as you do in England. I could by no means get any trimming to match the peach-coloured stripe, so I got a black velvet trimming for jacket and sleeves. I think the colour will be very becoming to you. How I should like to see you in it!

Do you remember my buying wools to make you an antimacassar when I was at Exeter with you? I did not finish it in time for the last parcel, so I send it now. You must have thought it a long time coming.

Biddulph sends Mr Boyce the skin of a duckbill, as a specimen of the natural curiosities of Australia. I have peppered it well, and I hope it is too dry to produce another crop of those gigantic maggots of which the last consignment from Australia seemed chiefly to consist. He also sends Mr Boyce a book of Australian views. They are not very splendid, as works of art, but you will like to see them. I have put a cross against the places we know among them.

We have sent Mama's likeness that Mr Boyce may copy it for you. I need not ask you to take care of it, and send it back again. The copy will be better than the original if the dress and hair are modernised.

I dare say that when Mr Boyce sees the box unpacked he will walk out in the garden in disgust, under the impression that Biddulph has favoured him with a present of a few of his old clothes which have become too bad for the bush. However, the ancient coat, trousers and waistcoat, which you will find packed up, are only sent as patterns. Clothes are so dear and so bad out here that he wants a lot from England. He means to get them from Manchester if he can, and has written to Mr Ellesworth about it, but if he cannot manage it Biddulph will ask you to get them for him, either from London or Taunton; the latter would be better, as Jeanes makes well and cheaply.

He wants three shooting jackets, one black and two coloured; two pair of trousers and three waistcoats; three suits in all, but you had better not do anything about it till you hear from him himself. I don't think he will write to Mr Ellesworth by this mail.

When the clothes come out we want several other things in the parcel.

December 21st. I wrote so far nearly a week ago, and since that I have written to you by the *Lightening*, which letter, I suppose, you will get first. Now I have to finish this in a great hurry, as I have just received a letter from Biddulph to tell me that he will meet me with a horse at Wollongong on Saturday, and as I shall have to start by the steamboat at eight o'clock tomorrow morning, I have to finish this letter tonight, as the *Wimera* will have sailed before I return to Sydney.

With much love to Mr Boyce and yourself,

RACHEL HENNING

REDFERN,
MARCH 3RD 1856

My Dearest Annie,[17]

I must write to you today, as it is your birthday, to wish you many happy returns of it. If anyone ought to have a happy life, you ought, but I am afraid the chances of it are small in Australia.

This is the third birthday you have spent in this country. I

17 Annie at this time was staying with Amy at Bathurst.

35

wish it could be the last you would spend here. Do you remember the last before you left home? We were at Ventnor; it was a fine, cold spring day, and we took a walk over the cliffs towards St Laurence's and found the first primroses by a stream. It was at Danehill in 1854, and that also was a lovely day, and Etta and Mr Boyce and I took a beautiful walk to Horsted Lake, in the afternoon. I have been looking back in my old diaries to see what we were doing, the first time I have ventured to look at them for months. Oh, Annie, if we were but all at home together once more!

I don't want this to be a dismal letter if I can help it, so I will leave the dangerous subject and tell you about Lizzie's christening party. Somehow it was not a very brilliant affair, as Captain Tucker did not keep up the dancing with much spirit, and the music was so wretchedly bad.

The Woolleys, Stewarts, Chapmans, etc., were there. Lizzie Tucker played the first quadrille, and a most doleful tune it was, like the Old Hundredth, as Captain Fix, with whom I danced it, said. Emily next played a polka, so hopelessly out of time that I fairly stood still, and so on all the evening. The only good music we had was a set of quadrilles that Caroline and Lizzie played, and some waltzes which Matty and Katy Woolley did. There was a little singing and a very nice supper in the passage.

"... Captain Fix, with whom I danced."

I went away with the Hirsts[18] directly after supper, as Caroline did not like leaving the baby any longer. We got home very comfortably, as the Woolleys'[19] carriage took us to Market Street,

[18] Mrs Hirst was formerly Caroline Tucker.

[19] A Mr Woolley started the first omnibus service between Circular Quay and Redfern. There were very few houses between Redfern and Botany at this time.

where we got a cab. Mr Stephen went with us. The party was kept up till about twelve, they had a few more dances after supper and Captain Tucker sang "The Whale". I am sorry to have missed the last; it is such fun to hear him.

Emily came up here on Saturday and said that Lizzie was none the worse for her exertions. Lizzie Chapman talked of giving a party, but I expect it has come to nothing; the music is the great failure, unless you hire someone to play as the Woolleys always do.

You seem to have succeeded at Amy's party. One thing certainly is that Lizzie's piano is an atrocious one, and that no human power of fingers can get any sound out of it. Old Mrs Stewart was there and enjoyed herself very much; hers certainly is a wonderful recovery, and it has made Emily quite a convert to homoeopathy, but I do not believe one word of it. She got well because the complaint had worn itself out and was best let alone. Most complaints are. I was so poorly all last week—weak and feverish and whatnot—that I dare say I should have sent for the doctor at home, but I let it alone and I am right enough now.

Biddulph writes word to say that the woodwork of the house will be up in "two months or ten weeks" (say three months, allowing for his sanguine calculations), and that will bring us into the middle of winter; and as the house will be built entirely of green wood, which will shrink about an inch to the foot with fire inside and sun outside, you may fancy how fit the place will be to inhabit for six months or so.

Besides, there is a stone chimney to be built and the shingles to be split and put on, for the carpenters he has engaged do not do that, and as the stone has to be quarried out before it is put up, that house can't be habitable till next spring or summer, and by that time it is ten to one that he will be obliged to give up the whole concern; and I have stayed about four months and may stay another six without doing him any good. I have been in a great fidget these last few days as to what I can possibly do with myself.

I am wearing myself as thin as a lath, that being a sensible proceeding to which I am much given, as soon as anything goes wrong. I do so wish I had gone home last autumn, for I have done no one any good by staying, and even if Biddulph stays on that accursed mountain, he is so used to being alone now that you could spend two-thirds of your time with Amy and other friends. But now that the Boyces have left Danehill and no longer expect me, it is too late.

37

I am very anxious for the next letters from England; we ought to hear something of the rest of Biddulph's money soon, and I want to know where Etta is and how she is getting on.

Kindest love to dear Amy. I do hope she will soon be in Sydney.

Ever your affectionate

RACHEL HENNING

BATHURST,
APRIL 17TH 1856

My Dearest Annie,

I have been longing to write to you, because from the last glimpse I had of your dear face at the railway station, I am so afraid you vexed yourself thinking I hated the journey so. It was not particularly pleasant, certainly, but like everything, far worse in anticipation than reality.

I got on famously and had nothing disagreeable anywhere. The ride to Penrith that night was rather pleasant, as it was very fine and there were only two people besides myself in the coach, an old farmer and a young digger. The latter went all the way, and was very civil to me in helping me and my goods in and out of the coach.

He was not quite a gentleman, nor yet a common man. The

"The ascent of the Blue Mountains on the Penrith side was almost impassable."

roads were in a most awful state. The driver from Penrith to Hartley said he had never seen them so bad. The ascent of the Blue Mountains on the Penrith side was almost impassable. We went along for four or five miles with the axle-tree buried in mud. I cannot think how ever the horses did it at all.

We passed a carriage stuck in the mud, which two horses had not been able to pull out, so they had been taken out and were standing by the side of the road, while a gentleman, up to his knees in mud, and a stupid Irishman were trying to fasten four bullocks to the carriage. Our coachman got down and helped them, remarking that very likely we should want to be dragged out soon. However, we managed to get along, and only came to grief once. We went through the bush to avoid the sea of mud in the main road, and one of the leaders got frightened and turned off among the trees, dragging the coach against some saplings and nearly upsetting it. The restive horse was taken out of the harness, and the passengers got out while the coach was backed out of the scrape.

The road was better when we got to the top of the mountains, though bad enough everywhere. It was a cloudy day and yet there was no rain, or none to speak of, and as we did get along I preferred the mud to the dust.

There were only three passengers besides me: the young man going to the diggings, and two women. One seemed like a shop-keeper and the other was, I think, a girl going to service. Both were going beyond Bathurst.

The view down Mount Victoria was very fine, certainly, but not equal to Snowdon by any means.

It has rocks and woods and is more extensive perhaps, but it wants water. I should have enjoyed it more, also, though I am no great coward, if we had not been going at a hard trot down that steep hill with an unguarded precipice on the left down which a coach was upset some time ago, and eleven passengers either killed or maimed.

I was fortunate in getting a comfortable room to myself at Hartley, while the other two "ladies" had to sleep together, and as it was clean, I had a good night's rest. Supper I had none, as there was nothing eatable—raw beef and bad pork, but the biscuits and wine were a resource. The last day's journey was the most tiresome, as the sun came out very hot and gave me a headache, and in the afternoon there was a heavy thunderstorm. It did not last long, but it come down a pelt while it did. I was not very wet, however, owing to the shawls and umbrella, but you may fancy I got in a great state of mud.

How curious those Bathurst plains are, when you first see them, so many miles without a single tree. Although there had been so much rain elsewhere, the road was quite dusty within fifteen miles of Bathurst. Mr Sloman did not drive to meet me, as he could not leave the office, but he met me at the coach office and walked home with me. Amy was looking very well and very glad to see me, and I was rejoiced to be there and have some tea and go to bed early, which I did. I was not so very tired, however. I can bear shaking about better than most people, all my bones are set so loosely!

Bathurst is an ugly place enough. All brick and dust. Amy's house is not beautiful, but it is comfortable inside, and I think I shall like being here for a time very much.

The piano is a capital one. I had no idea it was so good. Amy has a very bad servant who does not know anything, and has just made an open tart without putting any fat in the paste. Of course it has dried up to a cinder.

Ever, my dearest Annie, your affectionate sister,

RACHEL HENNING

BATHURST,
MAY 14TH 1856

My Dearest Etta,

Thank you, dear, for the parcel you have sent us by Theophilus.[20] It was very kind of you, and yet I am almost sorry you did; you must have so much to do with your money. I shall be delighted to have a ring of your hair, and I am so much obliged to you for sending me one. We have not received the parcel yet, because Theophilus has not come up to Sydney from Melbourne, but I hope he will either come or send it soon.

Thank Mr Boyce very much for sending me *Hiawatha*. I should like to see it, though neither he nor anybody else speaks very well of it.

It is so pleasant to find you both speaking as if you would like to have me in England, and you can never know how much I wish to be there. Sometimes I think I shall spend next winter with you. Amy will soon be comfortably settled in Sydney within a few hours' reach of Annie, and Annie likes nothing better than Sydney life; and Biddulph has now been so much used to being alone that I do not think he will mind it while Annie visits her Sydney friends—and I do not think it could now be wrong of me

20 Theophilus Biddulph.

40

to come home—before I am too much acclimatized to this country and everyone has forgotten me in England, both of which would happen if I stayed for the ten years that I believe Aunt wishes.

I should have certainly returned with Tregenna if I had been in Sydney when he went, but he made up his mind very suddenly, and I was here at Bathurst, so that it would have been the greatest scramble to get off, and I should not have liked to leave Amy to do the packing alone, and I should rather see her safe over the journey, which she rather dreads.

It seems absurd to talk of dreading a journey of about 120 miles, which in England we should do in about four hours, but it really is no trifle here. We take three days about it, the roads are so bad that we get nearly shaken to pieces, and the inns at which we have to stop are in general so swarming with insects of all description that sleep is nearly out of the question.

I left Sydney on a Monday and arrived at Bathurst the Wednesday afternoon following. It is a disagreeable journey to make alone, to say nothing of the open coach and the jolting.

I cannot say I admire the "city" of Bathurst. It stands in the midst of the Bathurst Plains without a tree or shrub near it. It is all built of red brick, stone being unknown in the district, and it blazes away in the sun, being the most boiling place in summer and the coldest in winter that is to be found in Australia. It looks large at a distance, because the houses are scattered about at long distances from each other, as if it had rained brick buildings. There is an immense square, or rather open space, in the middle of the town on which are scattered a church, which is called "Norman", though I hope the Normans were never guilty of such architecture. A Romish church, with a big square tower of no particular order, and a Scotch church all over pinnacles, a Dissenting chapel, a prison with a huge brick wall round it; a bank and various shops; all one mass of red brick.

What they call "plains" are in fact low hills, covered with tufts of brown grass. In England we should call them downs, and they must be like the American "rolling prairie", only the latter is said to be covered with the most beautiful grass and flowers, while nothing can be more barren than these are.

I sometimes go up a little hill that is near this house and the view from the top is not exactly beautiful, but very curious, being so utterly un-English. There are these undulating hills, stretching round you for miles, without a tree or shrub upon them, in a hollow below you lies the red town, scattering itself over a large space of ground. The Macquarie River winds along near it, and you can trace its course through the treeless landscape by the fringe of swamp-oaks that grow here and there on its margin. There being no water in it except a pool here and there; you would not know there was a river save for these dismal trees. They are the most melancholy of vegetable productions. Cypresses are gay to them. They are quite black at a little distance, and only grow in muddy, slimy places. The background of the whole scene is the best part of it, as it consists (on two sides) of the beautiful "Blue Mountains". They are clothed with bush to their very summits and make a beautiful contrast to the weary plains.

In one part of the road, as I crossed them, the scenery was magnificent. Annie says better than Snowdon, but there she was wrong. However, it really is very fine for Australia.

I suppose Annie and Amy have told you all about the latter's house and cabbage garden, for at present there is little but cabbages in it, and "Bathurst burrs", an uncomfortable sort of vegetable, something like a thistle with sharp spiny leaves and little hooked burrs which stick on to everything. The plant grows in the very streets (?) of Bathurst, and we never go out without coming home stuck all over with them.

Amy has a dull Irish servant who the other day, coming home from chapel, fell into the "creek", a dry watercourse, some seven or eight feet deep, and as it is utterly unguarded, it is a perfect trap for the tipsy inhabitants of Bathurst—by far the largest part of the population. Mary was not tipsy, but she fell in in the dark, and having been fished out by some benevolent individual, she came home one mass of burrs and in a highly disconsolate condition.

Ever, dearest Etta, your most affectionate sister,

RACHEL HENNING

[*Later in 1856 Rachel, terribly homesick, left Australia for Eng-land by the* Star of Peace, *and arrived on 15th October 1856. She stayed for nearly five years with the Boyces and other rela-tions in different parts of England. While she was away Biddulph sold his Bulli property (in 1857) to Henry Osborne, for he had been offered the chance of going to Queensland to gain station experience, with the prospect of getting a property himself. "Osborne," wrote Biddulph, "was buying all the land he could about, with a view to the future value of the timber and the coal underneath. I realized all I had expended on the property."*]

My Dearest Annie,

I have left my Australian letters very late this time, and they must be posted this evening. I intended to write yesterday, but had a bad headache and could not. It is now half past eleven o'clock a.m. I am sitting at the round table in "The Mount" drawing-room, having pushed into a corner sundry and various ornaments, books, etc., to make room for my writing-desk, a very nice Russia-leather machine, which Mr Boyce gave me on my last birthday.

Aunt and myself are just returned from St James's Church, where we have been to see Tregenna and Bella united in the bonds of holy matrimony. So I cannot do better than tell you all about it.

Tregenna has been a very assiduous lover, much more so than I expected; he has been continually at "The Elms", also riding with Bella a great deal. She also has been up here a great many times and I like her much, so I think will you when you see her; she is good-tempered and agreeable.

Although Aunt would not go to the breakfast, she took it into her head to go to church as if she was one of the wedding party, so when I came down to breakfast this morning, which was at eight, an hour earlier than usual, I found her in no end of a get-up, as Tregenna expressed it, in a blue flounced silk.

Tregenna also was there, looking very gentlemanly in a black morning-coat and grey trousers, and looking much better than his brother, who appeared next, very fine in a claret-coloured coat and lilac waistcoat, also grey trousers. Then Rachel,[21] with some difficulty, got her hoops through the door, in a light blue silk over which she had put on the white silk jacket she wore at her own wedding, and finally, very late, came Mr ——, whose collar had slipped down so as to be invisible, and who was vehemently assailed by Rachel because he had white pearl buttons in a drab waistcoat like a coachman, as she averred. Rachel's little girl came in with a clean white frock, so short and starched to such an extent that when she leaned out of the window the consequences were awful.

Tregenna was armed with the licence in his pocket, duly addressed "To our well-beloved in Christ, Thomas T. B.", etc., the ring on his little finger for security and eight guineas neatly

21 A relative of Rachel Henning's

done up in white paper. He was in capital spirits and neither shy nor nervous.

We had breakfast—veal pie and beef, if you are curious on that score—and then we all began to fidget because the clergyman who was to perform the ceremony—a Mr Coleman, who was a schoolfellow of Tregenna's at Bromsgrove—had not arrived. However, he came when we had all done breakfast and pitched manfully into the pie. Then we went up and dressed.

Rachel, who was going to the breakfast, was a great turn-out, and looked very well in the aforesaid blue dress and white opera cloak and lace bonnet. Tregenna's groomsman breakfasted at "The Elms". He, Tregenna and Mr Coleman preferred walking to church, through the by-lanes, which they did, Mr Coleman carrying his surplice in a carpet-bag.

All Aunt's servants turned out to see the fun, carrying baby between them, and Mrs Durin was left to take care of the house. Two carriages came up for our party, with postillions in white favours, etc., and very absurd it was. Into one of them got Uncle and Aunt, the latter in white gloves and an old bonnet with a white veil to hide it, and drove off. Rachel, Mr —— and I got into the other carriage, when to our horror we found it had only one seat, being meant for but two people.

Mr —— refused to sit on Rachel's lap, and with her hoops it was impossible he could sit between us, so he stood up with his back in a sort of arch. We pulled down all the blinds that the people might not see, and of course laughed all the way.

We found the church tolerably full. Tregenna was in the vestry taking a lesson in the marriage service from Mr Coleman, and Chapman—you remember him—generally paraded the church, very affable, with an astonishing shirt-frill and what looked like a white peony in his buttonhole.

Well, we waited about ten minutes, when a single carriage drew up, and presently Chapman ushered up the aisle two bridesmaids, a large one and a little one. They looked very awkward, and, finding no one else arrived, they decamped again, to wait for the rest of the party in the porch. Not long after, the wedding party appeared, Bella walking with her father and six bridesmaids next.

Bella wore a worked muslin, with a mantle of the same, a chip bonnet with water-lilies and the same inside, mixed with green grass. The bridesmaids were very prettily dressed, in white tarlatan and jackets of the same, white lace bonnets and rosebuds inside. They were Bella's three sisters, Georgy and two other young ladies.

44

Mr Coleman read the service very well, but bestowed the whole of it upon them, homily and all, a great mistake, I think. Bella behaved very well, and Tregenna said afterwards he never felt less nervous in his life.

We went into the vestry, saw the names signed and I think Uncle shook hands with all the bride's party; then they filed

"Then they filed down the church."

down the church and departed and Uncle, Aunt and myself came home.

I expect Rachel in directly, as she said she should not stay a moment after Tregenna and Bella were gone. They leave by the express for London, where they will stay about a week and then go to Preston. I believe they mean to come back here again before they leave England.

I came here on May 28th by the express. I always go by the express when I can. I think it is the Australian coaches that have given me such a love for fast travelling. I like being here very much.

And believe me, dearest Annie, your most affectionate sister,

RACHEL HENNING

25 PORTLAND SQUARE,
JANUARY 6TH 1858

My Dearest Annie,

I was very glad to get your letter by the *Red Jacket*. It is very kind of you to write so often, my own Annie, when you must be so very busy between taking care of dear Amy, and of your home on the mountain.

You must have a great deal on your hands, and yet it must be pleasant to you to feel that you are so useful, and helpful to everybody. I was sorry to hear that Mr Sloman had taken a house at Paddington instead of the one he had in contemplation at Redfern. It is so very lonely for Amy, when he is away and so far from all her friends. I dare say, however, that her baby will give her employment enough now.

Bristol does not supply much that is amusing to tell you. We went the week before last to hear *The Messiah* performed at the Victoria rooms at Clifton, and I was very much pleased, for, though the solo singers were not first-rate, the choruses were very good. They gave the "Hallelujah Chorus" with great energy.

I have lately accompanied Mary on some secret missions for the benefit of Mr Cates. He wished to have a photograph likeness of her.

We went to an awfully stupid evening at the Hollins's Monday night. Mr Hollins is the incumbent of St Clement's. They had invited a number of rather underbred young people to meet us, and the only entertainment of the evening was music, each young lady singing rather worse than her predecessor. I hardly ever heard such inferior performances. Mr Boyce was so disgusted he said he would not go out any more, and I am sure I hope he will not, for I hate that sort of party.

I have been reduced to the unhappy necessity of taking a district! Fancy me, and the good my visitations are likely to do the people! However, they have not visitors enough, and I could not help myself.

". . . each young lady singing rather worse than her predecessor."

January 7th. I am finishing my letter, having just finished packing the box for Australia. If it gives you one half the pleasure to receive it as it has us to get the things and send them, it will be welcomed in Australia.

I hope you will like the silk dress we have sent you. I wanted a blue, as I think you look well in that colour. I tried for a larger pattern, but could not get one. There are fourteen yards, so make the dressmaker put you a double skirt or a very full single one, if you cannot get a trimming to match well. Nothing looks prettier than rows of black velvet. Etta has a light green trimmed so and Kate had a blue. Those pink braces are to wear with your white dress, the bow goes behind and the ribbon over the shoulders, like capes, and the ends cross in front, fastened with a broach or bouquet. They are fashionable here, but should you not like them, the ribbon will do for something else.

I send back a portrait of Papa which belongs to you, and which was packed in my flower-chest and brought away by mistake, also a picture of Biddulph's, and two antimacassars, which last I am afraid you have wanted in the new house.

Mr Arnold sent me the *Press* lately to read a review of his on the life of Miss Brontë (author of *Jane Eyre*), which has just been published. I should much like to read the book itself, but we never get any new works here, for we only subscribe to the Athenaeum library, and they are deep in debt and cannot afford to purchase new books.

Miss Brontë is said to have been just what she describes Jane Eyre, little and plain, and quaint in dress and manner. Perhaps you will see the book in Sydney. I must make an end now, my own darling sister. You cannot think how I want to see you and Biddulph sometimes. I feel as if I would give anything for a sight of you. With very much love, believe me,

Ever your most affectionate sister,

RACHEL HENNING

[*In February 1861 Rachel Henning decided to return to Australia after an absence of nearly five years. The next few letters are addressed to her sister, Etta Boyce, with whom she had been staying in England.*]

ANGEL HOTEL,
LIVERPOOL,
FEBRUARY 14TH 1861

My Dearest Etta,

I hope you received this morning the little note I scribbled in the railway carriage on hearing from one of the passengers that we should be just in time to post it as we drove to the hotel. We got through the journey very well and comfortably and without at all feeling the cold. It turned out a much better day than we expected.

The "black country" between Dudley and Wolverhampton was most curious. The whole country ploughed up for miles by mines and covered with furnaces and tall chimneys and wretched brick houses. We got all the luggage safe, and drove to the Waterloo Hotel, which was full, so we went on to the Angel in Dale Street, which is very comfortable and clean. We had tea and poached eggs, settled accounts and went to bed. Mr Boyce said he was hardly at all tired. I was rather.

This morning Mr Boyce went out to Baines's office, where he met with Captain Gray, and on his mentioning my name to him he remembered me perfectly at Melbourne and said he would call on me, which he did, and very kind it was, considering all he must have to do on the eve of his ship sailing. He is a most jolly and genial-looking sailor, speaking broad Lancashire. He talked much of Annie and Biddulph, and seemed to be greatly struck with the wonderful cleverness of the former in learning navigation; said she could calculate the latitude from an observation much faster than he could.

We went to the wharf at three, only Mr Boyce and I, took all my luggage on board, except the carpet-bags, and saw my cabin. It is a comfortable little place enough, the berths look very much so, and my cabin companion has been so ill advised as to take the upper one, which I am very glad of.

I heard at Baines's office who my cabin companion was—a Mrs Bronchordt. They said she was a nice lady-like person, but I shall have to find out about that.

The last steamer, which is only for the first-class passengers, goes off at five o'clock tomorrow evening. I do not suppose Mr Boyce will be allowed to go on board with me, as it is against the rules

February 15th. Since writing the above we have been on board the ship again. Neither Mrs Bronchordt, my cabin companion, nor her luggage had arrived, so we took possession of the cabin and I unpacked and I put some things in order, while Mr Boyce screwed up the little cupboard in a convenient corner and made things look quite comfortable.

Captain Gray was on board and was very kind to me. We came back in the "tug" about three o'clock, with him, and he then informed us that I need not go on board till nine o'clock tomorrow morning, a reprieve for which I was very thankful. The evening is a dismal time to go among strangers, especially with the knowledge that the ship is lying near shore and that I might as well be there. She will probably sail about noon, but nobody seems to know exactly. Mr Boyce will see me off, and then start for Kirby Lonsdale at 11.30.

The Angel Hotel is very comfortable. We dined at four today, after returning from the boat, and since that Mr Boyce has been taking a nap and is now reading *Punch* while I write.

I do not like to end; it seems like saying good-bye again, but I cannot write for ever. Everything is well, and I am going out under the best circumstances. Captain Gray is most kind, and I am sure I shall be taken care of.

Kiss those darling children for me, and farewell, my own dearest sister.

Ever your most affectionate sister,

RACHEL HENNING

"GREAT BRITAIN",
SUNDAY, FEBRUARY 17TH, 1861

My Dearest Etta,

You will be surprised to hear from me again, as no doubt you are thinking today that I am half-way down the Irish Channel; but, although we seemed to start yesterday, the ship only went a short distance down the river and then anchored again. There was some hitch about her papers, the captain said.

I am very much afraid we shall not put in at St Vincent's. I have not had an opportunity of asking the captain, but the passengers say that she never stops anywhere now, so do not be uneasy, dear, if you do not hear, as I am afraid there will be no opportunity of writing till I reach Melbourne. Of course, if there is the smallest chance, as a passing ship, etc., I shall write.

After I sent off my letter yesterday, we were called to dinner. By the steward's advice Mrs Bronchordt and I sat down at the top of the captain's table next him, but I do not think that otherwise we have got among a very interesting set of people. There are several commercial gentlemen, or rather not gentlemen, and a little Scotchman, who looks more polished, also a pretty German, wife to one of the commercials, and who cannot speak a word of English. They are all very civil and unoffending, however.

The first evening was sure to be rather dull and dismal. However, we got books and sat round a candle in the saloon (where they have candles in dishes instead of lamps. I should think, in rough weather, the consequences would be disastrous), till nine o'clock, when Mrs Bronchordt and myself betook ourselves to bed.

I had been busy all day arranging my goods, so everything came to hand very easily, and Mrs Bronchordt is very civil and accommodating. I think we shall get on very nicely.

The cabin is so light that I can read well in bed, and the lamp shines into my berth, so, that being the case, I have nailed up a moreen bag just within reach of my hand, and put a little store of books into it; also my lantern matches, camphor, etc.

It was not to be expected that we should sleep very soundly the first night, especially as a baby cried in the next cabin considerably. What a life its poor mother will have when we get to sea and she and the children are all seasick! Of course the ship is now as steady as possible, but that will not last long. The stewardess called us at eight and brought a jug of hot water, an unexpected luxury, and we managed about dressing very well, as I got up first.

I am so well provided with everything I want that there never seems any difficulty; my dress and jacket are warm and comfortable and everything just right. How nicely you helped me in all that shopping. The bag of tools is worth its weight in gold. I have driven innumerable nails for Mrs Bronchordt and myself, and though the steward did come and inquire if the carpenter was in our cabin yesterday, as he was particularly wanted, no one has found any fault with the nails, and the cupboard which Mr Boyce screwed up behind the funnel has never been seen and is most useful.

They do not feed you so well on board this ship as they did in the *Calcutta*. There is a quantity of food, but it is coarse; great joints of pork and underdone mutton and chiefly cold. However, the first day is not a fair sample, and when the captain is on board and we are fairly off, no doubt all will go on smoother. I have not see Captain Gray since I came on board yesterday. They say he is to come off at twelve, and that we shall sail with the top of the tide at three today.

Some of the gentlemen went on shore again last night, to return this morning. The people are very impatient to be off now; it must be very tantalizing for those who have friends in Liverpool.

I am very well content, dear, though a little lonely. There is nothing to complain of in the ship or passengers so far, though I do not see many who *look* as if I should care about them. Mrs Bronchordt is very kind and pleasant, but I do not think there is much in her.

I am writing in the saloon, after breakfast, with a great many people writing round me, for the last mail. The doctor appeared at breakfast today, a droll little man, extremely like Vincent Macey, when we *first* knew him, and covered with yellow buttons to express his being an officer. I hope I shall never want him, and it is most unlikely.

There is no clergyman on board, which I am sorry for; there

is a Scotch minister in the second class, who will hold a service, I believe, in the saloon this morning and preach, but I like our prayers and shall presently read them and the psalms and lessons to myself, while you are in your corner at St Werbey's reading the same. How I should like to be there with you!

The captain sits at the top of the dining-table, next the mast. Mrs Bronchordt sits next him at his right, and next her I sit; then a Mr Brand, a Scotchman; the pretty German and her husband sit opposite, and the "commercials" down the same side. I can tell you nothing about the inhabitants of the different cabins, as, of course, I know none of them. I rather like a stout, good-natured woman, who inhabits, with her husband, the one opposite to ours; but she is not a lady.

The "ladies' boudoir" which they talk about is a nice little room enough, but rather dark and chiefly used by the children. I shall probably sit in the saloon, most likely where I am sitting now by the table just opposite the entrance to my cabin. I shall begin the pinafores tomorrow. I am so glad to have them to do.

I know you will think of the *Great Britain* when you pray for "all that travel by land or by water". Oh, how I should like to see your dear face once more before going! But all is right, and I am going hopefully and cheerfully. This letter seems all about myself, but you will like to hear all I can tell you about my new abode.

Ever your most affectionate sister,

RACHEL HENNING

OFF QUEENSTOWN,
FRIDAY, FEBRUARY 22ND, 1861

My Dearest Etta,

Unless you have heard by the papers that the *Great Britain* has put into Queenstown, you will be nearly as much astonished at the sight of my writing as you would be if I myself were to walk in. How I wish I could. It seems so tantalizing to be detained, perhaps for days, within a few hours' sail of Bristol. Still, the *Great Britain* might set forth again without me if I paid you a visit, perhaps.

I must tell you our adventures in due order, and most thankful I am to be able to tell them you, for when we lost a boat overboard yesterday I was quite miserable to think of the state of anxiety in which you might be kept for months as to the fate of this ship, for the boat and oars had the name of "Great Britain" on them, and, if washed ashore, might at least have given rise to great apprehensions as to what had become of us in the awful gales we have met with since leaving Liverpool.

We sailed, as you know, on Sunday the 17th, had a quiet night enough, and Monday was tolerably calm till the evening, when it began to blow; and during the night we had such a gale as is seldom met with. It *did* blow with a vengeance. The captain and all the officers were on deck all night; indeed, the former has not been in bed since we left Liverpool, such has been the weather. I saw him to speak to in the morning, and he said he had never had the *Great Britain* out in such weather before. However, there was no great damage done beyond making everyone, nearly, extremely ill and sorely frightened, and the wind went down in the course of the next day.

We had very rough weather during Tuesday and Wednesday, but still nothing remarkable, but yesterday morning it began to blow again, and for about six hours we had such a hurricane as no one on board ever saw before. To say that I never knew anything like it is nothing, but all the oldest sailors say a West Indian tornado was the only thing it was like.

Providentially it came by daylight; began about nine, and the worst was over by three. I could never give you the least idea of the force or roar of the wind, and some of the passengers who ventured on deck said the *Great Britain*, big as she is, looked like a cockleshell among the waves, and that it seemed impossible but she must be buried in them.

She behaved admirably, took in very little water, and came up as stiff as possible after every roll. Several seas came on board, however; one broke into the saloon and thence into the cabins, one of which was three feet deep in water. The steward mopped and dipped it out in buckets. Some water got into our cabin, and, on going in to investigate, I found that one of my boxes was standing in a puddle; and remembering that the children's likeness was at the bottom of that very box, I determined, gale or no gale, to unpack it and get the picture out, which I did.

It was not the least hurt, but it was so strange and sad to see their little smiling faces in such a scene. I was glad enough to think they were safe at home, and probably just going out for their walk, for the sun was shining, notwithstanding the fearful wind and sea. Nothing in the box got wet, so it was all right.

When I came back to the saloon I found all the passengers grouped about, looking grave and somewhat frightened, except one group of young men, who pretended to laugh over a game of cards, but who looked more alarmed than anyone when a harder squall than usual came on. I betook myself to a sofa at the end of the saloon to try and console some girls who were crying with terror, when the door opened and Captain Gray's cheerful face appeared. I asked him if the gale was abating, and he said yes, the worst was over and that he had never seen such a one before; and from then the wind went gradually down, leaving only a heavy swell, which has tumbled us about all night and is now making this writing almost illegible.

There was considerable damage done to repair which, we are now running into Queenstown as fast as steam can carry us. The foreyard was sprung and a sprit-sail hook broken; the bulwarks smashed in in one place and a boat stove in and half knocked away by a wave, and they had to cut her away as she was beating in the ship's side. This boat was a great affliction to me as the name of the ship was on her, but it will be all right now you can hear we are safe.

They report that one of the masts is sprung, but I cannot make out if it is true. How they ever stood at all I cannot imagine. The captain expected some of them to go, for he had axes laid all ready to cut away the wreck if they went overboard.

We have had a great escape, for which we are not half thankful enough.

We hope to be at Queenstown tonight, and this letter will go tomorrow morning. I do not know how long it will take to repair the ship, probably some days; so if you write by return of post the letter will probably reach me, and it will be such a pleasure to hear from home again. Put your full address, and if we are gone, the dead-letter office will return it to you.

We have made so little way that we have not been more than a day's sail from Liverpool all this time. I do not suppose they will leave Queenstown till a fair wind comes; it is no use beating about like this. We shall hardly be in Australia till the middle of May. It is very wearying prolonging the parting from England like this, but it is sure to be all right. It is such an inexpressible blessing to feel that it is all in better hands than ours; in a gale such as yesterday's it makes one not fear anything that may happen.

Although the voyage cannot be considered a very prosperous one so far, I have had more than my usual good fortune as to seasickness. I have generally been unwell for a few hours, but now I have not for a single hour of it, notwithstanding the bad weather. Mrs Bronchordt, too, has never been seasick at all, which is fortunate for me as well as herself, but she is headachey and poorly and seldom gets up to breakfast. I am rather glad she does not, as dressing with the ship at an angle of forty-five degrees is quite difficult enough for one person. We get on very comfortably together, as she is pleasant and accommodating, but there is no one on board of whom I know much as yet.

I rather like an old widow lady—a Mrs Ranken—she is Scotch and the coolest, quietest person I ever saw. She is going for the fifth time, and minds gales no more than nothing. Curiously enough, she is aunt to that Miss Ranken with whom I came home in the *Star of Peace*, knows Bathurst and Mr Sloman and has seen Annie and Amy there. She is very good and kind to the sick people, nurses roaring babies whose mothers and nurses are ill.

I have also made acquaintance with a rather dismal young lady, who is going out by herself and is sorely frightened, and a Scotch lady with two children and a sort of turban headdress, who is more frightened; besides a speaking acquaintance with a great many people.

The commercials I mentioned before have resolved themselves into rather a gentlemanly little German, with whom I play cribbage, a large and radiant squatter, whom may Biddulph never grow like, though he is the picture of good nature; and an intelligent sort of man, who really is a merchant, I believe, and comes from Bristol, besides the Melbourne merchant with the pretty German wife.

These are the people among whom Mrs Bronchordt and I sit at dinner. They are not a very aristocratic set, but they might be worse, and it doesn't matter for two months.

Most of the people have been frightfully ill and some have not yet appeared. The old Scotch lady and myself were the only ladies that appeared for a long time. I think we fraternized because we neither of us mind anything much. I believe she is a good woman, too, though stiff and silent and "Scotchy".

The cabin is wet just now, but all my things are in pretty good order, thanks to my exertions that first day. Mrs Bronchordt's are rolling about in sore confusion. She is not very tidy. The berths are very comfortable and I sleep well, when the ship does not roll beyond measure.

I am at the end of my paper, and the difficulty of writing is extreme and of reading it probably greater. I shall be able to write again from Queenstown, perhaps more than once.

My kindest love to yourself, Mr Boyce and the children and Sophy, if still with you.

Ever, dearest Etta, your most affectionate sister,

RACHEL HENNING

My Dearest Etta,

It was quite pleasant to wake yesterday morning and find the ship quiet, and then to look out and see that we were steaming up the beautiful harbour of Queenstown. The sun was shining, the sea quite smooth and numbers of white-sailed ships dancing about and getting out of our way.

We were soon surrounded by shore boats, and the whole *Great Britain* population seemed to turn out upon Ireland. I went on shore with Mrs Bronchordt and a party of gentlemen

"*. . . swarming with children and pigs.*"

to see what was to be seen. We had a pleasant row across the harbour and soon got to Queenstown, which is built on a sort of precipice, the white houses rising, tier above tier, all up the hill and looking very well from a distance; but we soon got into a narrow, filthy street, swarming with children and pigs. Some parts of the town were much better, but we had soon seen all there was to see, and then we set off in a steamer for Cork.

The sail was most beautiful between low green hills covered with woods and gentlemen's houses peeping out, or sometimes wild heathy hills and downs. We were about an hour going to Cork, which, though rather dirty, was a better town than I expected. The population generally despise bonnets and go bareheaded, or put up hoods when it rains—not that they seem to have much to do.

We went to the Imperial Hotel and dined, and then set off in a real Irish car to visit the ruin of Blarney Castle. The country round Cork is beautiful, something like Devonshire. We had a real specimen of an Irishman in the driver, who would have blarneyed the head off your shoulders, to say nothing of the money out of your purse.

We walked up a hill and I saw the furze in blossom, and the hedges budding as I did not expect to see them again in England for a long time.

Blarney Castle is a most picturesque ruin, and we went to the top and saw the famous Blarney stone.

We drove back to Cork intending to return to Queenstown by train, but were too late, and so had to get back by a most circuitous route, by train to Passaje, then a mile in cars to Monkstown, then we crossed a long ferry, then performed a night march of two miles over some very dirty roads, to Mrs Bronchordt's great horror, and at last got to Queenstown about eight, when we took a boat for the *Great Britain*.

The moonlight row across the harbour was lovely and sea like glass, the Queenstown lights reflected in the water and the ships dotted about and all showing different lights. It was a pretty scene. I thought as we came along that Mr Boyce was probably about then arrived at home, and was telling you about his adventures and our Liverpool experiences. I will not say I wished myself back in your drawing-room, but I thought very lovingly of it.

We got on board the *Great Britain* about nine after a very pleasant day's excursion. The weather was beautiful and quite mild.

This morning we had service on deck. There is a Presbyterian minister on board; he read a chapter, prayed and preached very nicely and to a most attentive audience. Perhaps it was more suited to them than our long morning's service, though I did not like it so well.

A great number of the passengers are on shore staying at hotels. Perhaps I shall get on shore again tomorrow, but there is some report of the ship sailing at noon, though I hardly believe the repairs can be done by that time.

We have not seen much of the captain till today, when he appeared at breakfast. He has had a terrible life of anxiety since we sailed. Now I hope we may make a fresh start under better auspices. Do not be uneasy that we have met with such weather; such a gale is quite an exceptional thing, and there has been none such since the *Royal Charter* was lost, nor did it blow so hard then, only she was inshore, while, providentially, we were in the open sea.

We may make a good passage after all. I have no fears myself. No ship could have stood a gale better. There are some in the harbour sorely battered with bulwarks gone, masts down, etc.; far worse than we are. Of course we cannot arrive in Australia till May, so you will not hear of us till July.

The saloon is full of visitors come off to see the ship, and I was surprised to hear my name called just now, and on looking up, to see Mr Humphries, one of our *Calcutta* passengers. I could not remember his name at first, and cannot imagine how he knew me, for I have not seen him these five years. He is living near Cork, and came to see some friends he has on board. He has sorely hindered my writing, and this has to go ashore by five o'clock.

Some of the passengers have talked of giving up the voyage, so dismayed were they at the weather, but I do not think any of them have done such a foolish thing. We have nothing to complain of on the whole, in the ship, though we amuse ourselves by grumbling a little at the table, which is not over-good for what we pay. The provisions are plentiful enough, but rather coarse in quality. Still, we have good appetites.

I have not made any great acquaintance with anybody except Mrs Bronchordt. I do not think we have a very eligible set on the whole, but perhaps they will improve as we go on, and it is only for two months, I hope, at all events.

You cannot think how dirty everything gets; hands, clothes, everything is black. The white in my dress is in a most disastrous state. I never saw such a dirty ship. We are well supplied with water, however, and as yet no animalculae have made their appearance.

Ever yours very affectionately,

RACHEL HENNING

SURRY HILLS,
SYDNEY,
MAY 15TH 1861

My Dearest Etta,

I suppose the newspaper telegrams will have told you that the *Great Britain* has safely reached Australia before you receive this. We landed in Melbourne on the 2nd of May after a very good run from Cork of sixty-two days. I wrote to you from Queenstown the day we sailed, so you know my adventures up to that point. After that we had a calm passage on the whole; of course there were rolling days and stormy nights, but nothing that could be called a heavy gale. The passage was a pleasant one, take it all together.

After leaving Ireland we soon got into warm weather, and very warm weather it was. Some days the thermometer was up to 90 in the saloon, but we were fortunate enough to steam through it, while the unhappy sailing-ships we passed were flapping their sails helplessly in the calms on the Line, while their inhabitants must have been nearly roasted alive.

We crossed the line March 17th and rounded the Cape on April 6th. After that we had some cold weather, of course, but nothing very intense, as we did not go very far south. We never had very favourable winds. Once we made a run of 315 miles in the twenty-four hours, but only once, and it was chiefly owing to the screw that we made such a good passage as we did.

I liked some of my fellow passengers very much, but not my cabin companion, Mrs Bronchordt. At least, I did not dislike her, for she was good-natured enough, but a more helpless, childish, complaining mortal it was never my misfortune to come across. She could not do her hair fit to be seen, nor mend her clothes, nor keep her things in any sort of order. However, as she spent most of her time in bed, I gave up the cabin to her and followed my own devices elsewhere.

I think I told you about Mrs Ranken. I found her most pleasant all through the voyage, and now I am going to travel up to Bathurst with her tomorrow, and she has asked me to come and stay with her there.

Of the young ladies, the one I knew best was a Miss Shering.

59

She was going out under the captain's care to be married, as were two other young ladies on board. She was a gentle, dark-eyed girl from Bristol, of some tradesman's family, I rather imagine, not very clever, but very kind and good. The young ladies, in general, were a very dull set.

We had some pleasant people at our table. My next neighbour, Mr Brandt, was a German Jew, but who spoke English very well, and we kept up an incessant skirmish on the relative merits of England and Germany; below him were the Friend family, some Sydney people; opposite me were Mr and Mrs Feldheim—he was another German and rather a well-informed man. Then there was Mr Gifford, a flourishing-looking Adelaide squatter, who told the most amusing stories about the bush; Mr Uphill, a merchant, but *not* from Bristol, as I first thought, but he knew the place very well; Mr Payne, a young lawyer, clever and amusing and a thorough Englishman, who used to join in the battles with the Germans; and a Mr Compton, who, I think, was a little cracked—he used to come out with such extraordinary statements. We had far more fun going on at our table always than at any of the others, and the captain used to say it was the only one he liked taking the head of. He took them all in turn.

Somehow there was good deal of stiffness and party feeling on board the ship. I hardly know how it arose, but half the people were not friendly with the other half. I enjoyed the voyage myself. I was always so wonderfully well; I never had a day's seasickness nor illness of any kind, and never was absent from a meal from the time I left Liverpool till I reached Sydney. It was a thing to be very thankful for; so many people were unwell at various times. I was more often than not the only lady at the table, except old Mrs Friend.

I will not say more about the voyage, however, as you will find plenty about it in my journal if you have patience to read that document. I am going to send it, together with the pinafores, to England by Captain Gray, and as he sails on the 29th of this month, it will probably be in England at the end of July, a short time after this reaches you.

As soon as we got to Melbourne we heard that there was no steamer on to Sydney till the 7th of May, and when I found that I must have missed Annie anyway I did not regret the detention, as I rather wanted to see something of Melbourne.

Soon after we anchored, a Mr Frew came on board and inquired for me. He brought a letter from Annie, who knew his brother in Sydney, and very kindly offered to see to my luggage, etc. I was very much disappointed to find that Annie had been in Sydney for three months, but that, expecting the *Great Britain* nearly a fortnight before it arrived, she had settled to go to Rockhampton by the steamer of the 4th of April; as there was no possibility of letting Biddulph know, and she did not like to disappoint him and make him come sixty miles for nothing, she went on the Saturday *after* I came to Melbourne. I think she was quite right, though it was very vexing, and the disappointment, I am sure, was as great to her as to me, but I hope I shall see her in a few weeks now.

I rather enjoyed my stay at Melbourne. About twelve of the passengers were going on to Sydney, and of these six besides myself had taken their passage through and were therefore entitled to stay on board the *Great Britain* if they liked. We were quite a pleasant little party there; Mr and Mrs Paul, Miss Parkins, the latter's sister, Miss Dyson, Mr Golding, Mr Osborne and myself, besides the captain, the doctor and Mr Turner, the first officer. We used to go ashore in the captain's boat every morning after breakfast, spend the day on shore and return to the ship to dinner at five; and in the evenings amuse ourselves with music or whist or chess afterwards.

We spent one day in seeing Melbourne, its shops and streets and grand buildings, and a very fine town it is, far better than Sydney. Another day we went up the river to the Botanic Garden and Zoological Gardens, and another we made a picnic to a place called Gardener's Creek, about seven miles up the Yarra Yarra.

You cannot think how kind the captain was to me during the voyage and especially during my stay in Melbourne. He always took me under his especial care in all the boating and railway travelling backwards and forwards, for we had to go up by rail to the town; the ship was lying about a quarter of an hour's pull from Sandridge pier, and then there was about a quarter of an hour's journey by rail to Melbourne.

I was very sorry to say good-bye to the *Great Britain* and her captain when we sailed from Melbourne. She is a splendid ship, and I am sure we all have reason to speak well of her.

We left Melbourne at two o'clock on the seventh in the *Wonga Wonga*, a pretty little steamer, but rather different in size from our old ship. We had a very calm passage. We took two days about it, entered Sydney Heads very late on Thursday night, ran up the harbour and anchored at the wharf at twelve o'clock at night.

I did not the least expect anyone to meet me so late, but as soon as we anchored, Annie's friend, Mr Macmichael, came on board; he had been waiting at the wharf all that time for me, and very kind I thought it of him. He wanted me to come out to the Surry Hills at once, but I would not knock up the Hirsts at such an untimely hour, but preferred sleeping on board ship one more night. I had not slept on shore for more than eighty nights, and had got rather to like small cribs.

The next morning I got up early, and a most lovely Australian morning it was, the sun shining and everything looking bright and beautiful. Mr Hirst and Emily Tucker came on board for me soon after eight o'clock. The former looks older and more careworn than when I saw him last, the latter exactly the same. I do not see that these three years have made a pin's difference in her. I was so glad to see her again. She is a very old friend after all. Mr Macmichael appeared again soon after, and after some research I found most of my luggage on the wharf; part of it was sent to Mr Hirst's stores and part of it was put on board a cab, wherein Emily and I set off to the Surry Hills.

There I found Caroline looking just the same as ever, the picture of a comfortable, well-to-do matron, stout and rosy and as pleasant as ever. The boys were grown out of all knowledge, of course. Edith, the baby when I was last here, is now a very pretty little girl of six years old, with fair skin and dark hair and eyes, not unlike Lucy Macey; she often reminds me of her. The youngest have been born since I left. Wilfred would be a very fine little boy, as he has beautiful dark eyes and pretty features, but the mosquitoes have devoured him till he looks as if he had the measles, and Caroline, having had the mosquito curtains to his bed washed and put away, cannot be prevailed on to take them out again.

Emily is most useful to Caroline in the house, makes puddings, dresses Edith, reproves the boys, and is, in fact, a model aunt. They have a nice comfortable house, with plenty of rooms of a good size. I sleep with Emily, and many a talk we have together about old times.

Of course I have heard a great deal about Annie and Biddulph —they are all full of the former here, as she has only just left. She seems to have been excessively popular in Sydney. She was escorted to the steamer by nine gentlemen and three ladies, all armed with pocket handkerchiefs, and several of them have been out of spirits ever since she departed. She must have dressed beautifully according to Emily's account, and she has taken up such nice things to the bush in the way of hats and

"She was escorted to the steamer by nine gentlemen and three ladies."

cloth habits and new dresses that I am afraid she will be quite alarmed at my shabbiness.

Biddulph, too, seems to have made quite a sensation here. He was here for two months at the beginning of the year. They say that he is not the least roughened or colonialized by his long residence in the bush, but that his manners and appearance are "first rate", so very simple and yet so very gentlemanly. That he is most polite and attentive to all the young ladies and a great flirt! I do long to see him and Annie again. I am sure we shall be very happy together. I fully mean to try.

We shall have some furniture at Marlborough,[22] which is a

22 A station near Rockhampton, Queensland, taken up by Biddulph jointly with the Tuckers in 1858.

blessing, for Biddulph bought a great deal of Captain Tucker's furniture when he went to England. Emily says he would have bought the piano only he was then uncertain about my coming out. I wish he had; it would have been such an amusement in the bush.

Emily was very much obliged for the coronet you sent her, and likes it very much; they are nearly new here. My large cases, of course, I shall not open till I get to Rockhampton. My watch came quite safely in company with Mr Flemming's. I took it out as soon as I arrived here and wound it up and it goes beautifully; it is certainly a very pretty watch, and it is a wonderful thing to me to know the time again. His Lordship, as they always call Mr Flemming here, called for his property the day after I arrived. He is rather a gentlemanly young man, more so than I expected, and with a most perpetual tongue; he spent yesterday evening here and was so good as to volunteer another call before I go.

I have walked about with Emily a great deal since I came; the weather has been perfection, bright and clear and just cool enough to be pleasant. Certainly the Australian winters are lovely; but the summers!

My bonnet is very pretty—that was your taste—and very new-looking, for very few of that shape are worn here yet. Emily and Caroline both wear the round fronts. My black one has survived the voyage, and Emily is at this moment pinning in a clean cap, preparatory to my wearing it to Bathurst tomorrow.

We went over to the North Shore yesterday to see the William Tuckers and the Stewarts. That north shore is most beautiful, in some places the wild bush goes down to the water's edge, or cliffs and water-worn rocks, with the clear blue water washing over them, and the houses have such lovely views from all the windows.

I do not know how to give you any idea of the beauty of Sydney Harbour. I certainly underrated the Australian scenery, but, then, it is winter now; I should tell a different story in the heat and dust of summer.

I set off for Bathurst tomorrow, and that is the reason you will get these letters dated so long before the mail starts. I wish I could have ventured to leave writing to you till I had seen Amy, but I shall not be at Bathurst till Saturday evening at the earliest, and if it goes on raining as it is doing today I do not know about getting there at all, as we shall probably stick in the mud on the Blue Mountains.

I should have gone up before probably, but I wanted to go

64

with Mrs Ranken; it is so much pleasanter than travelling
alone. We shall be a party of four; Mrs Ranken, her sister, her
son and myself. We start tomorrow evening by train for Parramatta, sleep there and set off next morning by the coach, travel
all day, sleep somewhere on Friday night, then on again till
Saturday evening, when, if we are lucky, we shall get to Bathurst,
and very glad I shall be to see Amy and her children.

I shall not get my luggage till some days after I get there
myself. It is such a dreadful plague to move luggage here, where
a cab costs ten shillings and you cannot get a porter to carry a
box to an omnibus.

I shall probably stay with Amy about a month; then come
back here and spend a few weeks, as Caroline will not be satisfied with the six days' visit I have paid her, and I shall probably
get to Marlborough about the end of July. They say it is a dreadful voyage up to Rockhampton, as the boats are small and bad
and take eight days on the passage. I am longing to hear that
Annie is safely and comfortably at her new home, for she is a
very bad sailor and dreaded the voyage very much.

Ever your most affectionate sister,

RACHEL HENNING

BATHURST,
SUNDAY, MAY 19TH 1861

My Dearest Etta,

I came up to Bathurst rather suddenly, as I was coming with
Mrs Ranken and she did not let me know till a day or two
before we started. I set off with her, her sister, Miss Hutchinson,
a very funny old lady, who talks such broad Scotch that I can
hardly understand her at all, and her son Tom.

We left Sydney about five o'clock and got to Parramatta by
train about six. It is only seventeen miles, but the Australian
railways do not go at express pace; though otherwise they are
very comfortable. We slept at Parramatta, and the next morning
set out at seven o'clock in an American coach,[23] which has lately
been set up in opposition to the old mails. It is a machine built
very strong and very light, hung upon a peculiar sort of spring
and with seats inside for nine. Three on each side and a canopy
over, supported by little wooden pillars and drawn by four
capital horses, changed every ten miles, at every stage.

The Bathurst road was *bad* when I was here before, but now

[23] A Cobb and Co.'s coach. The New South Wales service was established
in 1861, and headquarters set up in Bathurst.

there is no word that I should like to use that would the least express its state. We got on pretty well to Penrith, where we crossed the Nepean in a punt, the bridge having been lately carried away by a flood. The coach, horses and all, was driven on to a sort of floating platform, to the infinite terror of Miss Hutchinson; and then we were towed across. Then began the ascent of the Blue Mountains by a long pull up Lapstone Hill.

I wish I could give you the least idea of the beauty of the scenery here. It was a lovely morning, and we wound along one side of the hill with a deep ravine on our right, and, on the other side of the ravine, a wall of rock that seemed to rise up to the sky with trees growing out of every crevice and the sun shining on the top, while all below was in black shade. I had forgotten how magnificent those Blue Mountains were. We travelled among them all day, over such roads as I never saw before. We had a capital driver, fearless and yet careful, and he took us safe over rocks and ruts and deep holes and fallen trees. Once we certainly took off the head of a sapling and then got aground on the stump, but the united exertions of the gentlemen lifted the coach off and we got under way again.

The coachman drove very much by voice. "Hie, good horses! Pull then! Hie Chance, hie Jemmy! Hie a-l-o-n-g"—the last word with a good roar, when the horses would make a desperate effort and pull us out of that particular boghole in which we were at that moment stuck, and with a lurch, and a pitch, and a tumble (enough to break the springs of anything but an American coach), we would go on a rock and then descend into another hole. We took *six hours* to do the last twenty miles that night, and we arrived at Black Heath, a solitary inn among the mountains, where we were to sleep, about eleven o'clock at night. Here we had supper in company with a few coachmen, etc., and slept as well as we could till six next morning, when we made a fresh start.

There were ten people in the coach—six ladies and four gentlemen. The latter were always getting up and down to help the coach out of difficulties, and were covered with mud before the end of the journey.

We went down Mount Victoria just at sunrise, and some of the views were lovely. You looked down on seas of forest and fold after fold of mountains covered with wood. I should have enjoyed it more perhaps if I had been walking, instead of in a loaded coach coming down a steep hill over the worst road you can imagine, and with a precipice rising up on the left and another on the right going sheer down I don't know how many

66

hundred feet, and no parapet, so that a shying horse, or a wheel coming off, or an overturn, would have sent us all into another world most likely. There are many such places on the road through the Blue Mountains. Luckily I am not nervous, nor is Mrs Ranken, but Miss Hutchinson did nothing but groan and say "oh!" at every fresh lurch the coach gave.

Fortunately we had good horses down Mount Victoria, but at "Solitary Creek", the next inn, they put in a team that nearly did for us. The coachman tried to start them, when the off-leader turned short round and bit the horse next him, the latter, a colt, who had hardly been in harness before, reared on his hind legs, while both wheelers jibbed obstinately and, when exhorted with the whip, began backing and kicking.

We were all but overturned, and obeyed the order "to get out as fast as possible" with great alacrity. We lost nearly a quarter of an hour in trying to start those horses, and at last the whole team had to be taken out and four splendid horses substituted that had been kept for the down mail. How that latter vehicle got to Sydney I do not pretend to say, but about seven o'clock last evening we rumbled into Bathurst, very glad to be at the end of our journey, though I was wonderfully little tired to what others were.

In writing to Amy I had made a mistake between the mail and the American coach, so there was no one to meet me when I arrived at the inn. (Mrs Ranken's carriage met her before we got to Bathurst, and she lives four miles from the town.) But while I was inquiring for someone to show me the way to Mr Sloman's, a gentleman whom I had seen standing at the door came up and said he lived just opposite his house, so I walked with him for about half a mile, a most lovely starlit night, till we came to a pretty-looking house with a veranda before it, and knocked at the door, which was immediately opened by Amy.

She was looking very well, and I was so glad to see her again, for, kind as they all are at Sydney, it is not like being among one's "own people". Mr Sloman, too, is looking well, though I am not sure that he is improved by a beard that he has grown since I last saw him.

The two little girls had been kept up to see me, as they expected me later. They were sitting up at tea when I came in, and seemed quite delighted to see me. I think Amy had been talking to them about "Aunt Rachel". They are very neatly dressed in crimson French Merino dresses, made high with long sleeves for the winter, and white pinafores of the old shape;

they wear little cloth jackets out of doors and brown felt hats —a broad shape not turned up.

The baby I did not see till this morning; he is a very large, fine child for eight months old, but not pretty. He seems very lively and intelligent, takes notice of everything and held out his arms to come to me as soon as I saw him. He must have recognized me as his aunt, for in general he will not go to strangers.

The house is very comfortable; they have a pretty drawing-room, nicely furnished and with all Amy's knick-knacks that she used to be so fond of about it, a roughish sort of dining-room, where the children play also, then Amy has a large bedroom with a dressing-room inside it. The bedroom also serves as a nursery, for the baby is generally there when not in the dining-room.

Bathurst agrees with both Amy and Mr Sloman, I think. The climate is more like England than Australia; just now, for instance, it is like our very best autumn weather. There was a sharp white frost this morning, and it was quite cold enough to make fires very comfortable; then it came out into the most splendid day, clear sunshine, no wind and such a cloudless sky.

There was no service here this morning, and Mr Sloman got a dog-cart and drove us over to a church on the other side of the river about three miles off. It was quite a pleasant drive this beautiful day and we heard a very nice sermon.

The church we went to[24] stands on a hill with a beautiful view round it, but it is a very ugly contrivance in itself, red brick with a little square tower and an article on the top thereof exactly like a tin extinguisher.

Constance went with us and was very good. Amy dresses very nicely; she is wearing a tweed dress and she has a very handsome black silk mantle, one of the large ones, which Mr Sloman brought her on his last return from Sydney, and a straw bonnet trimmed by herself with black velvet. She says Mr Sloman also gave her a mohair dress, but I do not think she has had a silk one for some time, so I hope our present will be a useful one.

I mean to be very happy at Bathurst this time, so don't think of me as otherwise.

Your most affectionate sister,

RACHEL HENNING

[24] At Kelso.

My Dearest Etta,

July 3rd. I am beginning my letter very early this month as I
have a good many to write, and I think your way of writing by
degrees is a very good one. I am still at Bathurst and likely to
be so for some time to come, as I do not suppose Biddulph's
house will be finished till the end of August or beginning of
September.

I had a very nice letter from Annie a few days ago, in which
she says that the framework is up and two carpenters constantly
employed upon it, that it is to be a nine-roomed house with
two sitting-rooms, five bedrooms and office for Biddulph and
a store-room. I suppose also that it will have windows, but
of these I have not heard yet. I expect it will be a very comfortable abode, and I hope it will be done before the very hot
weather comes on. I am looking forward to some rides and some
gardening; they say English flowers do not grow very well there,
but flowers of some sort must; at all events, I shall try them.

Annie seems to like the sort of life she leads very much, and
to be very busy. She says she does something in the way of
cooking every day and also makes her bed, etc. I cannot exactly
see the necessity of this last operation, as if you have a servant
she may as well do the work herself. But the Australian servants
are very bad in general. She says she does not ride much, as
Biddulph has not time to ride with her often and she does
not like riding alone.

When I am up there, I hope we shall ride every day. Mr
George Hedgeland is up there now. Annie says he is rather
pleasant and gentlemanly, more so than the others. I dare say
you will remember him. Amy says I have seen him, but I have
not the smallest recollection of him. Perhaps Annie will write
by this mail herself, however, and tell you all the Marlborough
news, so I will return to Bathurst.

We went to the Subscription Ball on the 20th of last month
and were very well amused, for two or three hours; we came
home about 1 a.m. There is a very good ballroom here, and it
was very tastefully dressed up. Some of the colonial girls are
excessively pretty, while they are very young—such complexions
as you hardly ever see.

There certainly is a curious state of society here. The richest
man in the district, who was the chief steward of the ball, and
who was so good as to escort Amy into the room, met with "mis-

fortune" many years ago, and was transported for life for horse-stealing. That was in the palmy days of the colony, and he soon made a fortune, got first a conditional pardon, then a free one and now is a great man here!

We are having an exceedingly cold winter for Australia, and when it *is* cold you feel it more here than at home, as there is less protection from it, the wood fires are not so warm as coal ones, and the houses are built for warm weather. They say the seasons generally follow England: that when there is a severe winter there we have a severe one here afterwards, and you know how wet last summer was at home, and the past summer in Australia was just the same.

Baby has taken to crawl, and of course makes himself as black as possible. He is a dear little fellow, very lively and full of fun, and getting to that lamentable age when he takes up everything he sees and proceeds to eat it, so that Amy lives in a constant state of terror lest he should choke. If he is playing with ever so large a thing she labours under an idea that he might swallow it—a silver spoon, for instance, or a brass candlestick, which he got possession of yesterday.

Another great fear of hers is the well in the backyard. It is covered with a heavy door, which I do not think they, the children, could possibly lift, as I cannot, but it is only since I have been here that they have gone out to play in the paddock at all, and we keep a very sharp look-out after them. The most objectionable things in the paddock to my mind are the "Bathurst burrs", which are a real nuisance.

Amy got the fringe of her shawl full of them the other day, and it took her the whole evening to pick them out. It is not an indigenous plant, but was introduced from Valparaiso in the wool of some sheep that were imported. Now it has spread everywhere in this district, and is an awful nuisance to the wool-growers, as it spoils the fleece.

Another unlucky importation was the Scotch thistle, which a patriotic Scotch lady near here planted in her garden and which, like most of its compatriots, took so kindly to the country that it grows everywhere. The paddock is half full of it. We have, also, rather too much of even such a good thing as sweetbriar. My friend Mrs Ranken first planted it about twenty years ago, and it has spread so on her land that some of her paddocks are a mere jungle of sweetbriar. It must be lovely when in flower, but is not exactly "adapted to the wants" of sheep and cattle, and it is extremely difficult to extirpate. However, I have not taken warning, but have collected some seeds to sow at

Marlborough. I saw it growing wild in the bush as I came up to Bathurst, and rejoiced greatly, as it is the only approach we have in this country to wild roses.

I was looking in my diary this morning to see what I was doing at home this day year, July 3rd, and it was the day when, after waiting a long time for a fly in which we were to take a drive, and that did not come, you and I took little Constance through the avenue to a field beyond, where we got a quantity of wild roses and then we went on to a hayfield and sat in the hay. I remember it so well and how pleasant it was. I dare say you have been to the same place with the children this year.

July 11th. We have just got the telegram from King George's Sound with the English news. We shall get the letters, I suppose, in about a week, though I am terribly afraid mine may have been directed to Marlborough, as, of course, you never thought of my staying here so long. There is no very remarkable news except that the Southerners appear to be getting rather the worst in the American contest, and that the Princess Alice is betrothed to Prince Louis of Hesse, and the *Marco Polo* has run on an iceberg on her homeward voyage and has put into Valparaiso much damaged.

This is one of the cold, wet days of which we have had a great many lately. Most serious of all, the road to Sydney is all but impassable, the mail comes in later every night, and it is expected that it will be shortly swallowed up altogether in the morass it has to go through at the foot of Mount Lambie.

Yesterday it cleared up in the morning, and, as we wanted something in Bathurst, and the children had not had a walk for a long time, we thought we would take them into the town, which is about half a mile off, but we had no idea of what the mud was like, and they were soon over their goloshes and plastered up to their knees.

However, we persevered till we got to the great square. The middle of it looked tolerably dry, but before us was such a morass that after Annie had stuck in the mud and lost her golosh and been only extricated by the assistance of a passer-by, and Amy had got nearly up to her ankles in the attempt, and Constance had roared under the impression that she was going to be then and there buried alive, we thought that perhaps we had better turn back, which we did, and were very glad to get the children safe home again, making a great many vows that they should only go on the hills and never on the roads till the weather was better.

Pavements and causeways are things unknown in Bathurst, and, as the roads are never mended, you may imagine what it is like when it does rain. Fortunately there is very little wet weather in this part of the country.

One evening last week Mr Sloman brought home two gentlemen to tea, one of whom was a Mr Millar, of the Sydney Mint, rather a clever, agreeable man. I mention it to tell you of a very curious speciment of Chinese ingenuity which he showed us— a sample of what looked like very fine "nuggety" gold, which they had manufactured out of copper, mixed with gold, and which was so like the real thing that they had taken in a great many of the Sydney storekeepers till the imposition was detected at the Mint.

He showed us that it burnt green under a blowpipe, which was almost the only way of detecting it. He was here on some Mint business, and was seized upon by some Bathurst gentlemen to go and see a copper mine, which they fancy they have discovered, about twenty miles from here and which they are all crazy about. Mr Sloman has a share or two in it. I believe Mr Millar said there was plenty of copper there, but he doubted if it would pay to smelt and send it home. I never have the smallest faith myself in fortunes to be made out of the "Peruvian mines".

Those Chinese are dreadful rascals, though I do not think they ought to be treated as they have lately been by the mob at Lambing Flat diggings. There are lots of them in Bathurst. We met some the other day, evidently newly arrived from China, with broad flat hats with a little point in the middle, like ancient shields, and carrying their property slung at each end of a stick and balanced over their shoulders, exactly like the little men crossing the bridge on the willow-pattern plates.

July 19th. By this mail we heard of the safe arrival of the *Duncan Dunbar*, in which the Tuckers went home, after a very long voyage. I dare say you soon received Annie's and Biddulph's likenesses, and if they are as good as those they sent Amy, I am sure you must be pleased with them. Biddulph looks quite handsome, and Annie's is a very pleasing likeness, far better than the one she sent me. She appears hardly altered at all, and, where she is, has only for the better.

Just about this time, also, you will get my first letters. I wished I could put myself into the envelopes.

I quite hope and believe that I shall return home some day, though it may not be just yet. I always look forward to it when I think of the future and perhaps living, if not with you, near you somewhere and Constance and Leighton being very fond of their old auntie. But it is in better hands than ours, dear, and we will leave it there. It is enough that we are sure to meet again, I trust. What a difference that makes. I have never regretted having come as I used to fear I should. I think it was right and best, and there really is a great deal that is pleasant in this country when one is willing to see it, though I can never understand people liking it better than dear old England.

I should like to go to those church defence meetings with you. They would be very good things out here, where dissent is very rampant. I have taken to going to church once on a Sunday, as some old Sydney friends have offered me a seat, and Amy has gone several times with me. I went by myself last Sunday morning, it being the Sacrament Sunday here and heard really a very nice sermon from Mr Sharpe.

All the people in Bathurst have lately been going to see some wonderful caves that have been discovered about fifty miles from here. Mr Brady, one of Mr Sloman's partners, first made them known many years ago; he was out after a noted bush-ranger, and he tracked him to the entrance of these caves.[25] They are said to be most magnificent, running for an immense way under the mountain, and some of them are so large that there is no roof to be seen. In one part they slope down to a subterranean river, but they are of unknown extent and have never been thoroughly explored. Some of them are full of the most beautiful stalactites.

Several parties have been formed to go and visit them, and the week before last Mrs Machattie, the doctor's wife here, got up a party of twenty-seven, chiefly young ladies, to go and see them. They all rode, as there is no road for any vehicle, and took three packhorses with provisions, and each carried a blanket for a bed. The journey took two days each way, and when they got there they camped in the outermost cave, where a tent was pitched for the ladies and the gentlemen slept round the fire. They were out exactly a week and enjoyed themselves exceedingly.

Besides the wonderful caves, they say that the mountain scenery out there is most wild and beautiful. Mrs Machattie asked me to go, and Mr Sloman said he would get me a horse and saddle, but though such an expedition would have been delightful with one's own people, as the Irish say, I did not care to go with strangers.

We went to hear a lecture on Astronomy, which was given in

25 The accepted discoverer was Charles Whalan.

the courthouse here. The subject was "Comets" ("Cummats", as pronounced by the lecturer). He was mounted on a sort of platform while the audience sat in the gallery. We betook ourselves to the jury-box. A most uncomfortable seat, built, I should think, to produce short verdicts, and some little boys looked through the bars intended for the prisoner. We sat in the dark, as the lecture was illustrated by a magic lantern which presented comets of portentous appearance and gigantic tails, careering about among the planets in a most unpleasant manner.

The lecture was rather amusing, though I regret to say that a gentleman seated near me went to sleep in the middle of the Ptolemaic system and snored audibly. The room was very full, and it is a good thing that the colonial mind should be informed that there are things in earth and heaven besides money-getting and the price of hides and tallow. I was amused to see that the English telegram this month was half taken up with the "firmness" or "depression" of those savoury articles; wool, of course, is another matter, as Biddulph "grows" it.

With best love to yourself, Mr Boyce and the darlings.

Ever, dearest Etta, your most affectionate sister,

RACHEL HENNING

BATHURST,
SEPTEMBER 10TH 1861

My Dearest Etta,

We heard from Annie again on the 2nd of this month, and their plans seem now to be pretty well decided: namely, that Biddulph, directly after Christmas, must go out to see his new station on the Bowen,[26] and from thence to Port Denison, and that, at the same time that he goes, Annie will come down to Sydney, where I suppose she will spend three or four months; that Biddulph will then come down to fetch her, and then ("if nothing unforeseen occurs", as Grandpapa used to say) we shall all go back to Marlborough together, some time next winter.

But this latter move seems so distant that I do not think much about it. I believe the only way is to live on in the present from day to day, and do what is to be done and enjoy what is to be enjoyed, and there really is plenty of both here.

Amy and I walk most days, and lately we have taken to gardening. There is a large green paddock round the house with a wooden paling to fence it off from the hill; and after a

26 Exmoor station.

great many wishes that we had a garden, we one day got a line and marked out a long border at the top of the paddock under the fence.

Mr Sloman was incited to dig it up before breakfast in the mornings, instead of walking on the hill. I raked it over, and a benevolent lady gave us a quantity of plants and cuttings, which we planted. By dint of a good deal of watering and shading, they are growing very well, and we have now a beginning of a garden. It is a very good time for sowing seeds, and I shall put in some as soon as Mr Sloman has dug up some more of the border. Unfortunately all those I brought from England are packed up in a box at Sydney, but I believe we can buy them here. I have a box of scarlet geranium and petunia cuttings outside my window which will come in for planting out by and by.

Scarlet verbena grows like a weed here and lives out all the winter; so will most of the English greenhouse plants, with very little shelter. A beautiful garden might be made round the house as there is so much land to it, and the paddock is so green and so thick with clover that it would make a pretty lawn near the house, but it is not worth while to have much done to a house not your own. A gardener charges ten shillings a day for his work, but if we can raise a few flowers ourselves it will be worth all the trouble.

It is quite warm now, as warm as many English summer days. All the gardens about us are full of peach- and willow-trees, and the light green of the willows and the masses of peach-blossom look so very pretty together. The paddocks are full of clover, and the flowers are beginning to come out in the bush; the yellow wattle is beautiful, and there are some pretty little white shrubs like heaths in flower.

I must tell you about the drive for which the children endured their new frocks. It took place on September 6th, Amy's wedding day, when we "did repair", not in a chaise and pair but in a dog-cart to make two or three distant calls which had long been owing. The baby was providentially left behind, but Annie and Constance went, to their great delight. The former sat on a little stool between Amy and Mr Sloman, and I took care of Constance behind. We drove first of all by the river, which was full after the rains, and the black sheoaks and light green willows that fringe its banks made quite beautiful pictures.

We called first on some people called Piper who live in a pretty veranda house, with a grove of wattle-trees round it, which were one mass of yellow blossoms and scented the whole air. Here we partook of biscuits which tasted strongly of turpentine, discussed Bathurst news with the old lady and her son and daughters, and then departed for Mrs Ranken's. I was very glad to see her again, for I had not been there since the beginning of June, when I was staying with her. She lives too far off for a walk, and she never goes from home herself. She showed us her sewing-machine, which they have just set up. Amy is wild to have one, and they are now on sale at Bathurst, but £10 is a good deal of money.

Here the children laid in a fresh supply of biscuits and figs, and then we started again on a long drive over the plains through endless green paddocks, where the unfortunate Mr Sloman had continually to alight and let down sliprails for the carriage to go through, and past hedges and jungles of sweet-briar, which grows like a weed here, and swampy meadows full of iris-leaves, for the iris has also run wild on these plains. The farmhouses looked so pretty standing in the middle of peach orchards, which were just coming into flower. These sunny plains are beautiful in spring, but terribly hot in summer.

At last, after about ten miles, we reached our last house of call, just as it was beginning to get dusk. It was the prettiest house we had been to yet, with a lovely garden round it, but we had to cut our visit short and make haste home, as the children were tired.

On our way we passed a "haunted house", a little staring red-brick building, without an atom of romance about it, but it has not been inhabited for years, and the ghost is undeniable, for a few nights ago a tipsy man wandered to the door and was immediately knocked down by the ghost, and could not get up again till the morning.

After a beautiful drive of about twenty miles, in which we made three calls (I don't cotton to calling in family parties) we were very glad to have tea and put the children to bed; and so ended Amy's sixth wedding day.

September 12th. I have been drawing a good deal lately, copying some beautiful little vignettes of Creswicks that I found in an illustrated edition of Tennyson, which was lent me. Of course I enlarge them a good deal. Yesterday I had just finished what I considered rather a satisfactory copy of "Where Claribel low lieth" (how I do like that poem!)—moon, oak-tree and all. Amy was practising in the drawing-room, and I went in for a minute to tell her something about her music, leaving my concerns on the table. When I came back I saw little Annie covering my drawing with a paper and tumbling off my chair in a great hurry, and on investigation I found that she had helped herself to my blackest pencil and scrawled my drawing all over with it! It was pretty well spoiled, as the lines were deeply scored in and tinted paper won't stand any rubbing. I gave her a good scolding and put her in the corner, where she roared with all her might, and Amy, coming in to see what was the matter, gave her a whipping. I was rather sorry for it, but I cannot say she was much hurt and she deserved to be frightened to prevent mischief another time. She is my pet of them all and is very fond of me. And just at this moment she is displaying her affection by bringing me, continually, handfuls of grass, clover, etc., from the paddocks, till I have a heap beside me that would delight the heart of a rabbit.

The Bathurst people are wild about bazaars just now. The Roman Catholics had one last week to help pay for the building of their new chapel, a lofty red-brick building faced with white, which quite overtops the church. One of Amy's servants went to the bazaar, and came back in a state of great delight and excitement, carrying an enormous doll which she had won in a raffle for 2s. 6d.; the price of the doll was £3. She was dressed as a bride, in white tarlatan, hooped petticoat, veil and wreath of orange flowers, and was so large that she would require to be kept in a good-sized box all to herself. Jane says she shall take her to Sydney with her, and she certainly is a highly useful article for a general servant.

The said Jane is going away next week. She is a good servant —for Australia—at home you would not keep her a week—but she has a little weakness for giving warning whenever she is told to do anything. So at last Amy looked out for somebody else, and last evening engaged a stout young person, who is so good as to undertake to do as much of the work as she feels inclined for the trifling consideration of 12s. a week and everything found.

That is the regular sum for a general servant up here. Amy gives her nurse 9s., but then, except her unfailing good nature, she has no single qualification for a servant. So whenever your servants trouble you, think of the unfortunate housekeepers in Australia.

I am teaching Rachel, the nurse, to read and write in the evenings. She is native-born, and her education was utterly neglected. But she is quick and most desirous to learn. Amy began with her and got her on very well, but Mr Sloman did not like her leaving the drawing-room of an evening to teach Rachel, so the education was at a standstill till I came.

77

". . . a highly useful article for a general servant."

You have no idea what a plague the servants are here. If a few married ladies meet, it is quite ridiculous to hear the chorus of lamentation that they strike up. One has had a new American stove knocked to pieces; another every scrap of crockery broken; another her gowns pawned; another, bills run up in her name at every shop in the town. All the buckets have been let fall down all the wells and the name of the "followers" is legion. I suppose it is an evil that will mend itself as more servants come out here.

September 18th. The English news is come at last: that is to say, the principal items have been telegraphed from Adelaide; the letters will not be here for nearly a week, but it makes no difference to me as all mine will go to Marlborough. I hoped to have had your June letters back in time to answer, but the Rockhampton steamer is not yet in.

There seems to be nothing very remarkable in the English news, except that France wants Sardinia, and the Americans are calling in the Indians to scalp and tomahawk for them. There seems to be some chance of the war being ended by a compromise; what a good thing it would be.

I see you are still building iron-clad vessels at home. I hope they will answer, for they cost a good deal of money.

Your letters that come out by this mail will be in answer to the first I wrote home; it is very vexing to have to wait so long before getting them.

You will be sorry to hear that I have returned to my old state of ignorance respecting the time. My watch has failed me, and I much regret the £12 I spent on it. It is a most unaccountable thing how it could have broken, and the worst of it is, it will probably be spoilt in the mending; they treat watches so ill out here. Annie's has never kept time since she had it cleaned in Sydney, and yet it was a first-rate English watch and went beautifully before.

Our only timepiece here is an old silver watch of Mr Sloman's which hangs over the chimney-piece, but it gains frightfully and requires putting back half an hour in the morning and a quarter of an hour or so toward the afternoon before it will do you credit. Sometimes it stops, and then I exercise my old talent for guessing the time, which, when I had no watch, I used to astonish Aunt Vizard by coming home to dinner to the minute, after long walks on the hills.

The Bathurst dogs are a perfect pest. I do not think Constantinople can be worse in this respect. There is no dog tax, and everybody, rich and poor, seems to keep about five. Most of them are curs and mongrels of the very lowest description and endowed with supernatural powers of yelping. The chorus they raise at night is quite heartrending, and when we take Prince, our old brown pointer, who is of rather a quarrelsome disposition, into the town we generally get a whole pack after us. Every now and then I make demonstrations of picking up large rocks to hurl at them, but this only stops them for a minute, and a few of the most persevering generally follow us home and howl at the gate. I am fond of dogs, but there may be too much of a good thing.

Another peculiarity of this country is the incessant galloping that all the horses keep up. You never see anyone ride at a trot or walk; it is always a hard gallop uphill and downhill, all the same. I should think it must wear out the horses very soon, and you do see lots of skeletons lying about in the bush and by the waterholes and creeks. Some of them are bullocks, but the greater number are horses.

The other day I came upon one quite recently dead, under a gum-tree. I have avoided the spot since, for there he will lie till his bones are bleached white by the Australian sun. I am afraid Prince knows the place, for sometimes he comes in smelling anything but sweet.

September 19th. I must finish and post my letters this morning. Amy's new servant came last night in a flounced muslin dress and eardrops, but she seems to understand her work and looks very tidy this morning.

It is a rainy day, a great affliction out here, as the children yell in the house instead of being out from morning to night, as they are in general.

I have just seen among the English news that Mrs Barrett Browning is dead. I feel quite sorry. An author whose works you are fond of seems almost like a friend, and I like her poems so very much. Amy does not know them. I said her "The Romaunt of Margret" one day when we were sitting in the bush and she liked it very much. I wish I had bought her poems in England.

I shall not be able to write to Aunt Henrietta this month. Will you, therefore, tell her that about a fortnight ago I received a nice, pleasant letter from Theophilus. He is living with Mr Wood, of Brundah, as tutor to his boys, and seems pretty comfortable and jolly, though he says he hates teaching. He is making a garden round the house in place of the potato-ground that formerly existed, and had introduced Mrs Wood to Dickens and *The Old Curiosity Shop*, which certainly ought to be put down among his good deeds.

The Slomans asked him to come over here, but he says it is too far to come at present as he could not leave for long. Brundah is forty-seven miles from Cowra, the nearest town, and that is upwards of sixty miles from Bathurst. I am sorry he cannot come, as I should like to see him and be able to tell Aunt about him. I have at last sent him his parcel; it took nearly a month coming up from Sydney, and I am afraid he will hardly get it in time to write home about it by this mail.

Your ever affectionate sister,

RACHEL HENNING

My Dear Mr Boyce,

I have two letters to thank you for. One dated October, which duly arrived by the December mail, and the other dated September, which made the usual tour to Marlborough, and reached me the last day of the old year.

You will see in the papers the result of the cricket match between England and Victoria. I thought England would win, but nobody expected such a victory as it turned out—that, 11 men to 18, they should win the match in one innings, with a hundred to spare. The numbers were: Victoria first innings, 117; 2nd innings, 91; total, 208. All England first innings, 305; winning with 97 to spare. This ought to take down the colonial "bounce" a little.

The English players are coming to Sydney next, I believe, as the Sydneyites wish for a beating also. There was some talk of getting them up to Bathurst, but since the result of the Victorian match came out there has been nothing more said about it. It was a most audacious thing of the colonists to challenge the first players in the world, and to imagine that they could teach their respected Grandmother.

The English mail-steamer was telegraphed yesterday, and, as usual, the chief heads of the news she brings. We seem likely to have a blow-up with America. The disunited States must be insane to tempt a war with England when they have as much as they can do to run away fast enough from the Federalists. Unless the danger from without makes them patch up some sort of peace, they will have to get the same sort of lesson as the colonial cricketers did, before they will learn to be civil. I suppose new countries are conceited for the same reason that very young men are, and when they have seen a little more of the world they will learn to know their real standing—as John Bull does.

The Australians have nothing to boast of just at present, for a most awkward paragraph is going the round of the papers about a coachful of passengers was stopped by two bushrangers, who ordered them all to get out and be robbed, and were meekly obeyed by all the Australians, till they came to two little Frenchmen, who made such a sturdy fight for it that the bushrangers decamped—one of them badly hurt.

How the *Patrie* and the *Constitutionel* and the rest of the enemy will boast if it comes to their ears—but the people here are great cowards about bushrangers. Some time ago one man "stuck up", as it is called, and robbed a whole coachful of passengers on the Yass road. The main thoroughfares, such as the Sydney road, are pretty safe except as to overturns, as the mounted police look after them, but the cross-country roads are very dangerous just now. The bushrangers now are not escaped convicts, as they used to be, but disappointed diggers and general ne'er-do-wells.

Your very affectionate sister,

RACHEL HENNING

SYDNEY,
JULY 21ST 1862

My Dearest Etta,

I begin my letters early this month, as I have a good deal to tell you, and I shall be very busy at the time the mail goes.

Now for my Shoalhaven visit. I started that Friday night, just as I had finished my English letters. Mr Hirst saw me on board the *Hunter* steamer, and we sailed at eleven o'clock. A very pleasant night it was, blowing hard, and the ladies' cabin full of children, who alternately roared and were seasick. I was rather sick, also, but not very bad.

At daybreak we touched at Wollongong, where all the children landed, and I had the cabin to myself on to Shoalhaven. It was so rough that we did not get to the mouth of the Shoalhaven River till two o'clock on Saturday afternoon, and then the *Hunter* stuck on a mudbank, a fate which generally befalls the Shoalhaven boats, so I and three or four men, who were passengers also, had to leave her in a small boat, and row up the river in search of the little steamer that was to take us on to Shoalhaven, the town being built about fifteen miles from the sea.

I rather enjoyed the pull, though the river is very desolate-looking down there. Something like Eden, I should think—very wide, mud islands appearing here and there, the banks perfectly flat, the trees growing down to the water's edge, and dead trees torn up by floods sticking in the mud on the banks.

After about an hour's pull we found the little steamer taking in wood under the bank, got on board and steamed slowly up the river. It came on a pouring evening, so I retreated to the small cabin, which I had all to myself, being the only lady, and after watching the endless prospect of bush and river till it got dark, I went to sleep with my head on the table, and was only awakened by our arrival at Shoalhaven about six o'clock.

The inn was close to the wharf, and when I got there I was agreeably surprised to find that Bella[27] had ridden over to meet me, as she said I should find it so dull waiting for the steamer all by myself. It was so very kind of her, and I was delighted to see her.

We had tea and sat talking of Taunton, and old times and friends over the fire till bedtime. I expected the Terara Hotel would prove to be a log hut, but it turned out to be a most comfortable house, worthy of any town. We went to the Scotch kirk next morning. The Church seems to have forgotten the existence of Shoalhaven. It would be much better if instead of appointing new bishops in Australia they would send clergymen to some of these heathenish districts. Then we dined at the Prosper De Mestres', and at three o'clock we started for Eeree. It was rather late, considering that we had a 25-mile ride before us over a bush road, but we waited for Bella's English letters, and got them.

We called upon Honor by the way. She and her five children live at Nowra, about two miles from Shoalhaven. She is waiting to join Lindon. We had a very pleasant ride through the bush till we came to the river, and there we waited nearly an hour for a man who had promised to punt us over, and who did not come.

At last Bella routed out a couple of Irish settlers, who lived near the bank, to punt us over, then the anchor was stuck in a log, and would not come up, and the punt was half full of water, and the horses would not go into it, so that it was all but dark by the time we were fairly afloat. Bella and I perched on the edge of the punt with our knees up to our noses to keep our feet dry, and the horses and Irishmen splashing in the water.

When we got to the other side we could hardly see to mount our horses, and the worst part of the road was before us. Bella declared she could not find the way, which I was not surprised at, for there appeared to be no track whatever. However, I suggested that the horses should be left to their own devices.

It was a pitch-dark night in the bush. I really could not see my own horse's head, and could only feel that he was descending into gullies and scrambling over logs, and stumbling among rocks, and sweeping me against bushes and boughs of trees, and once, by a gleam of light on the water, I saw that we were riding along a narrow path overhanging the river far below us.

27 Wife of Tregenna Biddulph.

"Bella and I perched on the edge of the punt."

Bella and I kept shouting to know where the other was and invariably answered "all right", till at last Bella pulled up, and said it was all wrong, that her horse was at fault, and she did not the least know where we were. This was cheerful, and we began to discuss the probabilities of spending the night in the bush, and the consequent rheumatism that we should catch, when my horse, an animal rejoicing in the name of Skittles, after turning round and round several times, seemed to find the way.

Altogether it was a most pleasant visit, and I was very sorry to leave that beautiful country and return to the dusty streets of Sydney.

It took me three days to get back. Tregenna rode with me one fine morning over the mountain to a point on the river, where we met the little steamer. I got on board her—the only passenger again—and had a very pleasant afternoon's sail, till it got dark. The river scenery is beautiful.

We had to take in so many sacks of potatoes and corn by the

way that we did not get to Shoalhaven till past eight in the evening. I went to the inn again, and spent the next day there by myself. I wrote some letters, went up to the De Mestres' to dinner, and in the afternoon walked out to Nowra. I had a quite pleasant walk back from Nowra by moonlight along the river, slept at the inn that night, and the next morning the captain of the steamer knocked up the whole inn for my benefit, and at six I embarked for another voyage down to the sea.

It was quite dark when we left, and the dawn and sunrise were so very beautiful over the broad Shoalhaven River. We got to the sea at eight, went on board the *Hunter*, and I had a very pleasant voyage to Sydney, where we arrived about eight in the evening, went up the harbour by moonlight. It was rough and windy, but quite fine, so I stayed on deck all day, ate a good breakfast, dinner and supper and escaped seasickness for that time.

Soon after my return I received a letter from Biddulph with the welcome news that he will be at Rockhampton to meet us on the 15th August, so if all is well we shall sail on the 8th or 9th of August, as it is nearly a week's voyage from Sydney to Rockhampton.

I told you in my last letter that Biddulph sailed for Brisbane just as I left for Shoalhaven, from thence he went to Rockhampton, wrote to us from there fixing the time of his return, and then set off on his long ride to Exmoor, between 350 and 400 miles. He had to go there to make ready for the reception of 10,000 sheep and two sisters.

He will soon be on his way back again to Rockhampton, where I hope we shall meet him all right, and then we shall set off on the same bush journey of about 350 miles. He is going to drive the dog-cart, and take saddle-horses as well, to ride when the road is bad. We shall make stations at night, when there are any near, and camp out when there are not. If only the weather is fine the journey will be rather fun, but if it is wet we shall probably catch the rheumatism. It will take about ten days.

Biddulph has bought a quantity of things for Exmoor. No end of books, crockery, American-store cases of jam and honey, lamps and I know not what besides. All the pretty presents that were sent to him and Annie will come in now. They were sent off to Port Denison long ago.

I expect the house itself will be of the roughest, windows I know there are none, and I have great doubts about the floors; also the interstices between the logs may be large, but I dare say we shall manage to make it tolerably comfortable. Do not be uneasy about my catching cold, dear Etta, for I know you will think of that. The winter will be over by the time we get up there, rather unfortunately, and at Eeree we lived in a perpetual draught, front and back door always open, and half our time in the yard or veranda, and I never had the slightest cold, while I am always getting them in Sydney. I am sure it is quite right to go, and that we shall be preserved from all harm, as far as it is good for us to be so.

July 10th. My late letters about our Exmoor plans, and my letter to Aunt Vizard, which she ought to receive this month, will already have answered her very kind invitation for me to come home to live with her. I cannot bear to think that she will be so much disappointed as you seem to think, and you, too, seem to reckon on, and wish for my return, and I know you will be disappointed at the turn things have taken.

I need not say what it would be to me to see you and the darling children, and to be at home again. If I were still at Bathurst, uncertain whether Exmoor would ever be habitable or what I should do next, your letters would have caused me much deliberation at least, but now I think my course is perfectly clear, and I am sure you will think so, too.

Biddulph has a house which he thinks will be comfortable, and is most anxious that we should both come out with him—witness his travelling 700 miles to secure our company! I shall never forget his blank look when Caroline asked him if he would be much disappointed if we did not go. I came out on purpose to live with him, and his change of place need not change my plans.

The Australians are making a noble subscription for the starving Lancashire weavers. Blood is thicker than water, as the Yankee said.

Ever your most affectionate sister,

RACHEL HENNING

SYDNEY,
AUGUST 15TH 1862

My Dearest Etta,

I hardly expected to write to you again from Sydney, but our going up to Rockhampton has been a little delayed, as after Annie came down we decided upon going up by the *Boomerang* instead of the *Eagle*. Annie has had dreadful experience of the

86

rollings and pitchings and cockroaches of the latter boat, and the *Boomerang* is nearly twice her size, and, I hope, cleaner. Besides which, we thought Biddulph could hardly calculate on being back from a 700-mile journey exactly by the 14th or 15th. In fact, if the rivers are up he might be detained for a week or so, and it is better that he should wait than that we should, there being no inn fit for ladies at Rockhampton.

Annie has a great many friends here whom I do not know, and she and Emily have been visiting about together with great glee. Annie and I make shopping appointments together, and I go over to the Surry Hills, and then we proceed into Sydney and buy the thousand and one things we want for the station.

Annie has got herself a new habit—a very thin cloth one, and we have each got a black silk dress to wear till the hot weather comes. They do not spoil, and yet always look nice, and Biddulph has a mortal horror of seeing people shabby. We both have those green mohairs, almost new—I mean the one you gave Annie, and she has, besides, quantities of muslins and prints and ginghams, and two other thin dresses.

I have been obliged to get another mohair—thin—and also a muslin—rather a pretty lilac one, for, as usual, I am very short of garments, having bought but one dress since I came out here. I am going to make my two old prints do. I do not think they will ever wear out.

Bonnets, of course, are no use in the bush. I got a new hat when I first came down here, rather a pretty black straw, and I have had my old one cleaned and trimmed and have a riding-hat besides, so I think I shall do. I have that old brown shawl, you remember, and a thin one I got last summer, so I think I shall do very well, though Annie and Emily bewail over my deficiencies.

Annie dresses exceedingly well. She is looking very nice just now. The cold climate of Bathurst has done her good, now that the work there is over. She is in capital spirits, and is looking forward to another six or seven months' stay in the bush with great delight.

There is a very good opera company here now, and they have been playing some of the best operas; and the Chapmans have taken me five times, to my great delight. The singing and acting are exceedingly good. Not, of course, equal to London opera, but better, it is said, than in any provincial town in England. They have performed *Lucretia Borgia, Trovatore, Maritana, Satanella* and *Farouita.* I know it is a sort of thing I should get a great deal too fond of. I hate parties and abhor balls, but the music and acting, and all without any trouble to oneself, is what I greatly enjoy.

Last night a gentleman of our acquaintance took a whole box and invited Annie and Emily Tucker, Mr and Mrs Chapman and myself, besides several other people. So we all went together, and great fun it was.

Annie does not care for the opera, but she likes to see the people and talk to her friends, and it appeared to me that the effect of her presence was to bring some dozen gentlemen to the back of the box between the acts to talk to her. She has such a number of acquaintances here.

August 13th. I came back to the Surry Hills on Monday, and since that Annie and I have lived in a continual skirmish. We shop all day and go out every evening. It is like going to Australia over again. We are obliged to take so many things up to Exmoor, as it will be nearly impossible to get anything till we come back again. Annie made purchase of a large case yesterday, which stands on the back veranda at present, and is destined to hold an extraordinary assortment of goods. A little ironmongery, a little crockery, some of our clothes and endless odds and ends.

Annie was pretty well provided with necessaries at Marlborough, but she could not pack the things herself for Exmoor, and the chances are that everything useful has been left behind, or broken. Biddulph got a quantity of things when he was here. A breakfast set, dinner set, any amount of books, etc., but it is little things that we shall probably be short of.

I am staying at home to write my English letters and get my things in general a little forward and in order, but all the rest of the family are gone to Waverley to a picnic. They have a lovely day for it, and it will be very pleasant on the hills by the sea, but I would not afford the time to go. I hate to be "driven up" at the last, and the *Boomerang* may be in any day now, and then she goes forty-eight hours after arrival. Saturday she is expected to sail, and that is only two days hence.

We shall have an escort up, as Mr John Stewart, a brother of Biddulph's former partner, is going up with us, also a Mr Wise, a friend of Annie's, and popularly supposed to be rather more than a friend if he had the wherewithal. He has a station somewhere up in the north, but a non-paying one.

Biddulph, in an evil hour, invited Mr John Stewart to visit him, and now he has chosen to accept the invitation and accompany us to Exmoor. I think he hopes the warm climate will cure the asthma, from which he suffers dreadfully, but it will be rather awkward if he is ill by the way.

I am not looking forward to the voyage with any great pleasure. The probability is that we shall both be seasick. I believe it is the close air which makes me ill on board those coasting steamers. The ladies' cabin, as they call it, is a dreadful hole, and there is no escape from it unless it is fine enough to be always on deck.

August 15th. Our last evening has come, and we sail for Rockhampton by the *Boomerang* tomorrow afternoon at five o'clock. We have been terribly busy these last few days. Today we have been packing all the morning and shopping all the afternoon. Then we went straight from Sydney to Paddington to wish Lizzie Chapman good-bye. There was quite a party there to meet us, but we could only stay to tea and come away

". . . a friend of Annie's, and popularly supposed to be rather more. . . ."

directly after. We have so very much still to do. Then we missed the Paddington omnibus and had to walk back nearly three miles in the dark (Emily, Annie and I). We got back to the Surry Hills at nine o'clock, and now I have half a night's work before me in the way of writing and finishing up things.

The English mail is in, and the letters will, we hope, be delivered tomorrow, just in time for us to get them before we go. It will be very vexing if we cannot get them. Among other things, we have had each a carte-de-visite likeness taken. Annie has distributed any amount among her friends here. I have sent one each to Aunt Henrietta and Aunt Vizard. I thought you would not care about another, as you have a much better likeness, and I look remarkably hideous in a carte-de-visite.

I have also one for Amy and Emily Tucker. We have bought

ourselves some waterproof cloaks with hoods for the journey, for as we have to travel nearly 400 miles in an open dog-cart, we should certainly get the rheumatics if it came on to rain. We have also invested in a railway rug lined with waterproof for camping out, as we shall have to spend four or five nights in the bush and the ground may be damp.

Annie and I have given Caroline a very nice black silk dress as a sort of "testimonial" for her kindness. We really come and go and lumber up the house with parcels and pack and skirmish here exactly as if it was our own home. Nothing can be kinder than the Hirsts always are to us.

I am writing a most stupid letter, but it has been written under great hindrances. At this moment six people are in full talk round me, and I am dead tired besides.

Good-bye, my dearest sister. I feel as if I was going further away from you than ever, but we shall always remember and love each other and I trust meet again in God's own good time. We expect to be back again in eight or nine months if all is well. If possible I will write you a line from Rockhampton to tell you of our safe arrival there, and after there you will not hear again very soon, but I will write whenever there is a chance of sending.

My kindest love to the darling children.

Ever your most affectionate sister,

RACHEL HENNING

II.

EXMOOR RUN

[*On 16th August 1862 Rachel and Annie sailed in the coastal steamer* Boomerang *for Rockhampton, where Biddulph met them. On 24th August they set out for Marlborough station, which Biddulph had bought in 1858, later taking two partners of Tucker and Co. in with him. Annie had previously spent a good deal of time at Marlborough. On 29th August the party set out for Exmoor, the new property Biddulph had taken up. Biddulph himself described his acquisition of Exmoor as follows:*

"A Mr Stuart, employed by Lawson Brothers, of Bundoona station, came through Marlborough. He had a large number of ewes, and he wanted lambing country. I gave him the use of some of my run, and in return he told me of some good country in the South Kennedy district. He was unable to apply for it, as the district had not been thrown open to leaseholders.

"The South Kennedy district was soon after proclaimed, and I applied for a large area, being the watershed of the Bowen River, from its head to its junction with the Broken River, about thirty miles in length. A large party went out with the commissioner, Mr Dalrymple, to inspect the land applied for, or to apply for other portions. I went out with Mr Devlin, my superintendent. I was very pleased with the country, and arranged with my partners, Tucker and Co., to divide our property, they taking Marlborough, together with the sheep and half the horses, and I the new country, which I called 'Exmoor', together with the remaining horses and the cattle."]

MARLBOROUGH,
QUEENSLAND,
AUGUST 28TH 1862

My Dearest Etta,

We have got thus far on our journey, and I most unexpectedly have time to write to you, as we are luggage-bound here for two days.

I wrote to you from Rockhampton just before we started on our northward journey. We stayed there two whole days, and on the 24th Biddulph came over for us about the middle of the day.

It was raining when we left Rockhampton, but we were so tired of the place, and Biddulph was so tired of waiting also that we preferred taking the chance of bad weather, and the result proved we were right. Biddulph had our horses waiting on the other side of the river, and by a superhuman effort of packing we crammed our dresses and crinolines into a valise which he carried before him, while the rest of our property went into that little black bag we bought at Bristol and which I fastened to my saddle. All our other goods had been sent on the night before to the camp. The "camp", namely Mr Hedgeland, Mr Stewart and the horses, started before Biddulph came over for us.

I think I told you before that he had been encamped on the other side of the river for more than a week. We caught them up after a ten-mile canter, and then proceeded more quietly. The whole concern formed quite a cavalcade and looked so picturesque winding through the bush. We had five saddle-horses ridden by Annie and myself, Biddulph, Mr Hedgeland and Mr Stewart, five packhorses and six spare horses driven loose. We had to leave a good deal of our luggage at Rockhampton to be sent round to Port Denison, and the rest was packed in six "bushel bags" and slung on the said packhorses, to the sore discomfiture of our dresses, etc.

We made twenty-three miles that afternoon and got to a station called Yamba for the night. We had some storms by the way, but nothing to matter much. Annie and I went up to the house, where we were very kindly received by Mrs Macdonald; the rest of the party camped in the bush as usual. We saw quantities of blacks that day; a whole tribe seemed to be camped on the station. They are the queerest-looking mortals certainly, with their long lean legs and arms without an atom of flesh on them, more like spiders than anything human. Their costume is usually a shirt and nothing else. Men and women wear the same, and they laugh and show their white teeth whenever you look at them.

The next morning Biddulph came for us about nine o'clock. Fortunately it was very fine, and we soon joined the camp and set off again. We only made about twenty miles that day, as we had to stop about four o'clock, having reached the only camping-place where there was good feed and water for many miles. We made our first acquaintance with "camping out" that night, and found it rather pleasant than otherwise.

It was a very pretty spot on the bank of a creek, with shady trees and plenty of green grass. The blackboy they had with them had run away at Rockhampton, so Biddulph, Mr Hedgeland and Mr Stewart had to do everything themselves. They are first-rate bushmen—the two former at least—and in no time they had the horses unloaded, hobbled and turned out to feed, then a great fire was lighted by a fallen tree.

Mr Stewart went to the creek for water and proceeded to boil it in quart pots while Biddulph and Mr Hedgeland unpacked a very nice little tent, which was slung between two trees. Biddulph chopped down a sapling with his tomahawk and cut it into pegs, and in less than no time we had quite a comfortable little abode in the wilderness.

By the time the tea was boiled in the quart pots they spread blankets on the grass, and we each had a pint pot into which the hot tea was poured. We had some very good damper, fresh beef, cheese and jam and I was never so hungry in my life, having had nothing since breakfast and ridden twenty miles.

"We could hear the horse-bells as they were feeding round us."

When it got dusk we all drew round the fire, and I wished I could send you a picture of the camp then. Annie and I had a very comfortable sort of sofa made of a railway rug and the packs off the horses to lean against. Biddulph was sitting on a log in his shirt sleeves reading the *Home News* by the firelight, Mr Hedgeland kneeling on the grass manufacturing a damper for next day's consumption, and Mr Stewart intent on boiling some more tea for the refreshment of the establishment before going to bed. There was a tremendous fire, and it looked so pretty against the background of dark bush. We could hear the horse-bells as they were feeding round us, and the frogs croaking in the creek, else you may fancy it was quiet enough.

Annie and I betook ourselves to our tent about nine o'clock, where they had made us up a very comfortable bed of blankets and rugs, with our carpet-bags for a pillow, and you will wonder to hear that we slept as soundly as possible in our novel bed-room.

We turned out about seven the next morning and found the fire lighted and the tea boiled and Biddulph driving in the horses, wet up to his knees with the dew. Annie and I went down to the creek and washed our hands and faces; then we had breakfast, damper, beef, jam and quart-pot tea again. The others had slept by the fire under their blankets.

I do not think Mr Stewart much appreciated the opportunity, as he is new to this sort of thing; of course it is nothing to Biddulph and Mr Hedgeland.

Then the horses were loaded, a work of some time, the saddles put on, and off we went again. Annie and I did not always keep up with the packhorses. When it was very dusty we walked our horses some distance behind them and cantered up to them now and then.

We got to Princhester in the middle of the day and got some dinner there, the usual beef and damper and a higher table than usual. It is a remarkable peculiarity of the bush tables that the top is about on a level with the nose of a short person.

We did twenty-five miles that day and reached Marlborough in the evening, with ourselves and baggage none the worse for our journey. We took up our quarters at Biddulph's old house, a very comfortable sort of abode, and they say the house at Exmoor is better, so we shall do very well. There is no glass in the window, and certainly there are interstices between the logs, but they are not very wide, and then the climate is wonderful: the mornings and evenings are cold enough to make a fire pleasant, but in the middle of the day it is hotter than most English summer days. The thermometer was 78 inside the house at dinner-time and 115 in the sun.

The new house Biddulph built is a very nice one, ten good rooms with glass windows. What a pity we cannot put it on a dray and carry it with us to Exmoor!

We then took a walk down to the creek, where we picked branches of fire-tree; it bears a most beautiful crimson blossom and keeps some time in water. There is to be a township on Marlborough station, and all the part about the house is to be sold in allotments. All Biddulph's improvements are capital; the woolshed, meathouse, forge, kitchens, men's huts and dwelling-house are so very well put up.

We have been very busy since we came here, packing the things for Exmoor. Biddulph sent on some of the furniture by drays before he came down to meet us, but it has not yet arrived, having stuck in a creek and come to grief. By the way, the books, I am afraid, are nearly all spoiled, as the water rose in the creek.

Besides the packhorses we are going to take with us a spring-cart and the dog-cart. Some mattresses and bedding are to go in the spring-cart, as it is doubtful whether any has arrived at Exmoor yet. Mr Stewart is going to drive it. We should have been off today only that the said spring-cart wanted mending, and nobody could be persuaded to do it, so Biddulph and Mr Hedgeland have been tinkering at it themselves today. It is a matter of curious calculation how far it will hold together.

Biddulph will drive a tandem in the dog-cart himself, but I dare say we shall ride a good part of the way, as we have the horses with us. We shall have to camp out a good many nights going up, as what stations there are are mostly off the road. We shall take about ten days about it, as you cannot make more than twenty-five miles a day with two vehicles and sixteen horses. Packhorses cannot be driven very fast.

Our escort up the country consists of just Biddulph, who is looking very well and handsome just now and who is as easy and good-tempered as ever, taking strayed horses, damaged carts, unpunctual sisters (for we kept him waiting a week at Rock-hampton) with equal and imperturbable good temper; then there is Mr George Hedgeland, who has been with Biddulph a long time and is going to stay on at Exmoor with him. He is going to run some sheep on the station, and I dare say will do very well. I like him very much. He is Biddulph's right hand and works harder than Biddulph himself, being much more methodical. I do not think we should ever get through all the packing and arranging without him.

Then there is Mr Stewart, a brother to the Mr William Stewart you know, a quiet, good-natured little man with bad health; he is going up to see if the climate of Queensland agrees with him; and finally we are to take a certain "Tom" to cook for us at Exmoor and catch the horses, etc. We have seven revolvers among the party, for which there is not likely to be any need. Biddulph drives the dog-cart, Mr Stewart the cart, and Mr Hedgeland and Tom drive the horses, and we start early tomorrow morning.

And now I must stop as it is late, the spring-cart is packed, our "Sunday best", as Annie says, is once more deposited in three "bushel-bags", some fowls that we are going to take are cackling on the floor with their legs tied, the horses are in the stockyard ready to start, and tomorrow will see us on our way to the far north. We shall be able to write as soon as we get to Exmoor, as some drays are to be sent down.

With love from your affectionate sister,

RACHEL HENNING

EXMOOR,
PORT DENISON,
SEPTEMBER 23RD 1862

My Dearest Etta,

I wrote to you last from Marlborough, and now that we are arrived at Exmoor and a little settled, I will begin to tell you of our adventures by the way, as we may have an opportunity of sending a letter in a few days.

August 29th. We left Marlborough about three o'clock in the afternoon, after a great scrimmage to get off, and this was the cavalcade that started: first Biddulph driving a tandem in a dog-cart, the back of the dog-cart being packed with an infinity of things including a crate with some fowls in it, who cackled as we went. Annie and I took it in turns to ride on horseback or drive with Biddulph. I was in the dog-cart the first day and was exceedingly entertained by the second part of the procession, which consisted of Mr Stewart driving the spring-cart with the luggage.

He is a funny-looking little man, and had seen fit to array himself in a Crimean shirt which he put on *over* his other clothes, and he sat perched on a carpet-bag, holding the reins in his hands in the most helpless way, for he had never driven before and letting the horse go exactly where he pleased, to Biddulph's infinite disgust.

He kept shouting "Mind that gum-tree, Stewart! Look out for that log!" and then *sotto voce*: "I know that man will smash the cart before he has gone a mile." Behind came a mob of twenty-two horses, some of them packed but many driven loose, to change the draught-horses. Annie, Mr Hedgeland and Tom

96

rode behind them, the two latter driving them, and quite enough they had to do. Tom came up to Exmoor to act as cook and waiter; he was with Biddulph at Marlborough, has been steward on board a ship, and is a very handy fellow in everything but driving horses, which he performs as a sailor might be expected to do.

"Our only misadventure that first day. . . ."

Well, our only misadventure that first day was that Mr Stewart at last contrived to lock the wheel of the cart safely against a gum-tree; the horse was a powerful one, the gum-tree was strong, something must give way, and fortunately it was the harness, not the cart, and the horse walked off without a strap upon him. Mr Stewart tumbled out of the cart and stood looking on aghast while all hands patched up the harness with ropes, etc.

We camped about five o'clock. Annie, Mr Stewart and I lit the fire and boiled the tea while the rest were for two hours trying to catch and hobble a refractory mare belonging to Mr Hedgeland, which he was driving up to the station with the other horses.

She was unbroken and had a foal with her. The first thing done on coming into camp always is to hobble all the horses, which is fastening a strap round each foreleg with a short chain between; it is intended to prevent them straying far, but does not always succeed.

They caught the horse at last and we had tea, a talk round the campfire and such a sound sleep in our tent. We brought two small mattresses on with us from Marlborough and so were exceedingly comfortable.

August 30th. The usual bustle of catching the horses, packing and saddling. I rode today and Annie went in the dog-cart. Mr Morisset, one of the mounted police officers, joined us in the course of the morning, and we all stopped at the Tooloomba Inn and dined off sucking-pig! We had had nothing but salt beef since leaving Rockhampton, and you would have laughed to see how that sucking-pig disappeared. Mr Morisset left us at Tooloomba.

Our afternoon's stage ended rather unluckily; just before reaching our camping-place we had to cross a dreadful creek. These creeks are the great plague of Australian travelling; they are deep river-beds, sometimes narrow, sometimes very wide, often with the sides nearly perpendicular, except where drays have found some sort of passage.

Biddulph is a capital driver. If you could only see the places we took the dog-cart down into and out of again. I believe it was the first vehicle, except drays, that was ever taken up the country. Well, this Tooloomba Creek was worse than usual, the banks being like the roof of a house. Biddulph got the dog-cart safely into it—and then the getting out!

Two fresh horses were put in; Biddulph and Mr Hedgeland went at their heads, Tom and Mr Stewart ran behind with logs of wood to put behind the wheels the moment the horses checked. A tremendous strain, a shout and a tug and the dog-cart was safe on the opposite bank!

Then came the spring-cart that was heavier, and weak in its constitution besides; it was got half-way up the side when the horses jibbed and backed, and in a moment the cart was upset and lying in a smash at the bottom of the creek. Its bones repose there now. It was hopelessly broken, and there was nothing for it but to unload and leave it to its fate.

We camped that night beside the creek, and a very pretty creek it was, with pools of clear water lying about among the trees in it. Annie and I did a little "Dorothea" and washed our feet in a sequestered waterhole the next morning.

Sunday, August 31st. Sunday is not much like Sunday when travelling in the bush. Very early in the morning Biddulph packed the dog-cart with all that could be spared of the baggage, and took it back to the Tooloomba Inn to leave it there till the drays are sent down from Exmoor. A great deal of the furniture is also at Tooloomba, the dray that was taking it up having come to grief in the same creek.

Mr Stewart also left us here; he had had quite enough of bush travelling by the time he got to Marlborough and only accompanied us another day under protest till Biddulph could find a man to drive the cart. He was no great loss, as he was utterly unused to bush life and a most helpless individual, with ill-health into the bargain.

Biddulph did not get back from Tooloomba with the dog-cart till about twelve o'clock, so we only made a short day's journey with our diminished train. I went in the dog-cart, Tom drove the horses, which were getting used to the road now, and Annie rode with Mr Hedgeland.

We camped early, and were sitting round the fire resting and peacefully drinking our tea when Tom came running up to say that "the old black horse" had bogged himself in a creek; that is, had stuck in the mud, and, being hobbled, could not get out again. Off went Biddulph and Mr Hedgeland, and for two mortal hours they were all three at work up to their knees in water trying to get that horse out.

They caught the strongest horse of the mob, harnessed him to the other, and by alternately dragging at his head and tail extricated him at last, in a very woeful condition, covered with mud from head to foot. They came back wet and weary and we were all glad to turn in.

I never slept in my life as I did in that tent. Biddulph insisted on bringing on our mattresses, so they were rolled up and lashed behind the dog-cart, to the great improvement of its appearance. We had plenty of blankets and were as warm and comfortable as possible. Living in the open air and riding twenty-five miles a day is a great promoter of sleep. We used to turn in about nine o'clock, and got up at sunrise. We were usually waked by the cock we were taking up with us. Every night I used to take him and his wife out of the crate in which they were travelling and tethered them by the leg to the wheel of the dog-cart, "for exercise", and put them back again in the morning.

Mr Hedgeland slept in a hammock which he slung between two trees, and Biddulph usually took up his rest on the dog-cart cushions by the fire, while Tom made a little private fire of his own and rolled himself up in his blankets.

September 1st. Great tribulation this morning. Three of the horses were missing and could by no possibility be found. We camped all day to look for them. Two of our escort were perpetually out scouring the country while one stayed with us, as they did not like to leave us alone in that wild country. However, the day wore away and the horses could not be found. Annie and I improved the time by mending sundry rents in our habits and gloves, and generally polishing up our garments, which suffered grievously from the dust, which is dreadful. They gave up the search when it got dark, and we sat round the fire and discussed things in general.

September 2nd. We could not wait any longer. Biddulph was so dreadfully afraid of bad weather coming on, so we started with the dog-cart and horses, leaving Mr Hedgeland to go to Wilangi, the nearest station, and try and get a blackboy there to come and track the horses.

In the middle of the day we got to Waverley, Mr Macartney's station, where we stopped and dined. Mrs Macartney and her sister were at home, rather pleasant people. They had a comfortable little bush house with a veranda covered with passion-vine and a garden full of petunias in most brilliant flower. We begged a whole bundle of cuttings, and after dinner started again and made a long stage to get to the foot of the Collaroy Range, so as to climb the mountains in the morning. We did not arrive till dark, and Annie and I made the fire and boiled the tea, while Biddulph and Tom unloaded and hobbled the horses.

We camped in a sort of valley at the foot of the mountains near a creek, quite a romantic place. On our whole journey from Marlborough to Exmoor we never went to a station at night. The few there were lay off the road, and would have cost us several miles' journey, and we liked camping better. When we got in tired after a long day's journey, it was much pleasanter to pin up our habits and repose ourselves on very luxurious sofas made of blankets and saddle-bags in front of the fire, while Tom got our tea and Biddulph and Mr Hedgeland made fun of things in general—much pleasanter than to go to a station, dress and make ourselves agreeable—or disagreeable—to strangers all the evening.

September 3rd. All up very early. Biddulph and Tom directly after breakfast put the two best horses in the dog-cart and set off to get it up the Collaroy Range, an ascent of a mile long and about as steep as the roof of a house. Annie and I stayed in the camp to take care of the property and keep the horses in; the latter office we found it so troublesome to perform on foot that after two of them had led me a dance of nearly a mile through long grass I caught one of the riding-horses and we took it by turns to mount him and keep the rest together.

Biddulph and Tom came back about twelve, packed the horses and off we all set to climb the range. I never saw anything more beautiful than that mountain scenery. It was threatening for rain, and some of the mountains were in mist, some in sunshine, and you cannot imagine wilder crags and mountains rolling behind mountains. Annie got giddy about half-way up and got off her horse, but was peremptorily mounted again by Biddulph with the assurance that she would kill herself if she tried to walk up.

We reached the top at last, and found the dog-cart safe and the horses tied to a tree, and while they were being harnessed up again the rain, which had been threatening, came down. Such tremendous mountain rain; fortunately we had bought in Sydney some waterproof cloaks with hoods or we should have been wet through in five minutes. They kept us tolerably dry, and it was rather satisfactory that we had not bought them for nothing, for hitherto the weather had been lovely.

We had storms all the afternoon, but not settled rain, which was fortunate, for the road over and among the mountains was so frightfully bad that both Biddulph and Tom had to attend to the dog-cart, one at the head of the leader and the other of the wheeler, and in consequence Annie and I had to drive the nineteen horses, no sinecure among those ranges and gullies, where they kept bolting out of the road in search of "feed", and we had to gallop after them among rocks and roots and in all sorts of undesirable places. We had a long and tiresome day's journey, but at last got out of the mountains and camped by a creek at their base.

We had hardly stopped when the rain, which had ceased for a time, came down in a pelt. Mr Hedgeland overtook us just as we halted. He had found the horses by the help of a black-boy. They had not strayed at all, but had been "planted" by some miscreant, in the hope of stealing them when we were gone. They were found in a creek, each with one leg tied up, and with the bell silenced that was round the neck of one of them. He only got them that morning, and had ridden hard after us, leading them three in a string, as they objected to being driven.

Biddulph was in great tribulation for fear we should catch cold by camping in the rain, but I was not the least afraid of it; however, they pitched our tent in a twinkling, covered the ground with branches to keep the mattresses off the wet, hung our waterproof cloaks over the tent where there was a hole, and very soon we were sitting under shelter wrapped up in our blankets, and as warm and comfortable as I ever was in my life. Of course they pitched their own tent, which they never did in fine weather.

Tom lit a great fire and made some beautiful "johnny cakes" —thin soda cakes which are baked in about ten minutes and are the best bread you ever ate, and with johnny cakes and jam and hot tea, which was brought us in the tent by shiny mackintoshed figures, we continued to do very well. A tin pannikin of hot wine and water was put under the curtain the last thing with the remark from Biddulph that it was to keep off the rheuma-tism, and we slept as sound as if we had a dozen roofs over our heads instead of the rain pattering upon the canvas.

September 4th. Rainy morning, and Biddulph had some thoughts of camping all day, but a council being holden round our tent, and we being decidedly of opinion that we would rather ride in the rain that sit there all day, the order was given to saddle up and, the rain having abated, we set off again.

We were still among mountains, though off the Collaroy Range, and the scenery was very beautiful. We had storms all day, but not settled rain, so we thought ourselves very fortunate. I cannot tell how often the waterproofs were put on and taken off, nor what queer objects we looked in them on horseback. We had to camp again in the rain, but it did not last very long, and we had a dry night. The camp was in the prettiest spot we have had on a sort of range chosen for its dry and stony properties, with mountains all round us, the mist rolling over them.

September 5th. A beautiful morning, and the rain quite over,

102

so we thought ourselves very well off, for after the long dry weather we have had we expected at least a week of it.

We got clear of the mountains today, and took to the dog-cart again. Annie rode the first half of the way, and I the latter. Camped on a plain by a very muddy waterhole, where washing was the pursuit of cleanliness under great difficulties, as we had to stand in the mud to wash our faces, which I fear come out rather dirtier from the process. No one would drink such water in England, but it was not so bad in tea.

You must travel in the bush to know how good quart-pot tea is. About five quart tin pots are filled with water and set to boil before the fire. At the moment of boiling a pinch of tea is poured into a pint pannikin, and, thirsty and dusty as you generally are, it is the most delightful draught you ever tasted in your life. You think milk would only spoil it!

We did pretty well in the commissariat department. The "ration bags" contained flour, sugar, tea, sardines, bacon, cheese, salt beef and salmon and jam; and we had two bottles of wine and two of brandy in a small box in the dog-cart. Tom made capital damper and soda bread, and that sort of outdoor life makes you hungry and thirsty as you never are in a civilized country.

September 6th. Very fine, and we made a good day's journey. We were out of meat, so in the middle of the day Mr Hedgeland was detached from the main body in search of supplies. He took with him a led horse and an empty ration bag and proceeded to the nearest station, where he obtained some mutton, which, however, was very lean, or, as Tom expressed it, "showful"—not knowing the derivation of the word I cannot say how it is spelt—some dried apples, flour, sugar and other necessaries, pipes included.

We camped by a very pretty creek this evening, and Mr Hedgeland joined us with the above refreshments just as we had unloaded. We passed some very bad creeks today. How the dog-cart has held together considering the places it has been run into and dragged out of is a perfect marvel to me. We had vegetables with the "showful" mutton, for Tom discovered some "fat hen" in the creek, and when boiled it is not at all unlike spinach. I think it is a species of goosefoot; it is exactly like the English plant of that name.

September 7th. A very hot day's journey, and at the end of it we seemed to be come to a standstill altogether, for we arrived at a creek to which there seemed no possible passage. They rode a mile or two up and down it, to find a crossing, and at last decided on trying the hopeful one before us. Biddulph led the horse down the precipice, Tom and Mr Hedgeland clinging on behind to hold the dog-cart back a little. Then came the getting out again, which I think took nearly an hour. Horse after horse was put in and jibbed, and two could not pull there. It was got to the top at last, and we were very glad to camp on the spot, for it was all but dark.

September 8th. Another hot day, travelling through the Fort Cooper station, so called from a queer pyramidal hill which looks almost as if it were artificial. Made a long stage that day, as we had to reach a camping-place where there was water.

Annie and I both rode in the afternoon, as we were going over the Exmoor Range, a range of low stony hills that separate Exmoor from the next station. Camped at half past five on the top of a small hill entirely covered with stones, very sharp stones, too, and the way that ourselves and the horses hobbled about was something dismal to look at.

The water that we had taken such pains to reach was contained in a small and very muddy hole at the foot of the hill, as we found next morning when we walked about a quarter of a mile to wash our hands and faces.

September 9th. We both rode, as the road was bad. Beautiful weather again, and the country very pretty, but very dry, and we hurried on to reach a creek where Biddulph meant to camp, as the horses had no water since the morning. We reached it about four o'clock, and desperately thirsty we all were. The pint pot was untied from the splashboard of the dog-cart, where it always travelled in company with spare hobbles, straps, pieces of hide and rope and a general arrangement of rubbish which would have had a cheerful and pleasing effect if anyone had been there to see it.

A double-barrelled gun was lashed on each side of the dog-cart and the mattresses were slung behind, the back seat being one that shut up. However, this fascinating vehicle was left in the road, and men, women and horses made a general rush to the creek—it was perfectly dry, not a drop of water left in it.

With very blank faces we were turning away when Tom called out "Look, sir, there's a mudhole chock-full of black snakes!" On investigation, however, it turned out that they were not snakes, but eels, which had taken refuge in the last remains of damp mud. In a moment Biddulph, Mr Hedgeland and Tom were armed with sticks and an exciting scrimmage ensued. More than a dozen fine eels were knocked on the head and deposited in a bag, which Tom hung on his saddle. Then instead of camping we all started again to get to the river, which was seven miles further, but there was no water nearer and it must be reached.

I was riding in the dog-cart with Biddulph, and a most extraordinary country we passed through: low hills covered thickly with small granite boulders from one to six feet high, and all smooth and rounded as if water-worn. We also picked up great pieces of petrified wood on another hill. The granite hills were pleasant for the dog-cart; how we did bump round and over and through the boulders! The country was so perfectly new that I quite enjoyed the drive, only I was so thirsty.

Just at sundown we reached the river, a deep precipitous bank, and at the bottom a small clear stream of running water. How the horses rushed down the bank and how they did drink: and how the tin pannikins came out and were emptied at a draught! You never know what thirst is unless you have travelled a whole day under an Australian sun without water.

We crossed the river—the Burdekin[1]—and camped on the other side in Biddulph's country. The eels were boiled for supper and were exceedingly good; and as we sat round the fire and discussed them I think we were rather sorry it was our last camp, for the journey on the whole was very pleasant: that outdoor life is so healthy, too. I was perfectly well from the time I sailed from Sydney till I reached Exmoor. Annie was pretty well, too, but she got rather tired with the daily travelling and "shaking up", as Amy calls it.

September 10th. Travelling through the Exmoor country, and very pretty it is, low undulating hills excellent for sheep, and here and there broad grassy plains. It was all very brown though, as we are sorely in want of rain.

Biddulph has fine natural boundaries to his station—a range of hills, or rather mountains, on each side; those on the eastward are rounded hills like the Quantocks; those to the west are most picturesque. On the side towards the station they are cut down from the summit into a precipitous wall of rock, which runs for miles and miles and seems to shut out the world beyond with a natural wall.

Annie and I both rode the first part of the day, as the road

1 Actually one of the Burdekin's many tributaries.

was bad, and Tom in the excitement of getting home drove the horses along so frantically that he shook off all their packs, and had twice to go back and look for bags that had been dropped off. We overtook the dog-cart at last; Biddulph was waiting for us by the side of a running creek, so we stopped there and had our lunch. We never camped in the day during the whole journey, but put some bread and cheese in our pockets which we ate as we rode along, and got some water with it when we could.

Annie got into the dog-cart when we overtook it, and I rode the rest of the way. We crossed a wide open plain at a gallop, for the horses knew they were getting home, and then a clearing through the gum-trees brought us in sight of a long, low building of dark slabs, with a deep veranda in front, with a variety of doors and windows opening into the same. A neat little building, evidently the kitchen, a short distance off, some tents and men's huts behind where there were slabs piled up, and various preparations for building. The rails of a very strong stockyard appeared between the trees further back still.

The house stands upon a low hill; the ground has been cleared in front, and the creek which supplies us with water runs at the foot of it; beyond there is an interval of bush, the whole closed in by the eastern range of mountains before mentioned; and a very pleasant prospect it is. At all times of the day they are beautiful, especially in the evening, when they take generally a deep violet hue.

Mr Devlin, the superintendent, was away at Port Denison; so was Mr Robertson, so we had the place all to ourselves. I was surprised to see such a good house and one that, though very rough, possessed such capabilities for improvements.

But rough it undoubtedly was at first. The furniture consisted of: in the sitting-room, a table and some wooden benches round it, a few stretchers made of rough wood were scattered about the establishment, one of which Annie had, while I, fearing aborigines [insects], put my mattress on a sheet of zinc supported on two boxes. However, we were prepared for all deficiencies of this sort, as we knew from Mr Hedgeland that not a stick of the furniture had yet arrived; indeed, we had seen it packed in the veranda at the Tooloomba Inn. The books only had arrived, in a state of soak, for they had been capsized into a creek and all spoiled as far as appearance went, and a great pity it was.

It seemed quite strange to sleep under a roof again, though it certainly was a very airy one. We sat in the veranda all the evening and discussed our journey, and ought to have been very thankful to have arrived at home safe and well.

With love from your affectionate sister,

RACHEL HENNING

EXMOOR STATION,
PORT DENISON,
SEPTEMBER 29TH 1862

My Dearest Etta,

I like Exmoor very much, and think we shall be very happy in our new home. I am so glad we have got here at last. You must fancy a long low building, built of dark-coloured slabs of wood with a veranda in front, and the doors and windows opening into it. It contains five rooms: the first is our bedroom, the next the store and the next the parlour. At the back of ours is Biddulph's and Mr Hedgeland's room, and at the back of the parlour is another bedroom wherein reside any other members of the "staff" who happen to be at home—more than half are always at the out-stations. The kitchen is next door to the house, and behind are men's huts, sheds and gunyahs, etc.

The house stands on a low hill at the foot of which runs the creek which supplies us with water, and a very pretty creek it is, with deep banks covered with trees and shrubs. We have a piece of ground fenced and dug for a garden at the foot of the hill, but at present it only contains some pines and pumpkins and some petunia cuttings.

If it would only rain we should sow lots of seeds, but it is a very dry season. The ground in front of the house is at present in a state of nature, rough and stony, with gum-trees still scattered here and there. Beyond the creek we look over about two miles of bush to a beautiful range of mountains, which form the eastward boundary of the Exmoor run, so we have a very pretty view. The country round is beautiful, broken ridges and the river and creeks, and, of course, any quantity of bushland, but we have not seen much of it as yet.

Besides Biddulph, Annie and myself, the inmates of the house are: Mr Hedgeland, Mr Devlin, the superintendent, Mr Taylor, the sheep overseer, Mr Cressall, Mr Robertson and young Simpson, Mr Devlin's nephew, but these are never all at home together; indeed, now being the lambing season, they are all busy, and the whole establishment are perpetually riding about the country to see after the lambs or to find grass and water for the sheep.

When we first came up the house was in a very rough state, as we had been fully prepared to find it; none of the furniture had come up from Marlborough, so we had only benches and a rough table in the parlour and some rough bedsteads for us. But three evenings ago the drays from Port Denison arrived.

The advent of the drays is always a great event on a station, and these, besides the ordinary stores, contained some of our cases and boxes from Sydney. It was about six o'clock on Thursday evening that the cracking of stockwhips was heard in the bush the other side of the creek, and presently the long train of bullocks came in sight. Biddulph was sitting on the veranda with us, but down he flew to help get the drays over the creek.

Young Simpson had just come in on horseback, and down he went likewise, and presently there was such a chorus of shouting and bawling as was never heard out of Australia. I suppose it helped the oxen to drag the heavy drays through the sand of the creek, for they presently appeared rising the hill and drew up in front of the veranda—first a very large new wagon drawn by twelve splendid bullocks (Biddulph is very proud of his teams), next a large dray with ten bullocks yoked in it, and finally a smaller dray with eight bullocks. This latter was driven by a blackboy named Alick, and his gin, Biddy, was perched on the top, such a queer object dressed in a Crimean shirt and, I believe, no other garment.

The drays were left for that night, the bullock-drivers took up their rest on the veranda and the blacks camped by a fire under the gum-trees in front of the house.

With love from your affectionate sister,

RACHEL HENNING

EXMOOR,
PORT DENISON,
OCTOBER 18TH 1862

My Dearest Etta,

After being nearly nine weeks without seeing a letter, on Thursday last, the 16th of this month, our eyes were gladdened by the sight of a dirty newspaper parcel which was conveyed to the station by an amiable individual who rode six miles out of his way to bring it.

We espied the parcel under Biddulph's arm as he stood talking to the man who had brought it, and instantly dispatched Mr Hedgeland to extract it therefrom, as it was impossible to say how long our respected brother might stand and "yarn" about the news from Port Denison, and the prospects of the country generally.

I untied the parcel, and to our great delight it contained letters from yourself, Amy, Emily Tucker, Bella and a few Sydney friends of Annie's; newspapers, the *Cornhill Magazine*, and some letters also for some of the gentlemen on the station, and one or two for the shepherds.

Of course the reading that ensued was tremendous. (I forgot to say that Biddulph himself had about a dozen business letters.) Yours came very quickly, considering the distance. It is dated July 18th, and arrived here October 16th, but I fear we shall not always get them so speedily.

This is your birthday, my dearest Etta. May you have many happy returns of it. I wonder where and how you will spend it. I wish I was with you, though I like being here, too. I certainly do like this place very much, and so I think would you if you were here. We are going out, so I must not write any more today.

October 19th, Sunday afternoon. Sunday seems so quiet in the bush. I should like to hear some church bells, but there is no bell near, except that on the blackboy's pony, which I hear tinkling somewhere in the bush. It is a beautiful afternoon, the warm air blowing in through the open door and window, and whispering among the gum-trees, cloud shadows gliding over the opposite mountain range, great Lion, the bloodhound, lying asleep in the doorway, quite regardless of being walked or fallen over. Biddulph arrayed in white trousers, white coat and regatta shirt (nobody ever sits in the parlour without a coat) is lazily reading in an armchair in the pleasant recess where the books are. Mr Hedgeland in a similar airy costume is writing to his aunts, the Miss Hedgelands at Exeter, at the table. Annie, in a very pretty black and green mohair dress trimmed with green silk lozenges, is also writing—to Amy. Mr Taylor and Beckford, who came in last night, one from the Seven Mile, and the other from a station forty miles off, are sitting on the veranda discoursing.

Away down the hill among the trees I can see the blankets of the establishment all hung upon a line, and as they are mostly scarlet ones, they have a very picturesque effect. Presently, when we have done writing, and Biddulph wakes up—he is not to say asleep—we shall go for a walk, probably to the site of the new house, and then on to the plains beyond, and up the "Blackwall", a curious range of cliff that bounds the station on the west for two miles, then we shall come back to dinner.

Tom always provides an extra good one on Sundays, and in the evening Biddulph will have in Tom and the Forsters, and any shepherds or bushmen that are on the head station, and will read the evening service. You cannot think how nicely he reads, reverently and distinctly, and yet very simply, and the people seem glad to come in and to have the Sunday made a little different from other days.

We have been taking some nice rides lately, when Biddulph or Mr Hedgeland goes to the out-stations with provisions, or rations, as they call them; we generally go too for a ride. The stations are named according to their distance very often. There is the Two Mile, the Five Mile, the Seven Mile, the Twelve Mile, Grass Valley, Running Creek, etc. We went out to the Seven Mile a few evenings ago; such a pretty place—a plain just under a range of such noble mountains and close by the Broken River.

If the shepherds had any taste for the picturesque they would rejoice greatly in such a station, but I am afraid they do not appreciate it. A shepherd's must be a lonely life. There are two at the Seven Mile, but their flocks are a mile apart. They each have a yard made of branches of trees, strong enough to keep the sheep in, and the wild dogs out at night, a tent generally, a pot for boiling beef, a sheet of zinc or bark, and the unfailing pair of red blankets for a bed, and a sheepdog. This is generally a shepherd's establishment.

During the lambing season some of the "staff" go out and live at the more important stations to look after the shepherds. Mr Taylor is at one, Mr Cressall at another and Mr Devlin and Mr Robertson are both at a very distant one forty miles off. Mr Hedgeland goes out with rations and helps when he is wanted, and he is here on a visit. He and Annie are great friends and may perhaps be more.

Mr Robertson is pleasant and good-natured and good-looking, fond of poetry, which he can repeat by the yard, always bringing home birds or fossils or wild fruit or "U.K.s" of some kind or other. Just one of those people who are generally described as "no one's enemy but their own".

Mr Taylor is English, a clergyman's son, and well educated, rather shy, but with a good deal of fun in him, a little of the Vincent Macey style in appearance, with a great deal of black hair that would be the better for cutting.

I have not seen Mr Devlin yet. He has never been home since we came. He went to Port Denison to give delivery of some cattle which Biddulph had sold, and has since been on a very distant sheep station. His nephew Beckford Simpson is rather a nice lad of seventeen or eighteen, who gets us flowers and is happy to do any small errands that may be wanted. Biddulph says he is very useful on the station.

Mr Cressall I like the least of the party. He is not ungentlemanly, but he thinks by far the most of himself. He is up here "to get colonial experience", though Biddulph pays him. I do not think he particularly enjoys the sort of colonial experience he is at present gaining on a lambing station. Biddulph says he never saw a man with such a capacity for losing himself in the bush.

On the whole, we are very well off in having such a gentlemanly set of men in the house, for some of the sons of the bush are very rough; but I do not think Biddulph would ever stand living with anyone who had vulgar manners or habits. Our visitors are few and far between, and the farther the better; for I consider them rather a bore, except when they bring up letters, but I think Annie likes to see people, and rather misses the Marlborough levees.

We are going to move the house. Biddulph did not choose this spot, and though it is pretty, there is one far prettier about half a mile off, and here we are upon the brow of a stony hill, where there is no good place for garden or paddocks. The new site is the ridge of a high plain, a rocky creek at the foot of the ridge in front, and a noble view over a wide sweep of undulating plains dotted with gum-trees and patches of scrub, like a park, beyond the thick bush and a panorama of mountains all round, peak behind peak.

There is plenty of room for a garden round the house, and a flat of rich soil close by the creek for a kitchen garden. To the right of the house is a rocky creek with pools of clear water and pretty trees growing in it; to the left is an expanse of sloping plain, where the store, men's huts, woolshed, yards and paddocks are to be. At the back of the house the gentle slope on which all the buildings are rises suddenly into a little steep rocky hill, crowned with gum-trees and rocks where you can sit down and survey a most lovely prospect.

When we go there to live there will be very few days on which I shall not mount that hill, about ten minutes' walk. It is a most eligible spot for a head-station, and the two carpenters have already begun putting up the store. It is not much to move a slab house; all the woodwork takes down and puts up again; some of the roof will have to be new, but nothing else.

We shall live in the store while the house is being moved.

111

There is a good deal to be done first, however, and I do not suppose it will be till January.

Monday, October 20th. Everybody at work again. I see Tom fetching water from the creek with a barrel mounted on a sledge, and drawn by an unwilling horse, for the sand is very heavy. Mr Forster has just walked off with a huge bundle of clothes, which require washing, and rather a hopeless speculation it appears to be, for we are short of soap till the Port Denison dray comes up, which we expect in a week or ten days.

Biddulph and Mr Hedgeland are stuffing saddles on the veranda, and Beckford and Mr Taylor departed after breakfast to their several stations. Annie is writing to Emily Tucker and wears a pink gingham morning dress, while mine is that identical green print like little Constance's which I bought at Snow's, and trimmed with white by your advice. It has washed so well.

By the way, Biddulph is not stuffing the saddle at present—he is shoeing a horse which he has tied up to the veranda. People turn their hands to anything in the bush. We have been making Devonshire cream lately, and Tom manages it very well. It is too hot to make butter, and no one eats it when it is made, so a tin dish of milk is set on the stove every day. The cream is exceedingly good, though not quite so rich or smoky as the English article.

The cows are only milked once a day. They run with their calves, and about sundown Jacky the blackboy sets forth on horseback and searches all the creeks and gullies round till he finds seven or eight cows. These he drives up with their calves, and the latter are shut up in the stockyard for the night, while the cows stand outside and bellow. In the morning the cows are milked, and the whole lot turned into the bush again.

Biddulph's old watch, which we gave him at Backwell, which once lay in the bush for three months, and which he lends the shepherds to time their night-watches by, is going like a brick, and it only cost about £6 at first, while mine was £14.

My kindest love to you all, and many kisses to all the children,

RACHEL HENNING

EXMOOR,
NOVEMBER 2ND 1862

My Dearest Etta,

It is getting very warm now, but I stand the heat very well so far—better than Annie does, I think. The mornings and evenings and nights are always cool, but in the afternoon the thermometer is often up to 95 and 96 in the parlour. It is wonderful to me that we do not feel such a degree of heat more, but Biddulph rides in it all day and we work and read and write without being at all melted.

It always gets cool about half past five; then we go out for a walk or ride. We take it by turns to ride, as this dry weather the horses stray so far that we can never get up more than one ladies' horse at once. I had a beautiful ride last week: the establishment was out of soap, and, as we had heard that a Mr Palmer, who was encamped on the other side of the Broken River, was in possession of some of that useful article, Mr Hedgeland set forth to borrow some, and, it being my turn to ride, I accompanied him.

We went through the bush and over the wide sheep plains for nearly ten miles till we came to the Broken River. More beautiful scenery I have scarcely ever seen in England: the river-bed is full four hundred yards wide, the banks steep precipices in some places, in others sloping down more gradually. We rode down the best place we could find, and I cannot fancy anything wilder and more picturesque than that Broken River when we were down in it; banks of sand and shingle, beautiful groups of trees, something like willows only much larger, tumbled masses of grey rock (from which the river has its name) rising into crags and ledges in some places and pools of the clearest water here and there among them. The river was still running in a channel on one side and tolerably wide in some places, but what a sight it must be when it is bank to bank and a torrent four hundred yards wide is rolling over the rocks and trees.

We rode down the channel for some way to find a narrow crossing-place for fear of alligators, and then we scrambled up the other side and proceeded through the bush in search of Mr Palmer's encampment. It took nearly an hour to find, as there was no guide except his dray-tracks, and he appeared to have been disporting himself by driving all over the country. At last we came to a bark hut and some cattle-sheds, the whole guarded by a great bulldog, the happy possessor of five squealing puppies who were rolling in the dust in a corner.

Mr Palmer was not at home, but we were received by an amiable stockman, from whom we extracted two bars of yellow soap; and very bad soap it was. However, Mr Hedgeland tied it up and fastened it in front of his saddle in triumph. The amiable stockman also offered to make me some tea, but I declined this refreshment, and then he showed us what he called a short way across the river, which was down a place which very much resembled the face of a precipice, but these bush horses will go up and down anything.

It was quite dark when we got home, but there was the soap. It might, perhaps, be considered a pursuit of cleanliness under difficulties, but I wish we could get everything we want by riding twenty miles for it.

I wish you could see the wildflowers here; they are not very numerous, but some are so very handsome. I found the other day a beautiful wild azalea, the blossoms quite as large as those paper ones I made for you, and pure white with deep crimson stamens. It grows on a large shrub or small tree with bright green leaves which are unlike those of an azalea, but there is no mistaking the flower or the powerful azalea scent. We brought home great bunches of it and put it in water, but none of the flowers up here will last more than twenty-four hours in water, and very vexing it is.

There is also a tree we find in the creeks that has a beautiful pink blossom in shape and size something like a Turk's-cap lily, and very sweet. Another beautiful shrub we call the fire-tree. It grows in the creeks and bears large upright branches of splendid crimson flowers. I dress a vase of wildflowers every morning, for if we do not bring any home, Tom, the cook, or the blackboys or some of the gentlemen are sure to bring home some. I often dress Annie's flower-basket, too; it looks very pretty with white azaleas and fire-tree blossoms.

Biddulph came home a few evenings ago with three young emus hanging to his saddle and a lame lamb carried before him. One of the shepherds had run down the emus for him. They are rather difficult to rear; two of them died, but one seems pretty flourishing, and I hope he will survive. He is about the size of a duck now, only mounted on very long legs. I feed him on soaked bread which is crammed down his throat. He also eats quandongs, a sort of wild plum that grows in the bush. They look very like the common black plums you preserve, but they are sour and bitter and harsh to an untold degree; sloes are nothing to them.

The emu is kept on the veranda, tied by the leg to one of the veranda seats. He met with a misfortune last night. He was put in the kitchen to be kept warm, as they very soon die of cold, and a pet lamb was also there, and in the night the lamb contrived to pick off and eat the whole of the down from one side of the emu. You never saw such a miserable spectacle as he

114

presented this morning, with his bare skin, and I am afraid he will catch cold and die besides.

Believe me, my dearest Etta,

Ever yours most affectionately,

RACHEL HENNING

EXMOOR STATION,
PORT DENISON,
NOVEMBER 22ND 1862

My Dearest Etta,

We have quite a houseful here now. The lambing season is over, and all Biddulph's "staff" are at home; six of them. So we generally sit down nine to table, to the great bewilderment of Tom, the cook. Mr Devlin, the station superintendent, is come in among the rest.

The shearing began yesterday, and everybody is busy in the woolshed all day. Biddulph has hired six shearers; they can shear from seventy to one hundred sheep a day each, but as there are about 8,000 to be got through, it is a long business.

The shearers have encamped down by the creek, where they have erected a tent for themselves. Some of the shepherds are in, too, with their flocks, and the whole place looks like an encampment, and you continually meet sunburnt figures, with flannel jerseys and trousers, held, apparently, by a very insecure tenure by way of costume.

Biddulph has just had an immense wool-press up from Port Denison; it was made in Sydney. It takes several men to work it, but the power of pressure is enormous. The wool is laid in a box some five feet high and is pressed into about a quarter the size. During their leisure time they make wool-bales. I am happy to say we are not expected to sew at the tough canvas, but Mr Taylor and Mr Hedgeland sit on the veranda and stitch away at them.

We dine later than ever now as the days lengthen, and they do not leave the woolshed till dark. So it is often eight o'clock before we sit down, and the evenings are rather short in consequence.

We have had more visitors than usual lately. Mr Selheim, the owner of the next station, was here last week. He is rather a gentlemanly German, but endowed with the most extraordinary stammer I ever heard. He says "apenhalt" before every word he utters. "Do you grow any apen-apen-apen-halt apenhalt pumpkins in your garden, Miss Henning?" I was speechless and did not dare to look up from my plate, but Annie and Biddulph were used to it and could talk without laughing. Biddulph is rather fond of him, but he lives forty miles off, so we do not see much of him.

Since the lambing season I have been quite overwhelmed with pet lambs; there is a flock of seven now lying on the veranda waiting for next feeding time. Two of them are large now, and can nearly feed themselves. They are rather troublesome at meal-times, as they thrust their heads into everybody's lap for bread. Chummy, the eldest of the family, is growing into a great butting ram, but he is so tame that we are very fond of him. His great delight is to drink tea out of a quart pot if he can find one on the ground, and then he gets his head stuck in it and walks about in that guise. The four smallest lambs have to be fed out of a bottle with a quill stuck in the cork, and a great deal of time it takes, but they have lost their mothers, and it seems a pity to let them starve.

We have had some nice rides lately. The day before yesterday we contrived to muster two ladies' horses, and Annie and I

"The dogs went after them, and we went after the dogs."

had a beautiful ride with Mr Hedgeland and Mr Robertson across the Bowen River and through a gap in the cliffs they call Blackwall, and over such noble plains.

The country on that side of the station is most picturesque. We saw some kangaroos on the plains, and the dogs went after them and we went after the dogs as hard as we could for a long distance, but the kangaroos got into a patch of scrub where we could not follow them.

There is hardly anything pleasanter than a gallop over a plain with the wind rushing by you and the ground flying under your horse's feet. We came home by Grass Valley, one of the sheep stations—such a pretty spot, but very lonely for a solitary shepherd; dense scrub nearly all round it, except where the wide plains go stretching away.

Sometimes there are two shepherds on one station, but if the flock is small there is only one, and a very lonely man he must be; he has a tent or bark gunyah, his blanket and pot for boiling meat; his dog and his sheep, from 500 to 800. One man cannot manage much more. He goes out with his flock in the morning and sits under a tree while they feed about; in a country where there are no fences, of course, they require constant attention lest they get lost. In the evening he drives them into the yard (made of branches of gum-trees) and pens them for the night and betakes himself to his tent.

About twice a week someone visits him from the head station with rations and to count the sheep. The rations are beef, flour, tea and sugar; everything else the men pay for. Their wages are very high, from twenty-five shillings to thirty shillings a week.

Sam Weller says that in England men of a misanthropic turn of mind take a turnpike. I think in Australia they must take to shepherding.

With love from your affectionate sister,

RACHEL HENNING

EXMOOR,
DECEMBER 27TH 1862

My Dearest Etta,

I wrote to you last on the ninth of this month. Biddulph took the letters with him to Port Denison, whence he meant to start by the steamer for Brisbane, but after waiting a week in the Port, which he describes as the dullest, hottest and generally most detestable little town he ever saw, it became evident that the steamer had missed this trip, so he came home last Monday, to our great surprise, when we thought he was at Rockhampton at least.

The steamer is expected again next week, and he is going off again tomorrow to meet her. I hope he will be more fortunate. It is very inconvenient that the *Murray* is so uncertain, as it is nearly a hundred miles from here to Port Denison. I expect you will get several of my letters together, but if so you must be sure and read those of the earliest date first, and then they will not be so stupid, but will come in the form of a journal.

I am writing now chiefly to acknowledge your seventeenth of September letter, which reached me on the 13th of this month. You see, you may reckon on your letters generally taking three months to reach us.

Christmas Day is come and gone. It was an unexpected pleasure to have Biddulph back here to spend it with us, and though we were but a small party we were tolerably jolly. The shearing of the large flocks on the other side of the river is not over yet, so Mr Devlin, Mr Robertson and Mr Cressall could none of them come into the head station. Mr Taylor managed to come over twenty miles on Christmas morning, carrying before him on his saddle a hind-quarter of mutton, which he had begged, borrowed or stolen from somewhere for a Christmas dinner. All attempts to shoot ducks or turkeys failed. We have had a great many lately, but on Christmas Eve they entirely declined to "come and be killed".

Mr Woodward, a gentleman who is camping with cattle on the other side of the Broken River, was invited over, and he came early in the morning and bestowed his company on us for the day. He has been rather a pleasant neighbour for the last two months—riding over to see us about once a week, and I am sorry he is leaving the district. He goes to Port Denison with Biddulph tomorrow on his way to Sydney.

Well, he, Mr Taylor, Mr Hedgeland, Beckford, with Biddulph and overseers, made up the Christmas party. We dined at eight (we have got later and later as the days have lengthened). The mutton was stuffed, and was rather approved of, being the first we have had since we came here—for squatters never kill sheep. Tom made a very superior plum pudding, apple tart and custard, and any quantity of tea completed our dinner, which I have described to you, that you may not think we are starved in the bush.

Christmas Day was frightfully hot, and there was thunder about, which made it oppressive; otherwise we do not care much for mere heat now, but a cool breeze sprang up in the evening as usual, and we sat on the veranda and were rather merry, and drank to our absent friends in lime juice, which the gentlemen warmed with a little brandy. Biddulph brought up two bottles in his valise from Port Denison for the occasion. He sent some to the shepherds in pickle bottles.

I thought very much of you on Christmas Day, and of my last Christmas at home. Do you remember how bright and cold it was? And how we went out on Christmas Eve and bought a great branch of holly and dressed the drawing-room? Here we hung up over the pictures some Australian mistletoe, a pretty parasite, with bright-yellow drooping branches—like willow in the autumn—which grows in the gum-trees here. Beckford Simpson, Mr Devlin's nephew, nearly broke his neck in climbing for it, as a branch gave way, and he only saved himself by catching the trunk of the gum-tree and sliding down.

On Friday Mr Taylor and Mr Woodward departed again after lunch, and tomorrow, when Biddulph is gone, we shall be a very small party—only Mr Hedgeland and Beckford in the house besides Annie and me. All the others are wanted at the new sheep station that is forming on the other side of the Bowen, twenty miles off.

You used to say at Danehill that "Rachel cometh with the sheep", and you might say so literally if you were here, for I am generally to be seen walking about with a quart pot full of milk and a train of nine lambs after me. They are such gentle helpless creatures that I am very fond of them, though it is rather a trouble to feed them three times a day.

To my great horror one of them broke his leg a few days ago. Tom knocked down one of the veranda benches upon him as he was bringing in dinner in the dark. Mr Taylor bound it up with splints and he hops about on three legs and does not seem to mind at all. Lamb's bones unite very quickly. The lame lamb is called Absalom, because he was found in the creek caught in a tree, not by his hair certainly, as it is of the shortest, but by his legs. One of the shearers found him and brought him to me nearly dead, but I got him round, and he was very flourishing till this accident befell him.

On the evening before Christmas Day Annie and I were taking a walk in the bush, and Lion, the great bloodhound, who always goes with us, was trotting along in front when he suddenly stopped and started back, and right in the middle of the path we saw a large brown snake. It coiled itself up and always faced Lion as he danced round and round it in a frantic state of mind

"Rachel cometh with the sheep."

between desire to kill it and a wholesome dread of its fangs.

I was rather afraid to go near it, and still more afraid that Lion would get himself bitten, so at last I made a dive and dragged him forcibly off by the ear, when he yelped dismally and the snake took the opportunity of gliding off among the grass.

He was about four feet long, and those brown snakes are very venomous. A black snake nine feet long was killed at Port Denison while Biddulph was there, but the snakes are not very numerous in this district. That is the only one we have seen in all our walks.

Our last pet was a young curlew, which Mr Taylor caught and brought in one day. Such a pretty creature, with long bill and long legs and bright eyes and grey downy feathers. We kept it for some days and it was getting tame, but one day Lion lay down within reach of its tether and I suppose it must have

"I dragged him forcibly off by the ear."

walked over him, and he put his great paw upon it, very likely by accident, for we found it unable to stand and it died.

Lion is very good-natured to his fellow occupants of the veranda in general. The lambs caper over him, and he only utters a faint growl of remonstrance. Sometimes he licks them all over. He is a great terror to us when we have clean dresses on out walking, for he just cools himself in a waterhole, then rolls in the dust and finally becames affectionate and comes slobbering up to be patted, and the result to a clean dress may be imagined. He is a most ferocious-looking dog, with his deep bloodshot eyes and great hanging ears and lips. I think the very look of him is a protection if one wanted it.

Mr Hedgeland has just been making for the veranda two of the easy-chairs called "squatter's delights". They are made of two straight poles, which are leant against the wall of the house ladder-wise. These are held together by two cross-bars, and to the bars is nailed a strip of strong canvas, such as we use for wool-bagging, and this forms the seat and back of the chair. The materials are simple enough, but I think it is the most comfortable kind of easy-chair I know. American chairs are nothing to it, as they do not yield as the canvas does. Try it if you want a garden chair.

No rain yet, and the country gets browner. Most of the sheep have been sent across the river, where there is better feed. We think nothing of the thermometer being 95, as it generally is that. If it gets to 100 we say it is hot. It goes down to 70 at night sometimes, as we know by Mr Hedgeland's registering thermometer.

It is wonderful how soon you get used to heat. I quite thrive in it as if it was "my native air". Annie feels it more, but she is quite well, and Biddulph does not mind it at all. They say this is a much hotter summer than last was. I cannot think how the trees keep so green, but they are most brilliant green. The bush flowers are all over, and we shall have none now till autumn.

Your most affectionate sister,

RACHEL HENNING

EXMOOR,
JANUARY 27TH 1863

My Dearest Etta,

Biddulph came home on the 14th, not having been to Brisbane at all, only to Port Denison. He found he could settle part of his business there, so he then and there "summoned" Mr Palmer, the man who had invaded his property; and Biddulph obtained judgment against him that he was to leave the territory immediately. So Biddulph remains in undisturbed possession of four blocks of fine country. Each block is five miles square. It was a most iniquitous attempt of Palmer's. Biddulph bought the station in question some time ago, cheaply, no doubt, and Palmer asked him to let him "lamb-down", as it is called, on some part of his country as he (Palmer) had no place of his own.

Biddulph gave him leave to go on this new station for a few months, and then the fellow claimed it on the ground of prior occupation.

122

Biddulph brought home with him a Mr MacDougall, a gentleman who is in treaty for the purchase of the above-named station, and I believe will buy it. Biddulph does not want to keep two stations in hand. Exmoor alone is eight blocks, or forty miles square—not square miles. Both Biddulph and Mr Mac-Dougall came in sorely afflicted with the "sandy blight". Biddulph could hardly see at all, and rode in twenty miles with his eyes shut, letting his horse follow Mr Devlin's.

The day after they came in arrived Mr Williams, the lieutenant of the Mounted Police, with four of his troopers; he, too, had the blight very badly, so there were three blind men here at once. Annie and I used to read aloud to Biddulph all day; it was so terribly dull for him to sit in the dark doing nothing. That sandy blight is, in fact, the Egyptian ophthalmia, and in summer people suffer greatly from it. We have an eye lotion that soon cures it if used in time, but it is extremely painful while it lasts.

We were a party of ten in the house for some time, and the station looked quite gay with the troopers camped about. The blight got better and Mr Williams and the troopers departed; they were in pursuit of two runaway blacks, but on their way back they are going to stop and clear our station of wild blacks. Mr MacDougall also left, but returned yesterday, and tomorrow he, Biddulph and Mr Hedgeland start together for Rockhampton overland. The little steamer to Port Denison is so very unpunctual and Biddulph is so tired of waiting about in the horrid little port that they prefer riding to Rockhampton, though it is near 200 miles further.

Biddulph has still to go to Brisbane on some other business, and then he will go on up the Burnett River to buy more sheep, so we shall not have him back, I am afraid, for two months at least. I cannot bear him to be away, but business cannot be neglected.

Mr Hedgeland is going down about selling some country that he has, and we and the station will be left in the care of Mr Taylor, Mr Cressall and Mr Robertson.

We have had some heavy rain lately, and the country looks quite green, the cattle and horses are getting fat and my lambs do not require nearly so much feeding; they run about and eat grass, but I do not like their going very far for fear of their being killed by native dogs. One was killed the other day, found dead by the creek. I believe I cried; I was so sorry. However, I also vowed vengeance, and I got Beckford to make a dozen "baits"—that is, a morsel of strychnine put into a bit of suet and each bait screwed up in paper; then Beckford, Mr Cressall and I set out in the evening, Beckford dragging an odorous piece of meat by a string behind him to make a "trail", I with my apron full of baits. Mr Cressall laid them at intervals along the trail under convenient trees.

Of course we tied up the station dogs that night. Next morning eight of the baits had been eaten, so we had probably poisoned four or five wild dogs. The same process was repeated yesterday, and seven baits were taken. So I hope the lambs are safe for the present. Those wild dogs are a terrible plague to squatters, but their numbers get thinned by constant poisoning.

My writing is not assisted by a little tame parrot which insists on sitting on my pen and biting the nib. Tell Constance it is a pretty little thing with blue and yellow feathers. It walks about on my shoulder and sits on my head, and eats bits of sugar out of my mouth. The lambs, too, are very tame; one follows me everywhere, and is just now lying under the table at my feet.

We have heard of the case we thought was lost. The agent never forwarded it from Rockhampton, where it still is, so my writing materials, summer dresses, etc., will arrive in time. The whole station is engaged in saddlery just now. It is wonderful how soon people learn to do everything for themselves in the bush. Mr Taylor and Mr Hedgeland are now lining the saddles, and Biddulph has made a quantity of new girths, stirrup leathers and surcingles.

We have been doing a little ironing lately, for our washerwoman has departed. Her husband, the carpenter, would not work, so they are gone, and Biddy, a black gin, washes at present. The things are of rather a remarkable colour when they come out of her hands, but she does her best, and we wash collars, etc., ourselves.

We have such a very easy life here that this does not hurt us. We shall have another servant in a month or two, as Biddulph will get one at Brisbane.

Ever your most affectionate sister,

RACHEL HENNING

EXMOOR,
APRIL 27TH 1863

My Dearest Etta,

To begin with my principal news: Biddulph is come home again, I am happy to say, much before we expected him. He arrived on March 30th, having been absent exactly two months.

He had satisfactorily accomplished his business in Sydney and Brisbane, but he had not been up the Burnett River, as he was obliged to be back here in April. He was looking very well; all the better for his trip and was in capital spirits.

He had a great deal to do when he came back in arranging and setting things in order on the station, particularly in getting rid of a lot of idlers who under the cook's auspices had quartered themselves in the kitchen, some under the pretence that they were waiting to see Biddulph about wages or work. One man said he was ill and could not "move out", another that he had met Biddulph on the road, who told him to "wait here" for him. I was amused to see the celerity with which four or five of them were packed off the next morning, and the remaining one was sent out to "shepherd" that he might work if he wished to stay. Mr Devlin, the superintendent, is a meek old gentleman, who said he had "no orders" to send people away.

Biddulph brought home with him, as a sort of supernumerary, a Mr Julian, a lad of fifteen or sixteen, whom he met with in the steamboat. He was only just arrived from England (Devonshire). I think he must be related to those Exeter Julians whom you remember in the old days. He expected to find some friends in Rockhampton, but they had left, so he was very glad to come with Biddulph and learn "colonial experience" here. Of course he gets no salary, but is expected to make himself useful for his lodging and board.

I am sorry to say that Biddulph is leaving us again next week; he has bought 7000 sheep at Dalgangal, in the Burnett country, and has to go there himself to take delivery of them. It is an overland journey of some hundred miles, and he will be absent for another seven or eight weeks. He means to take young Julian with him, I believe, and possibly Mr Taylor, who is the sheep overseer, to superintend the driving-up of the flock. Of course Biddulph will not wait for that process, which will take three or four months, but will come back directly.

I told you some time ago about the hopeful young lady we had as a servant; she has turned out much better than we expected, however, and made a very good laundress and housemaid. She has been here eleven weeks, and Tom the cook has fallen in love with her and announced that they were going to be married, which would have removed all objections, but Biddulph, not knowing this, hired in Brisbane an Irish family, recently imported, wild from the Galway bogs.

They consist of the father and five children; the father, a lame old gentleman, apparently very infirm, who scuffles about in slippers as if he was walking on hot eggs and always carries his mouth open, a practice which, it is prophesied, he will soon leave off in this land of flies; a daughter of seventeen, handsome, but who walks exactly as if she was carrying a load on her back. She says she can wash and iron. A good-looking boy of fifteen or sixteen, another about twelve; and two little girls, younger still.

I believe the old man is a good blacksmith; he shod some horses very well, but Biddulph set him to dig the garden a few days ago, and he was seen still in his slippers hoeing among the wet weeds, for it was rainy weather, till Biddulph ordered him back to the house, for he was doing no good, and only catching the rheumatics.

The "family" came up as far as the Twenty Mile station in one of the drays, and from thence Mr Cressall went to fetch them in a spring-cart. He gives a most entertaining account of the eldest boy getting down to get a drink at a waterhole, and presently they heard most hideous yells and howls from the scrub where he had gone. The father and all the family began to howl likewise and wring their hands. "Oh, Johnny's kilt entirely! To think of him coming all this way to be kilt and murdered!" But they never made the smallest attempt to go to the rescue.

Thinking that he had really either seen some blacks or got bitten by a snake, Mr Cressall took his carbine and went in the direction of the shouts. He found the boy with the perspiration streaming down his face and nearly frantic, as he said he had lost himself. The best of it was, the cart was in sight the whole time—if he had only looked in the right direction.

We have not got your parcel yet, but it is at the port. Biddulph brought it up from Sydney with him, but, as he rode up from Port Denison, of course he had to leave it to be brought up by the drays. He opened the pictures in Sydney and saw, and was very much delighted with, the likenesses. He thought the children's very pretty. I think he wrote to you while he was away, but I fancy it was from Rockhampton, before he got the parcel. The drays were to have come up before this, but we have had nearly a week of rainy weather, which has made the roads heavy and swollen the creeks and rivers so that they have been impassable. It requires a great deal of patience to get things up here.

Annie has just made a pleasing discovery in the garden. We have a kitchen garden down by the creek where things are beginning to grow now that the hot weather is over. Well, as there was no work for Methuselah, as the lame old Irishman

I was telling you of is generally called, he was yesterday set to dig. Part of the garden is covered with a thick crop of weeds. She and Mr Hedgeland, taking a stroll thither in the evening, discovered that he had rooted out all the watermelon vines, on which the fruit was just ripening, a goodly patch of Indian corn and two pines out of the three that survived the summer drought! Indignation is wasted upon him, as he only opens his mouth wider and ejaculates "Sure!" but it really is very provoking.

April 28th. Biddulph is come back at last and has brought your letter of January 23rd. I am glad you received all our Exmoor letters safely. I cannot say we have anything to complain of in the postal line. I do not think a letter has ever been lost on either side since we have been out here. I am glad we gave you a pleasant impression of Exmoor. It is not pleasanter than the reality, as I can still say after nearly eight months here. The unavoidable "crooks in the lot" are too small to mention, and a lovely climate, easy life and good health are no small elements of happiness.

I like your picture of home life, to know exactly what you are all doing just when you are writing.

Biddulph, Messrs Devlin, Taylor, Julian and Palmer came home yesterday afternoon. They had been detained for a week on the other side of the Broken River by a heavy flood, which swept away the canoes and entirely prevented horses from crossing. There they had to wait when every moment was precious to Biddulph; as it is he has just this one day to settle everything at home. Men have to be dismissed and engaged, the woolshed and paddock to be arranged about and he is nearly distracted. As it was, the party crossed by swimming beside their horses.

Your ever affectionate sister,

RACHEL HENNING

EXMOOR,
JUNE 29TH 1863

My Dearest Etta,

The parcel you sent out by Mrs Tucker has arrived at last at Exmoor. It has taken nearly nine months coming, for I see the date is September 2nd 1862, and the drays arrived at Exmoor June 20th. However, it was all the more welcome. Thank you very much, my dear brother and sister, for the beautiful photographic album you sent me. It is exactly what I wanted.

127

The same drays brought up Biddulph's long-lost case. I think I told you that he rescued it at Rockhampton just as it was going to be sold by auction, the direction having come off. It contained a teapot and coffee-pot, etc., a great many pairs of blankets, a variety of books of the green novel species, most of them stupid, which he bought at a sale, and three beautiful illustrated volumes of the *Vernon Gallery*, which he took a fancy to in Sydney. They are fit for a drawing-room table, and too good for the bush.

Annie and I also got a parcel from Emily Tucker containing some winter dresses we had sent for. She has very good taste and has chosen very pretty ones, but they are a great deal too good for the bush. They are made of some material resembling woollen poplin, if there is such a thing. Mine is a deep blue and Annie's green with a small black stripe, both beautiful colours, but as to wearing them for morning dress, it goes to my heart to think of it.

The drays brought up the usual amount of flour-bags for the supply of the station, and not at all too soon, for we had come to our last pound, pretty nearly, besides borrowing from the neighbouring stations. The drays had been delayed again at the river and could not cross till Mr Devlin went to the rescue, constructed a bottle-tree canoe and ferried the goods over, when the bullocks swam and dragged the empty drays through the water. Now the said drays are just getting ready to start again with the last of the wool. Three drays, with six yokes of bullocks in each. I should rather like to see them at the river or some of the bad creeks, where they "double-bank the bullocks", as it is called: that is, put the whole team, thirty yokes perhaps, on to each dray to drag it over. After these drays return from the Port I suppose there will be no more going down for some time.

I told you when I last wrote that a detachment of the native police had been stationed on the run. Since that we have had a visit from the commandant of the district, a Mr Bligh. Rather a pleasant, gentlemanly young man. He was accompanied by Mr Marlow, the lieutenant at Port Denison. They stayed two days and decided that the place chosen for the camp was not central enough, so I suppose the permanent camp will be formed about twenty miles from here, which I am rather glad of. A sergeant and two troopers only are left here at present.

A bad accident happened at the camp not very long ago. The sergeant came here with one of the black troopers to ask for some "plaster" for the latter, as his carbine had burst and hurt two of his fingers. Mr Cressall took off the coarse rag in which they had been bound and found that the upper joint of the two fingers had been completely blown off, leaving the bone sticking out. He bathed them in cold water and washed out the gunpowder, and then very carefully bound them up in wet linen rag, telling the man to keep them always wet. He also strongly advised the sergeant to send him to the Port to a surgeon.

He did not do so, however, and Mr Cressall dressed his hand again yesterday. It was actually getting better under the cold-water treatment, and the black said it had not pained him, though if it heals his fingers can only be shapeless lumps. The blacks cannot have the same susceptibility to pain that the whites have. When Biddulph tore his hand in the mill he had no sleep for nights with the pain of it.

We are nearly through the first month of winter and have never had a fire yet. Indeed, we cannot without moving all the books and the side table, as they are "located" in the recess intended for the fireplace. We have had a few cold mornings, when we have shivered and grumbled and condemned the books to return to their boxes, but by the time breakfast is over the sun is shining so warmly into the veranda, and makes us so warm, that we forget about the fire and put it off to a more convenient season.

June 29th. I told you some time ago that we had a large shipment of crockery by one of the drays, a very handsome dinner set and a pretty white-and-gold breakfast set. When Tom left we counted the crockery, and were quite horrified at the smash that had taken place. The dinner set, being strong, was tolerably entire, but the breakfast set had nearly all gone, and, to complete our discomfiture, a week or two ago John, our Irish servant, was bringing in the dinner when he stumbled over a bridle that was lying in the veranda, let fall the tray and smashed everything in it except the milk jug. I think we lost seven plates and six cups and saucers.

We ran out on the veranda, and it was impossible to help laughing at the capers John was cutting. He danced in an agony and smote his head, first on one side and then on the other, though nobody scolded him, as it was a mere accident. However, it reduced us to four cups and saucers, large and small. So when more than four people are at the table we have to return to the pristine pint pot. We have sent to the Port now for some strong earthenware cups and saucers; it is no use to have china in the bush, servants are so careless.

We had a very pleasant day last Saturday. Mr Hedgeland

"He danced in an agony."

wanted to count the flock at the Ten Mile station, so, as our horses were up, we thought we would make an excursion of it. Annie and I cut a quantity of sandwiches and we took some cake and tea and sugar, and at 1 p.m. we all started—Annie, myself and Mr Hedgeland and Mr Cressall.

We had a most lovely ride. We forded the Broken River under "Tent Hill"; such a beautiful spot it is, the green slopes and grey rocks almost hanging over the clear water, and soon we got on the Ten Mile Plain and a wide "prairie" covered with long grass, patches of bush here and there, and bounded on all sides by mountains. The Tent Hill Range, close to us, the others very distant.

We followed a bridle track towards the station, but on the main road, in the distance, we saw our wool-drays, which had left Exmoor the day before; they looked so picturesque winding along the plain. Three drays with loads of wool, each drawn by twelve bullocks.

Further on we saw a solitary traveller coming along the road in the opposite direction. Of course he was a source of great interest, and Mr Cressall galloped across the plain, so as to intercept him to see if he had letters for us. He had none, however, and we went on our way.

We did not go directly to the sheep station, but to a sort of green sloping meadow on the banks of the Bowen River, which is here a broad deep stream, flowing along between green banks, fringed with trees. We unsaddled the horses and let them feed about and then made a fire, boiled some "quart-pot tea", and sat down under a tree in the long grass to enjoy our dinner.

It was one of the cloudless Australian days, with a bright sun and just breeze enough to prevent it from being hot. I never saw anything prettier than the sunset by the river. About sunset Mr Hedgeland went up to count the sheep into the yard, as the shepherds brought them home from feeding.

There are nearly 2,000 in that flock, so the counting took some time, and it was nearly six before we started for home. We had a lovely moonlight ride back. I think our party must have looked quite picturesque fording that beautiful Broken River in the moonlight. We got home between eight and nine, and were not sorry for some tea, and my pet lambs came bleating out to meet me the the moment they heard my voice. And so ended a very pleasant day.

We are expecting Biddulph now *any* day and every day. He has been gone more than two months, and he expected to be back in seven weeks. We heard, however, that the man from whom he had agreed to buy the sheep had failed. He wrote to us from Rockhampton and said he did not know how much further he might have to go for them, so we have no way of calculating when he may be back. I do not like him to be away so long, though I don't think there is any reason for being uneasy about him.

We have had no letters from you since May 17th. I know there is a mail for us at Port Denison, but no one had brought it on to us, it has been there nearly a month, and it is vexing not to be able to get the letters. I hear that the Government have

"We made a fire and boiled some quart-pot tea."

advertised for tenders to run a mail from Fort Cooper to Port Denison, past Exmoor, and a very good thing it will be, but I am afraid it will not be till next year.

By the last drays that came up, the Irish family received a kind of ark, which was supposed to contain their worldly goods, but I am sorry to say that it had been left out in the rain at Port

Denison and nearly all their clothes spoilt. We were the more sorry as Mary Anne, our house servant, is ragged in the extreme. Her jacket is a sight and her petticoats usually hang in ribbons. It is no use to give her our old print dresses, as she splits them to pieces in no time. I gave her a cloth jacket which I thought might keep her whole for a time, but I saw her washing in it yesterday. I am trying to manufacture a dress for Biddy, the black gin, out of two stout blue linen shirts which I got out of the store. I think it will make her a very strong garment.

I am afraid this letter will hardly catch the July mail. I had no opportunity of sending before, but I shall send it to Fort Cooper today on the chance.

My kindest love to the darling children and with very much to yourself and Mr Boyce.

Believe me, dear Etta, your ever affectionate sister,

RACHEL HENNING

EXMOOR,
JULY 25TH 1863

My Dear Mr Boyce,

I have just been reading over your two letters before writing to you. You ask me if I have learned to tolerate your hand-writing? You do not know how glad I always am to see it. You tell me so many little things about Etta and the children that even she does not relate.

I am sorry Canon Hall is failing at last; he is a good old man, though it might be wished that his sermons were a little shorter and more lively. He must be very old now.

Etta told me, before your letter came, that you were very much interested in the revision of the Liturgy. Some parts certainly would be much the better for revision, but the difficulty seems to me to be "who is to do it?" There would be an awful quarrel, possibly a split, between high and low church, would there not? But here in the bush we can judge very little about it. We should be very glad to hear the service in a church in any form.

It is curious how far away one feels from all the disputes and controversies of the world. It is not that we do not feel interested in them, but they seem so distant.

But you will be expecting some Exmoor news, and, first and foremost, Biddulph is come back at last. He arrived the 14th of this month in high health and spirits, bringing with him some new horses and two freshly imported Irish emigrants, whom he hired from the ship. He was eleven weeks absent, and during that time he got through a good deal of business, bought seven thousand more sheep, and he also made extensive purchases of goods for himself, and I am happy to say bought a quantity of plants which are coming up by the drays.

Now that he is come back he has set to work energetically at improving the place. The new store was finished while he was away. The old store has been floored, and it makes quite a pleasant room, which we are inhabiting at present while the sitting-room proper is being floored. Our bedroom will come next and then the veranda, and very comfortable it will make the house.

There is a fence being put up all round the house so as to form a garden in front. The fence is of upright posts with unbarked saplings laced in and out between them, close together. They are put close to keep out the fowls, and it makes a very pretty fence, especially when we get some vines and pumpkins growing over it. I have a small flower garden already in front of the house and some flowers do very well, but the soil is very hard and stony. Now Biddulph has employed the newly arrived Irishmen to dig up and trench it, and they are at present hard at work upon it. It is also to be manured from the stockyard. We are going to plant some bananas and orange-trees and vines in it; all the other fruit-trees are going down in the kitchen garden, which is at the foot of the hill by the creek that supplies us with water.

As soon as the house is floored the new woolshed is to be begun, so in another year's time the head station will be very complete.

The two Irishmen work very well and look the picture of good temper, but as they have only just arrived they have the queerest ideas about Australia. They amused Biddulph extremely on the road up; he says they were most willing in helping him, fetching up the horses, etc., and he taught them to make very good damper and "johnny cakes", but they had a great talent for losing their way, and were most mortally afraid of blacks, who they thought lined the road on both sides all ready to pounce out upon them.

They mentioned that they thought the beef had a "wild flavour" in this country, and, having passed Mr Taylor on the road, who is bringing up the seven thousand sheep that Biddulph bought, Biddulph overheard them conversing by their own fire at night and expressing their unmitigated astonishment that "a gentleman, a 'rale' gentleman, who had thousands of sheep, should be travelling in this wild country and sleeping under trees like a tramp".

They were also very anxious to know from him whether, in case they did not like Australia, they could get to America without crossing the sea again. They appear very well satisfied here, but they opine that it is a "very lonesome place" though, as there are two sawyers, two bushmen, a carpenter and a blacksmith at work here, besides the family in the kitchen and the inhabitants of the house, I should not think they could suffer very much from solitude.

You would admire the scenery round here, I am sure. A few days ago we went for a beautiful ride with Biddulph to a place on the Bowen River, about five miles from here, which he thought would make a capital sheep-washing place. We were quite a large party, as, besides Biddulph, Mr Hedgeland, Mr Cressall and Mr Palmer were with us. We had a beautiful ride over the plains; saw the Five Mile shepherd with a flock of very fat sheep, and, having passed his lonely little hut among the scrubs, we got down to the banks of the river.

Such a beautiful spot. I wish you could have been there to sketch it. The river is very wide here, and almost bridged across in some places by long ridges of flat grey rocks with pools of the clearest water between, and here and there little waterfalls down to the lower level; both above and below the rocks long reaches of deep, still water; green sloping banks, covered with trees and all lighted up by the sunset. We tied our horses to trees and all got down and climbed about the rocks. You could nearly cross the river by them in some places.

While Biddulph discussed the capabilities of a deep pool into which a small waterfall descended as a place for washing sheep, I privately made up my mind that my pet lambs should never be terrified by being put under a waterfall.

As we came up from the river we found quantities of petrified wood on the banks, in some places large trunks of trees, half buried in the soil, which retained so exactly the appearance of wood that it was only by looking very closely you could see they were stone. We found one piece that had evidently been near the root and all the knots in it were as distinct as when it was fresh.

This is a most curious geological country. I often wish I knew something about it. Petrified wood is found almost everywhere; in one place, by a creek, they say there is a whole tree-trunk, roots and all, petrified. Then we get all sorts of curious fossils, shells and plants brought home sometimes. I wish some good geologist would pay us a visit and tell us about them.

I forget whether I told you when I last wrote to Etta that Biddulph has just got a large paddock made round the house. It is what is called a "dog's-leg" fence, made of unbarked saplings, but crossways, and it looks quite pretty as it goes up and down the gullies, across the creek and far away among the trees. It is very useful, as now there are always some of the horses about the place, instead of their all being miles away in the bush.

We have had a good many visitors here lately, and I suppose we shall get more as the outside districts get more and more settled. Sometimes they are great bores and sometimes they are pleasant enough. One of the latter sort was a Mr Dalrymple, who spent an afternoon and night here lately. He was pleasant and gentlemanly, and I have not seen anyone who travelled in such a comfortable way.

Instead of riding, he had one of the light American "buggies", a thing with four light wheels and a seat for two, and a pair of horses, and the whole concern so light that it goes over the roughest ground without any danger.

Of the former sort, namely the bores, were two atrocious young "overlanders"; first-rate specimens of the free-and-easy young Australia. They arrived on Sunday evening, while we were all out riding, came up and shook hands patronizingly with Biddulph, who had never seen them before in his life, and it presently appeared they had turned out their horses without "hobbling" them, evidently with the intention of not finding them so that they might make themselves comfortable here for some days. I suspect they had been told down the road that Exmoor was a very pleasant place to stay at.

Believe me, yours affectionately,

RACHEL HENNING

EXMOOR,
AUGUST 10TH 1863

My Dearest Amy,

The house was being floored when Biddulph returned, but now he has had the sitting-room enlarged by taking a bedroom that used to be behind into it. It makes it quite a pretty-shaped room, as it has a recess on one side where the books are to be and a sofa; and a low window is to be cut through to the back. Then it is going to be lined and papered and ceiled with green lining,

136

so it will be a very pretty room in time. Last evening the services of the whole station were pressed in to sew together the long lengths of "osnaburg" for the lining over which the wallpaper is to be pasted.

Biddulph, Mr Devlin, Mr Hedgeland, Mr Taylor, Mr Julian and Beckford, besides Annie and myself, were all hard at work. They really all managed very well, though of course they sometimes pinched their fingers and could not always manage to thread their needle. Mr Taylor did best; he worked as fast as Annie or I, only he persisted in pushing the needle outwards instead of towards him in the orthodox manner. It was great fun, and in the course of the evening half the lining required for the room was actually done.

In the midst of the working party John came running in to say that a "lot of rats" had jumped in his face in the pantry. Of course a general rush was made towards the said pantry, when it was discovered that it was not rats but a large "native cat" that had so alarmed John. Mr Hedgeland instantly fetched a long cavalry sword, Beckford drew a bowie knife, and Biddulph presented a revolver, and I got out of the way, for I did not like to see it killed; it looked such a pretty creature curled up behind the milk-cans. I believe it was finally transfixed with the sword, as I saw Mr Devlin wiping that instrument. They are pretty little creatures with soft spotted fur, about the size of a kitten.

The garden, too, is being very much improved. Biddulph bought a quantity of bananas, oranges, figs, vines and pines to plant in it when he was in Sydney. The trees have all come on very well and the kitchen garden has been trenched and manured, and they are all planted. If they thrive we shall be well off for fruit.

A good space round the house has also been fenced in for a flower garden, and the old hurdles taken down. We have a pretty fence now comprised of posts placed upright in the ground and unbarked saplings laced in and out between them close together so as to keep out the fowls. I have had some flowers growing in the front for some time, and I hope to have quite a pretty garden by and by. There are some rose-trees, chrysanthemums and the bulbous roots come up with the fruit-trees for the flower garden, also some watercress, which we are going to plant in the creek.

We are very well off now for outdoor labour as Biddulph brought up with him two workmen whom he hired from an immigrant ship at Brisbane. They are willing and industrious, though they opine that the place is lonesome. I suppose they mean in appearance, for as any quantity of bushmen, sawyers and carpenters and bullock-drivers are at work here now, the place looks like a fair.

We have seen that queer little Mr John Stewart again lately. You know he came up in the steamer with us and travelled with us as far as Tooloomba, where he got disgusted with the journey and turned back. He is to come up to Mr Selheim's now with some sheep and he and Mr Selheim's manager lunched here one day.

The latter gave us a very funny account of Mr Stewart's uselessness and helplessness in the bush. How he once lost himself on Funnell Creek close to the road and then wrote on two trees a certain distance from each other "Search down the creek", and rode up and down between them all night. He was afraid to dismount and light a fire lest the blacks should attack him. He found his way back to the camp in the morning, but he will never hear the last of writing his own epitaph. He has brought up, or rather accompanied, some sheep which Mr William Stewart has bought in partnership with Mr Selheim, but they all say he will never do any good in the bush; he is too old to begin. He must be nearly fifty, and looks sixty, in the thickest and hottest coat I have seen since I left England, and it was very warm weather when he was here.

We have had no winter this year, only two or three coldish mornings and evenings. The weather in general is lovely; this is the pleasantest climate I ever lived in. Far better than that of New South Wales. It is not much hotter in summer and we do not get the cold winters.

Nearly all the old party are assembled here again now, and we are quite a large party after being only four for so long. Mr Devlin is come back from Funnell Creek, where he went to fetch the load that has been left there so long. Mr Taylor and Mr Julian have come up with the sheep, and Beckford is returned from the Port. Mr Robertson is away up the country, and Mr Cressall has left for good. He only came here for a year's "colonial experience". Mr Devlin will leave shortly; I think he wants to go gold-digging again, and Biddulph does not want a superintendent at £200 a year now he is settled here himself.

The furniture came up much better than we expected; the dining-table and sideboard and looking-glasses are in capital order; the drawers are dilapidated but can be easily mended. Biddulph bought a great many "conveniences" in Sydney—a knife-cleaner, washing-machine, mangle, pump, etc., besides a new breakfast set to replace the one that has been broken since we came here. It is the same as the other, very pretty fluted white and gold. I hope we shall be more fortunate with this.

The house will be very pretty and comfortable when it is finished, though I cannot say that it has ever been uncomfortable in this beautiful climate. I wish you could come up and see it, my dear Amy.

August 17th. Yesterday I received your letter to me dated July 15th. Thank you for it. I was very glad to hear a tolerable account of yourself and, although I am afraid you are not very strong, you must be much better than you were. It is not very long before our visit to Sydney now, though I would just as soon stay here except that I want to see you and also to make a few purchases. I like the bush and don't care for Sydney. And now I must say good-bye.

With kind love to you all, believe me, dearest Amy,

Your very affectionate sister,

RACHEL HENNING

EXMOOR,
AUGUST 23RD 1863

My Dearest Etta,

We have been very busy since I last wrote improving the house and garden. All the plants that Biddulph bought in Sydney came up quite safely. They were packed in boxes of earth and I think they are all alive. The kitchen garden down by the creek has been trenched and dug up, and Biddulph has had quite an orchard planted there—oranges and lemon-trees, figs, guavas, vines, bananas, about five dozen pines, besides quantities of vegetable seeds and some English herbs, mint, thyme, etc. Biddulph actually bought some watercress also which is being culti-vated in the garden to be hereafter planted in the creek. I think I told you when I last wrote that we had a flower garden fenced in round the house.

The lambing season has begun and is highly prosperous so far, very different from last year. There is plenty of good grass and the lambs are thriving. On Sunday evening we took a walk with Biddulph to two of the lambing flocks and saw pens full of the pretty little things. I always long to make pets of them all, but there is no need this year as their mothers take to them, and now that the house and veranda are floored it would make a great mess to feed them.

I still have my two last year's pets, "Beauty" and "Blacky", and very fine lambs they are. They are shut out of the house and garden now, but I have a little house outside where I pen them at night, and they always go out walking with me and they generally lie under the parlour window where I can talk to them and feed them with sugar.

I have another pet now in the shape of a little pointer puppy which Mr MacDougall gave Biddulph as a great prize, the dog being nearly thoroughbred. He was handed over to my care: so I feed him and take him out walking, but as there is no use for a pointer in the bush Biddulph talks of educating him as a sheep dog.

Lion is still flourishing, but he is very lazy lately and sleeps in the sun all day instead of walking. The native dogs are getting very numerous and bold; sometimes at night they come up and howl for hours quite close to the fence. You never heard a more dismal sound than their howling. It is like children screaming and bewailing. Every now and then all our dogs are tied up (when they generally get up a little private concert of their own) and, a piece of bad meat being dragged for a mile or so round the station, lumps of poisoned meat are dropped at intervals along the "trail". This generally clears off a wild dog or two, but they come back again, or rather their friends do. It is almost impossible to extirpate them in a wild country like this.

By the last drays we had the *Saturday Review* for the first time. The four May numbers came. It seems a very clever periodical, and there are some very interesting papers in it. I think *Punch* is falling off very much. The *Illustrated* is always amusing, and was especially so about the Prince of Wales's marriage. I have been reading *The Heir of Redclyffe* again lately. I have never read it since we read it aloud together at Danehill when it first came out. It is very interesting, but a most aggravating story. I do not think there is such an objectionable character in fiction as Philip.

Except the magazines *Cornhill, London Society* and *All the Year Round* we have not had many new books lately.

We have had plenty of rides since Biddulph came back; either Annie or I generally go with him on his expeditions to the distant stations. I walk regularly every evening with the lambs and dogs, but Annie very seldom goes out. I have also been sketching a little lately. Yesterday I rode over the plain where those beautiful lilies used to grow last summer. I noticed a poem in *Bonar's Hymns* the other day that so exactly describes the flowers and their wild place of growth that I could almost fancy it was written for them. Do look at "Desert Lilies" next time you are reading *Bonar*.

Ever your most affectionate sister,

RACHEL HENNING

EXMOOR,
SEPTEMBER 21ST 1863

My Dearest Etta,

Since I last wrote we have actually had a visit from some young ladies, the first we have seen since we came up here. They were travelling up to the far north with their father, a stout old gentleman who was the proprietor of 12,000 sheep. They journeyed with the sheep, and had been five months on the road and expected to be six more. They drove themselves in a kind of spring-cart, but as they only went seven miles a day it probably did not require any great skill.

They were nice-looking girls; one of them I thought pretty. They were natives, and a little colonial, as might be expected. They had just left school in Melbourne, they told me. I formed my own opinion respecting the state of the fine arts in Melbourne ladies' schools from the specimens they exhibited.

They had an instrument with them which they called a harmonium angelica. Something between an accordion and harmonium, which, when pulled out, gave utterance to a yell. One of them sang to this machine, just playing each note as she sang it without the smallest attempt at the accompaniment.

The night they were here we had two gentlemen staying besides our own party, and it was quite a study to watch the faces round the table—in the struggle between good manners and amusement. One had rather a good but utterly untrained voice and the instrument was out of tune. The other sister had an album filled with her own and her schoolfellows' drawings, and there really was not one that was not, as Mr Hedgeland said, utterly below criticism. The worst of our "Mount" drawings in the earliest days of learning were works of art compared to them.

They had been exhibiting the music and drawings (they had several music-books in the cart which must have been for display, as they were all pianoforte music) all the way up the road, I fancy, for I told Mr Richardson, the lieutenant of the Native Police, that we had had a visit from some ladies. "Yes," he said, "I heard of them. They are very highly educated, are they not?" with a sort of tone which expressed doubts as to the style of education.

It is a shame to laugh at them, though; the elder was very pleasant, and they both had something frank about them, though not very polished. They are going to stop some time near Port Denison to shear the sheep, and it is my belief they will both be married there and never go any further north.

We have such beautiful flowers out in the creek now. The fire-tree, we used to call it last year. It is a small tree covered with beautiful crimson blossoms, bottlebrush-shaped, as many of the Australian flowers are. All the wildflowers will be coming out soon. We have them in the spring and autumn. In the winter there are only a few, and in the heat of summer none except the gum-tree blossoms. We have been here just a year this month. I can hardly fancy it, for it does not seem any time. Time flies so very fast in the bush. I suppose it is from the easy, free sort of life and from one day being much like another.

We shall probably go down to Sydney in January for a couple of months. Except to see Amy, I do not care much about it myself. I should have liked another visit to Shoalhaven, but I think the Biddulphs must have left.

I have been making a lampshade for the establishment of the same kind as the one I made for you. I foolishly left all my patterns of flowers in Sydney with a good deal of my other property, but I got some wild clematis in the creek, and drew a wreath of it and it cut out very well and looks very pretty. I have also taken advantage of some cloudy afternoons to make some sketches which I will send home to you when I go to Sydney, though it is beyond me to give any real idea of the country. You will be able to see how the house is situated and what pretty bits we have in the station creek, and that is all.

The house is so comfortable now that it is all floored and lined. We have a chest of drawers, too, in our room, which is a great convenience. You hardly know how much till you have had some months' experience of "rooting" in boxes for your things. Four looking-glasses have likewise been set up in the different rooms. We have a large one with a marble stand wherein I have discovered the interesting fact that I look very ancient and Annie more so under the influence of the hot climate, though it agrees so well with me.

Biddulph is and looks very well. I think he is pleased to have the house and place so pretty and comfortable. It is the exception, too, in the bush. The furniture was rather damaged in coming up, but one of the carpenters here is a cabinetmaker also, and he has put everything into capital order, mended sideboard, tables, looking-glasses, drawers and chairs.

142

A huge hair mattress which was over the things and sorely weather-stained has made three small ones for the narrow stretchers we all use here, and, except that there is no glass in the windows and I hope never will be, you would not call this an uncomfortable home.

I must conclude. Don't think that because I like Exmoor I can ever forget home and all it contains, especially Bristol. There is nothing like England after all.

Your most affectionate sister,

RACHEL HENNING

EXMOOR,
OCTOBER 15TH 1863

My Dearest Etta,

You have no idea of the trouble it is to get a dress here. I told you I remade my black silk. The winter dress Emily sent me did not fit in the least, and I left the making for another winter and did without, while of the two print dresses she sent me up, one I made entirely again, as it washes tolerably though not very well, and the other does not wash the least, so, as I cannot get into it, I have not thought it worth while to do anything to it. Annie wears the skirt of hers with a jacket. So you see such misfortunes are likely to make one contented with any wearable garment!

My Exmoor news is not extensive this time. I think the principal is that we have got the room papered at last. We finished it yesterday, Biddulph and I and Annie and Mr Hedgeland. We did about half each, and it really looks very well considering that it is extremely difficult to paper over strained canvas, much more so than over a good, firm plastered wall. The paper is an extremely pretty one, a very light green ground with a small white pattern of wild roses and ivy-leaves on it. I am afraid it is the true arsenic green, but in this airy abode I do not think we are likely to be poisoned. It is the greatest improvement to the house and sitting-room. There is paper enough for all the rooms, but I do not think we are likely to undertake any more at present. Our room is lined with white calico, and Biddulph does not care about doing his own or the rest.

Another improvement we have lately made is that Biddulph has put some arches of wire between the veranda-posts to train the passion-vines upon. They will soon be over the veranda now, and the shade will be a great advantage, as we have the morning sun in the veranda now, and a house looks so much prettier with creepers over the front. I have quite a gay garden now, larkspur and convolvulus and hollyhocks and pinks in blossom. It requires a good deal of attention, though, to make flowers grow in this climate. They want watering every night, and I have no watering-pot, but go to work in a cockneyfied fashion with a water-jug and two pint pots.

Biddulph has just had a piece of ground ploughed up down on the flat and sowed with Indian corn, and we have had our first green tomato tart from the kitchen garden. It tasted very much like a green gooseberry tart into which a little quinine or some other powerful bitter had been dropped, but it was very beautiful.

A few days ago we had a visit from Mr Prior, the Postmaster-General, who was travelling through this district to decide on the places whence a regular mail was needed. I suppose it does not require any great talent to be a "Postmaster-General". I hope not, for such a goose I have seldom seen. He talked incessantly, and all his conversation consisted of pointless stories of which he himself was the hero. The witty sayings that he had said and the clever things he had done. However, we treated him very respect-fully, and Biddulph gave up his room to him, and I think he left us under the idea that a mail to Exmoor was necessary for the good of the country, and the tenders are already out for it.

So we shall probably have it at the beginning of next year, and a great benefit it will be. He was very much disgusted at the treatment he received at Fort Cooper, the next station to this. I believe it is the dirtiest station on the road, and the overseer would not lend him a horse. I do not know whether this will stop the mail from running on to Fort Cooper or not.

Biddulph has just given me a new chestnut horse to replace Alice Grey, the mare that I used to ride and who is, we are afraid, permanently lamed. At least she will not be pleasant to ride again. He bought the chestnut when he was last at Rock-hampton, and it was then very poor, but after three months' run in the bush it is now fat and in good condition and a very pretty creature. So it was fetched up out of the bush one day last week and shod, and then a side-saddle was put on him, and Biddulph, with a red blanket, mounted him and cantered round the hill; and as he took the proceeding very philosophically and even did not mind when the blanket was shaken before his eyes, I put on my habit and took a ride upon him in company with Mr Julian, for Biddulph was too busy to go out that afternoon. I had a very pleasant ride, and the horse went very well and has very good paces. I am glad to have one of my own again, as hitherto I have been riding any chance horses since Alice Grey went lame. It was very kind of Biddulph to give me such a nice one.

I walk more than I ride, though. I take a walk twice every day. The first thing every morning after breakfast I go out on the flat with the lambs or else away into the bush with them and then sit down under the trees and read, while they feed, till it gets hot, and I come in again. I also take a longer walk late in the evening after it is cool and do not come in till dark. The mornings and evenings here are most lovely and fresh and dewy and beautiful.

We have been hanging the pictures again this afternoon, and they look so nice. There is also the advantage of them covering any little misfortunes in the papering. Biddulph has some very nice engravings, besides the two watercolours I brought out—the Danehill garden and Aunt's picture; and Annie has two watercolour drawings of the Bulli Mountains scenery besides the Danehill house and a warm bit of sunset landscape done by a gentleman at Bathurst. I wish you could see our sitting-room now; it is so bright and pretty.

October 15th. I must finish my letter today as I think there is a chance of sending it. Mr Hedgeland went away yesterday to see after his station at last, but he will most likely be back in a few months, as he is sure not to like roughing it on an unformed station, and with small means, after living for three years as a visitor on the most comfortable station in Queensland. I am afraid Annie will miss him very much at first.

I am just come in from a nice ride with Biddulph, along the beautiful Bowen. We rode in the bed of the river part of the way, among reeds and long grass, as now the channel is comparatively narrow, about as wide as the Tone at Bathpool. I am rather warm and lazy after my ride, so I will come to a stop.

Ever yours affectionately,

RACHEL HENNING

EXMOOR,
NOVEMBER 26TH 1863
(Finished December 2nd)

My Dearest Etta,

Shearing is begun—the great event of a sheep-station year. We commenced on Monday the 23rd. The new woolshed is finished sufficiently to work in, though not quite complete. It is

145

said to be the best in the north; it is very large, raised on piles so as to be always dry; the shearing floor is made to accommodate twelve shearers, then each shearer has his sheep-pen behind him, capable of holding twenty sheep. Then there is a place where the great wool-press is set up and worked (you would be astonished to see into what a small bale they contrive to press from 4 to 5 cwt of wool by means of the press); and then there is a place for stowing away the wool-bales.

Everybody is busy now, and, except at mealtime, we see nothing of them. Besides the shearing there are eight men employed at the wash-pool; they are short-handed there, and even John, the cook, is pressed into the service, and if he was only firmer on his legs, I am certain they would seize on the old blacksmith. The wash-pool is down at the weir where they have put up yards, etc., for driving the sheep into the water. Mr Taylor superintends operations down there, while Biddulph takes up his residence in the woolshed, sees that the sheep are properly shorn and rolls up all the fleeces. He has a large wire table at one end of the woolshed for this purpose. As each fleece is cut off, he takes it up, rolls it and ties it separately.

We have only Mr Julian and Beckford here now, besides Mr Taylor, as Mr Devlin is away on an expedition looking for country. I suppose the shearing will be over in about six weeks, and then I am sure Biddulph will be glad of a change and we shall be thinking of going to Sydney.

You may be sure I keep my pet lambs out of the scrimmage most carefully. They would be frightened out of their lives if thrown into the wash-pool and dragged about in the woolshed. Mr Taylor shore them for me a month ago. Two very handsome lambs were carried into the store one fine morning, and, shortly after, there emerged therefrom two little black objects that I hardly knew again; they are improving now that their wool is beginning to grow.

We do not get many rides or drives in shearing-time, but before that we made some very pleasant expeditions. One day we went to the river crossing at the Five Mile station. Biddulph drove the dogcart with Annie and Mr Taylor in it, and I rode on horseback with Mr Palmer and Mr Julian.

The Bowen is very beautiful at the Five Mile; a bar of grey rocks goes right across the river, which makes beautiful clear pools and cascades among them. We sat down under the shade of a wild-plum tree which was loaded with fruit. They are not bad, those wild plums; they are about the size of a medlar, quite black in colour, and when ripe they taste very like sloes. Then

146

Biddulph instituted a new kind of fishing. There were shoals of fish swimming about in the clear shallow pools, and Biddulph and the other gentlemen stopped up the outlet to a large pool, then drove the fish up into a corner among the rocks and caught them with their hands. It was great fun, and, of course, the fish were so nimble and so slippery that half the time they escaped.

Mr Taylor and Julian waded about in the warm clear water to drive the fish, regardless of damage to boots and trousers. They caught a good dishful of bream, a good-sized fish about 1lb. or 1½lb. in weight. We had them for dinner when we came home and they were very good, only somewhat bony. We also carried home a quantity of wild plums and had a very pleasant ride back in the cool evening.

Another evening we went out to pick wild limes for preserving. They are a little fruit about the size of a large gooseberry, but in colour, taste, smell and shape exactly like a small lemon. We went over some plains where there was no particular road to a "scrub" under Blackwall, where the limes grow. Annie preserved them the next day, and a very nice jam they make to my thinking, only they require a great deal of sweetening— nearly 1½lb. of sugar to 1lb. of fruit. Biddulph is not very fond of them himself.

We had a capital view of a lunar eclipse last night, November 25th. We did not know there was one expected and were surprised when we saw the moon, which ought to have been full, rise over the mountains a small crescent. We soon found out what was the cause of it, and brought a telescope and operaglasses to bear upon it. In this clear atmosphere we saw it beautifully. The eclipse must have been nearly total; only a very small rim of light was to be seen when the moon first rose. It lasted about two hours.

Biddy, the black gin, was rather frightened, and thought Alick, her husband, who is away on an expedition with Mr Devlin, must be murdered.

You should have seen the said Alick the other day. We heard screams of mingled laughter and terror from the Irish children in the kitchen, and, looking out to see what was the matter, there was Alick, with his black face plastered with white-lead and red raddle, hideous to behold, and he was running after them and saying he was "debil-debil". Finally he squatted himself on the top of a box and howled in a most unearthly and demoniacal manner.

I hope we may get some letters from you before these go, but we have waited a long time for this last mail. I hope it will come soon now. We also expect the drays up soon, and the sooner they come the better, for everybody on the station wants shoes and boots. We are all nearly barefoot. Biddulph says he has nothing left but a pair of Wellingtons, which will last about three days on these stones. Mr Julian's toes are out. Mr Taylor's ditto, John, the cook, has no shoes at all, and I mend my boots with bits of leather every day, and they will soon be beyond mending and I have no more till the drays come. This is the most dreadful place for boots, owing to the rocks and stones, which abound everywhere, if you go off the beaten roads.

A few evenings ago I came nearer to a snake that I ever was before or ever wish to be again. I was walking by the creek, accompanied by my usual "tail" of two pet lambs, a tame emu and a bulldog, and one would have thought that all these creatures would have made disturbance enough to drive away any amount of snakes. The grass was rather long, and I noticed the lambs, which were trotting on in front, give a violent start, and, while looking at them, I all but trod on a large yellow snake that was literally under my feet. I only avoided him by giving a great spring to the right. He was coiled in the path so that I could not jump *over* him as people generally do. He slipped off into some hole, and I looked very carefully in the grass during the remainder of my walk, I assure you. Annie was not there. She never walks further than to the kitchen garden to cut vegetables for dinner.

It is getting hot now. Some days it has been very hot, but we get such frequent thunderstorms this year that the whole country is greener than an English spring. You should see the way convolvulus grows here this year. It climbs to the top of the veranda, and the beautiful pink, white and blue blossoms look so very pretty mixed with the passion-vines. But most of the flowers are over now for the summer. We shall have fresh blooms in autumn.

December 2nd. I must finish my letter today, as there is a chance of sending to the Port. I wrote to Aunt Vizard and Sophy and sent their letters two or three days ago, but yours was not then finished. We hoped to have had your letters to answer. We heard from a Mr Grimaldi, who arrived yesterday afternoon, that a certain Mr Martin was bringing up the letters from the Port and would be here in the course of the evening. Later Beckford came in from the Nine Mile, and said that Mr Martin had been seen by the shepherds to pass both the Nine Mile and Two Mile sheep stations and ought to have been here before him [Beckford].

However, he never came last night nor this morning. It was a pitch-dark night and raining hard, and he must have got off the road between the Two Mile and this. We fired several guns last night and again this morning to guide him, if within hearing, and now the blackboy is gone out to try and track him, but it is almost hopeless to track, for the deluge of rain must have washed out every mark. He was an old bushman, however, and not likely to be lost so near the station, and in broad daylight. We think he may have camped out in the wet last night, and this morning struck the road somewhere past Exmoor and then gone to Mr Lack's, the next station—taking our letters with him.

Biddulph is rather disgusted at the wet weather we are having; thunderstorms every day, so that just as the sheep get dry enough to shear they got another soaking. It is a week since a whole day's shearing was done. This will delay our visit to Sydney till February, probably. If it was not for being out of everything in the garment line, I do not care about going at all this year.

Ever, my dearest sister, yours most affectionately,

RACHEL HENNING

EXMOOR,
BEGUN DECEMBER 20TH, 1863

My Dearest Etta,

When I last wrote we had begun shearing, but were sorely hindered by the wet; that all passed off in a week, though, and since we have had it tremendously hot, real tropical summer weather. The thermometer stood at 100 yesterday in the shady veranda, and for days it has been 95 of an afternoon in the parlour.

The wonderful thing is that people go on with their work just as usual. The shearers shear, and Biddulph and Mr Julian roll up and tie their fleeces, and Mr Taylor and his gang (about eight men) stand in the river and scrub the sheep all day. I think they have rather the best of it.

Shearing must be awful work stooping over the sheep the whole of these burning days, and yet several of our shearers shear one hundred sheep a day, and one man who is a "cracker" shearer can shear 150, working long hours. They get well paid, 4s. 9d. a score of sheep, but it is very hard work. Biddulph says he tried it when he was at Gin-Gin learning sheep-farming, and lumbago was nothing to the backache it gave him.

Everybody will be glad when the shearing is over. It is one perpetual drive of work, shepherds coming and going, flocks "camped" about in every direction (for they have not yards enough for half of them), and then they have to wait till all the sheep lie down, light several fires round the flocks and then camp by the fires to look after the sheep, and drive them in, if they begin to go away to feed in the night.

Biddulph and Mr Taylor are generally camped out somewhere, for the shepherds are not to be trusted at night, and Mr Hedgeland often goes out also. Mr Hedgeland came back on the 13th, having been away two months. I do not know how long he will stay, but I suppose till we go to Sydney. We expect to leave Exmoor about the end of January, and have already packed up and sent away some boxes to Sydney, as they had to go with the wool-drays. I cannot say there was a great deal in them, as we have not much clothes to spare just at present. It is coming back that they will be full.

What we shall want for the voyage down, and for our stay in Port Denison, we shall have to take with us on packhorses. Biddulph will want a change after all the bother and hard work of shearing, and Annie wants to go down, but for my own sake I think it is going through a great deal of trouble to arrive at very little. As the boy said when he had learned the alphabet.

Except Amy, there is nobody I care to see in New South Wales, and this easy out-of-door life with the shady house and veranda in the heat of the day and the beautiful evenings to walk in is far pleasanter than the dull streets of Sydney, dusty or muddy, as the case may be; besides, I feel morally convinced that some misfortune will befall my pet lambs while I am away, or they will be neglected. However, it is no use to grumble, and we hope to be back here again in three months, when the hot weather is over, and the beautiful winter has begun.

Sometimes I think perhaps we shall never come back to remain. Biddulph may at last find him a wife in Sydney; for his own sake I should be very glad, for I think he would be happier, and he is quite old enough to know his own mind, and well off enough to marry. Well, if he does there is a pleasant side to it even as far as I am concerned, for though I should be sorry to leave Exmoor I should see England again, and you and the children! Annie would mind more, but I suppose she would stay with Amy till married herself.

I do not know what tempted me to give you this dose of

speculation on possibilities, but, of course, one often thinks of the changes and chances that may come, and Annie and I sometimes talk of them.

Since I last wrote the drays have come in again and started once more with their second load of wool. Biddulph has nearly always two drays on the road going down with wool or bringing up supplies. The bullock-drivers are almost the best-paid men on the place. They get 40s. a week, as much a year as some clerks and curates have to live on at home. It requires a great deal of skill and practice, though, to make twelve or fourteen bullocks all pull together.

Biddulph had two very good drivers in his employ, but one of them died on the last trip up very suddenly. His dray had capsized in a creek, and, as a storm was threatening which would have spoilt all the cargo, he and the other driver and some men who were travelling up the road with them worked very hard at reloading it. It was a very hot day, and Miller, who was a very excitable man, over-exerted himself, they supposed. Whether it was that or a sunstroke or heart complaint nobody seems to know, but he sat down to drink some water and died in a few minutes.

Mr Gordon, a gentleman who was passing and who told us about it, tried to bleed him, but it was no use. They dug a grave on the bank of the creek. Lowe, the other driver, said he should like "a prayer read over him", and Mr Gordon got out a church service and read the English service over him, then they fenced in the grave and left him.

Everybody here was very sorry when the news came, for poor Miller was much liked on the station. He was a German by birth, and Biddulph is trying to get more information about his family and relations, if he had any.

I told you of the old shepherd Scotty's death. Biddulph could never hear of or trace any relations of his, and his wages, some·thing between £30 and £40, remain in Biddulph's hands. He is keeping the money towards a church at Port Denison, which has long been talked of, but they do not seem able to get funds to begin it. I suppose they will as the place increases. Meanwhile the police magistrate as the chief Government official there reads the service on a Sunday in the courthouse.

There is no clergyman, and no funds to support one at present. People are married at the registry office, baptised not at all and buried by anyone who is kind enough to "read a prayer", as the poor bullock-driver said. The English advocates of the voluntary system should come to Port Denison to test its efficacy!

We are looking forward to Christmas now, though the shearing will not be over; however, they will make a holiday Friday and Saturday, of course. How different from your Christmas weather! I dare say you have snow on the ground and hard frost perhaps. How well I remember the last Christmas I was at home. This morning was cloudy, and we were all saying how nice and cool it was, though the thermometer over our heads was standing at 85, which we should call very hot in England. We begin to shiver when it is 70 only.

Annie has been concocting mincemeat. She and Mr Hedgeland held a great chopping in the veranda yesterday while I was settling the week's accounts inside, and when I went out I beheld a black-looking mass like a huge dirt-pie. It was made of dried apples and currants, raisins, spice, brandy, etc., and I dare say will prove very nice, though it looks queer. Of course it would be bad in a day if you put meat or suet with it.

We have doubts about the plum pudding, as we have no eggs at present, and the fowls refuse to lay. Mr Taylor wrote to Mr Woodward, whom Biddulph invited to come here for Christmas, and requested him to bring a few eggs with him, as he keeps fowls, but if he comes he will have a thirty-mile ride on horseback, and it is very doubtful in what case the eggs will arrive.

We have actually had another lady visitor since I wrote last. Gentlemen visitors are nothing, they come so often. There are three reading now in the room where I am writing, and as I have to talk to them now and then you must excuse any mistakes I make, but our last week's visitor was old Mrs Lack, rather a pleasant, quiet old lady who wore a large sunbonnet and made her own gowns.

Mr Lack bought a run[2] off Biddulph, about fifteen miles from here, and his father and mother and several brothers are living there with him. We always intended to call on the old lady. Mr Lack used to say he thought she would rather wait till they were more settled. However, last week he brought her over to see us and she stayed three days. We rather liked her, but it is rather troublesome to entertain a lady. They cannot go up to the woolshed or betake themselves to the store as gentlemen do. I took her out walking with me in the evenings, and she greatly admired the "black lamb"—in fact the whole posse of pets that followed us, even dogs and lambs. Then she meandered in and out of the veranda and worked a little and read a little and so got through the day.

She talked a great deal about her family, as old ladies like to

2 Blenheim station, now called Tiverton.

do, gave us the histories of her six sons and two daughters, both of whom are married in the colony, and finally departed, taking with her some beef and two live fowls wherewith to commence a poultry-yard. They have no cattle on their run as we have, so they live entirely on mutton. They are going to send over here for some beef and suet the day before Christmas Day.

Our gardening is nearly at an end for this year—this summer, I mean—the sun has burnt up everything. You should see how the pumpkins and cucumbers and watermelons droop in the heat of the day, and though they revive in the evening they do not grow. We can get flowers and vegetables for three-fourths of the year, but in the three summer months, flowers none, and of vegetables okra seems to be the only one likely to do, that being a West Indian production, rather prefers to be scorched. When we come back from Sydney I hope to do much in the gardening line.

December 25th. Christmas Day, and a very wet Christmas, too. The weather changed the day before yesterday and today it is a regular downpour; warm rain, however, so we do not much mind. I have been thinking of you much this morning and hoping you will have a very happy Christmas. We are quite a large party here as, besides the rest, Mr Devlin got back yesterday evening from his expedition, having travelled about 800 miles in five weeks. Alick, the blackboy who was with him, got very nearly killed by the wild blacks while he was out. Mr Devlin left him in the camp one day while he went round to explore the country, and a whole mob of blacks came out of the scrub and attacked Alick by throwing spears at him. He had a revolver and a double-barrelled carbine with him, and he kept firing and wounded several. They evidently had never seen firearms before, for they did not mind them till one or two of them were wounded and then they all ran for their lives. Alick had a narrow escape, for Mr Devlin picked up eleven spears that had been thrown into the camp. Two went through his trousers, but without wounding him.

Annie is busy about the Christmas dinner and Mr Hedgeland is helping her. It consists of roast beef, two brace of wild ducks, which Mr Taylor shot yesterday, plum pudding, apple tart and mince-pies, with pumpkin and okra for vegetables and watermelons for dessert. Not so bad a bill of fare for the Far North.

Biddulph was busy yesterday distributing fresh beef and currants to the shepherds, also rum in judicious quantities. It is a great blessing that there is no public-house near here, so that they can only have what is given them. At Marlborough nearly every shepherd got tipsy on Christmas Day, and were all lying helpless under the trees while their flocks were meandering at will over the country. Biddulph, Mr Taylor and Mr Hedgeland spent their Christmas Day in hunting for lost sheep, which they afterwards had to shepherd.

A black grinning face has just appeared at the window with "Me want master." The face belongs to Alick, who has been following Biddulph about all day with entreaties for "grog" which he does not get. I hear a sort of babel in the kitchen, in the midst of which Mary Anne and John are preparing a Christmas dinner for their own family, and also for four Irish labourers that we have employed on the station.

The shearers, nine in number, have a cook of their own and buy their own extra rations, everything except flour, beef, tea and sugar. They pay a man about £2 a week to cook for them while they are shearing. Christmas Eve, yesterday, was signalized by a chase and capture on the station. One of the shepherds came in the night before and said that his hut, which is near the road, had been robbed, while he was out with his sheep, and his blankets, clothes and rations stolen. Biddulph gave him some more blankets. Yesterday afternoon Julian came in in a state of great excitement to say that the man who had stolen the things had just passed the station, and that the shepherd had recognized the blankets he was carrying.

Biddulph mounted Julian's horse and went off through the bush at a gallop. Pat, Mr Palmer's man, followed, also on horseback, and everybody else on the station ran.

Biddulph presently came back with the culprit mounted on Pat's horse. He conducted him up to the stockyard, and the whole of the property was found in his possession. Moreover, he had borrowed Pat's horse the day before, promising to leave it at Exmoor, where he said his own horse was left, and then had ridden it on past the station evidently with the intention of stealing it.

Biddulph said he could not have the trouble and expense of sending him to Port Denison in custody, 110 miles, and afterwards appearing against him at Rockhampton, 370 miles off. So he had him then and there tied up to a tree and soundly flogged, Pat, who is a stout Irishman, being the executioner; and he bestowed two dozen with hearty goodwill, stimulated by the remembrance of his wrongs about the horse.

Justice being administered in this summary manner, Biddulph gave the man some rations that he might not be obliged to rob

". . . then and there tied up to a tree and soundly flogged."

any more shepherds at stations and sent him off, at the same time warning the shepherds all down the road to look after their huts.

There has been a great deal of robbery on the road lately. I do not mean bushranging, but stealing of horses and robbing shepherds' huts. I suppose you have read in the papers about the bushranging in New South Wales. On the western roads the bushrangers are getting so daring that they robbed one of the Bathurst banks in open day, and went to a country house some short distance from the town, captured the owner thereof and sent his wife into Bathurst for £500 ransom for him, or they threatened to shoot him, and she was obliged to get them the money.

Amy does not seem much afraid of them; I think she is too much taken up with the children and changing her nurses to attend to their exploits. She never keeps a nurse any time. Certainly the Australian servants are not good, but she and Mr Sloman are awful fidgets about the children. Amy writes in good spirits, and seems well for her. I hope we shall see her again soon now.

I have just been hearing the exploits of Ned, the shearers' cook: how he borrowed our three camp-ovens and sat up all night cooking for today, when he could have had the said camp-ovens.

The productions of his genius were beheld this morning by the wondering eyes of Mr Taylor. Two great cakes, six jam tarts, small cakes and unlimited plum puddings and beef. I think it is fortunate that the weather is so wet, and that they will not be required to shear tomorrow.

December 30th. I finish my letter today, as there will be a chance of sending it as soon as the river is down. It has rained ever since Christmas Day, and both the Bowen and Broken rivers are in flood and the road to Port Denison impassable for the present. A man was sent out yesterday on horseback to try and swim the Bowen to carry rations to the shepherds at the Nine Mile, but he came back with the news that the river was "bank to bank", and so much timber coming down that he was afraid to risk swimming his horse. Of course the shearing is stopped and the wash-pool is washed away. The rainy season has set in early this year.

Your very affectionate sister,

RACHEL HENNING

EXMOOR,
MARCH 4TH 1864

My Dearest Etta,

We have a regular mail now, but we have hardly felt the benefit of it yet, for owing to the floods the roads have been impassable, and even the steamer was stopped at Rockhampton for three weeks. The Fitzroy was a mile wide, and coming down such a torrent that no vessel could go down the current for fear of being swept on shore or against sandbanks.

Such a wet season as this was never known within the memory of the oldest inhabitant; that is to say, for about five years. I suppose it is the counterbalance to the drought of last year. Besides various thunderstorms and minor rains about three weeks ago, it poured incessantly for three nights and two days, real tropical rain, and accompanied on the second day by a perfect hurricane of wind.

The "Station Creek", which is generally a small stream, came down a roaring river; such a torrent that it carried away and swept down with it the whole of the paddock fence which crossed

156

its bed, though it was built in that part of entire trunks of trees, large thick ones, too. What we call the "Little Creek", which runs into the other, overflowed the whole of the flat at the bottom of the hill and formed a lake. Both the creeks have plenty of rocks in them, and the roar of water all round us was something fine, especially when we were quite safe from them; for nothing but an unusual deluge would reach us at the top of this hill.

A few old sheep, about twenty-five, I think, died from the continual cold and wet. Some iron was blown off the roof of the store, and the drays were stopped for three weeks on the bank of the Bowen; and that is all the harm we took by the rain. Exmoor is a capital run for sheep, as besides the rich plains where they can feed in dry weather there are plenty of dry stony ridges where they flourish when it is wet.

But on some of the low-lying runs in the Broad Sound country the losses have been frightful. At Fort Cooper, seventy miles from here, 2,000 sheep were washed away by the sudden rise of a creek, and most of the other stations to the southward have lost great numbers. At Mr Palmer's station on the other side of the Broken River he had left two men to take care of the place while he went to Sydney; and these unfortunates were short of provisions when the flood came, and there they had to stay for a fortnight, hemmed in between the Broken River and the Dart, with nothing to eat except meat. They were obliged to kill the calves, as it is a cattle station, and eat as much as they could while it was fresh; for they had no salt.

The moment the current was a little abated they contrived to swim the river, and get over here, one of them very ill with scurvy. He soon recovered under the influence of the kitchen physic, but the Irish family we have as servants were so alarmed at the idea of getting scurvy also, though there is no earthly reason why they should, that the two little girls for some time devoted their leisure to picking "pigweed", rather a nasty wild plant, but supposed to be exceedingly wholesome, either chopped up with vinegar or boiled. John, the cook, used to boil a large milk-bucket full of it every day and administer it to the kitchen in general by way of vegetable.

There are generally twelve or fourteen people who have their meals in the kitchen, and I wonder the said John does not go distracted. Our Irish family number six, and there are two shepherds, a bullock-driver and two or three blackboys besides. The blacks are not allowed to dine with the white aristocracy. They "takes their meals in the wash-'ouse", or, in other words, on a bench outside the kitchen door.

To the north, the floods have done great mischief. The Burdekin River overflowed the country for miles, and there are reports of herds of cattle being carried away, but they are probably exaggerated, as cattle have more sense than sheep, and can generally take care of themselves. It is certain, however, that the township on the Burdekin to which the steamer runs (for the river is navigable some way up) was nearly all washed away. The steamer had just brought up supplies for the squatters about there; and these, being left on the quay, were all lost. So there is every probability of a scarcity of provisions in those regions.

There were two small vessels anchored in the Burdekin when the flood came on. One of these was washed from her moorings and carried away into the bush, where she now lies high and dry among the gum-trees. A man on board jumped into the water to try and save her, and was taken down and killed by an alligator. Only one tent was left standing in Port Denison. A great part of the population there dwelt in tents; and very desirable abodes they must have been in that wind and rain.

All this rain has still further delayed our visit to Sydney by delaying Biddulph's journey to the Flinders. He talks of starting next week if there is no more rain. I suppose he would be home about the end of April, and in that case we might start from here about the middle of May; but it is impossible to reckon on very long beforehand. On a station so many things turn up which require immediate attention.

It is just as well that we were not going in February, for unless we liked to swim the Bowen on horseback or to cross in a bark canoe we could never have got to Port Denison. Biddulph crossed the Bowen in a canoe last week-end, and he said he took off his boots before starting, fully expecting to have to swim for it, such was the leaky state of the boat. By the same token, he left his spurs in the canoe and lost them.

Biddulph is just the same careless mortal as to small properties that he used to be. The country round must, I think, be supplied by the knives he loses. A shepherd brought in two silk handkerchiefs the other day which he said the master had used on two different occasions to tie up hurdles with, and left behind him; and the disappearance of whips, saddle-straps, saddle-cloths, hobbles and all minor articles of saddlery is something marvellous. But that, I believe, is always the case on a station. Everybody takes what is good in his own eyes, saddle-straps especially.

We got the mail a few days ago after a month's delay. All the English papers came, but as I said before, no English letters. We have written to Sydney, and asked them to forward the February and March letters. We have come to the end of the summer, and though it has been a wet one it has been a very cool one and nobody seems any the worse for it, though it is said that people feel the second summer more than the first in a tropical climate.

I do not suppose we have had what you would call much rain in England. We often have none for a fortnight or three weeks, but when it does come it is in such torrents that it floods the rivers and makes the roads impassable. We have not been riding much lately, the roads have been so heavy; but the lambs and I have been walking every evening, and very beautiful the evenings are now. I often go a short way in the bush before breakfast, too; and the early mornings are, if possible, better than the evenings.

All the gum-trees are in blossom now. Such masses of white flowers; and when the dew is on them they smell like honeysuckle. I go and sit under a flowering gum-tree and watch the lambs feed and they come up in their turns to be petted and have their noses rubbed! "Beauty", one of my last year's pet "lambs", is now grown a very handsome sheep; and she yesterday presented us with a lamb of her own. Such a pretty little creature.

I often think I would much rather stay here than go down. I know I shall often wish I was feeding the lambs in the beautiful bush when I am grinding about the Sydney streets shopping, or trying to keep Amy's children quiet at Bathurst.

I wish had some letters from you to answer, but we cannot hear for a fortnight, and that only provided the river does not rise again. How I wish I could see you all, instead of hearing from you only! Now I must say good-bye, dearest Etta. My kind love to Mr Boyce, and Constance, and Leighton—but they cannot have the slightest remembrance of me—and with very much love to yourself, believe me, my dear Etta,

Ever your most affectionate sister,

RACHEL HENNING

P.S. *March 5th.* I finished my letter rather in a hurry yesterday, expecting the postman to come; but he did not arrive; and as it poured all last night, he is not very likely to make his appearance today. It is a beautiful morning after the rainy night, and I have been paddling about in very old goloshes ever since breakfast to enjoy it. This hill is so gravelly and stony that it never remains wet, but the long grass is just damp enough to be cheerful. I have taken the lambs out to feed, and left them enjoying the short grass on a dry ridge while I went down to survey the creek, which rose about five feet last night, and looks very fine this morning tumbling over the rocks and sweeping round the sandy points, much wider than the river at Bathpool. In the last flood it hollowed out a hole in its channel about eight feet deep, which is a source of great rejoicing to all the inhabitants of Exmoor, as they go there to bathe. I often wish we could bathe, too. There are some beautiful flowers out by the creek this morning, almost like a wild holly border, large pure white blossoms with a crimson eye; but they die off in an hour or two. The different kinds of convolvulus are most beautiful of a damp morning like this. It is to be hoped the postman will come today or you may have more "last words" inflicted on you. Good-bye once more, my dearest Etta.

EXMOOR,
MARCH 23RD 1864

My Dear Mr Boyce,

I received your November letter a few days ago, and one from Etta also, for both of which I am very much obliged. Four months seems a long time for them to have been on the road. I know our letters must reach you most irregularly, but though we have a mailman we have no bridges, and when the two rivers are up that are between us and Port Denison (and they have been so more or less ever since January) the letters are sure to be delayed.

I have heard from Sydney by this mail of the safe arrival of my case. Mr Hirst has taken charge of it and stored it safely in his office till we come down. When that will be I am less capable of saying than ever. Biddulph has not started for the Flinders yet. He has been waiting this three weeks for Mr Taylor's return; and Mr Taylor has not made his appearance yet. We are getting almost uneasy and wondering what has become of him. He certainly may have been unable to cross the river all this time. Now Biddulph talks of starting before he comes back, and if it does not rain much, may go next week.

We are not likely to go to Sydney till June at the earliest, and I think it will very probably be later. I cannot say that I care much about it myself. I like this place far better than Sydney, which I always find very dull. Annie does not care to leave Mr Hedgeland, so we must endure the delays with great equanimity, especially as the weather is getting very pleasant now. All the heat over, and though there is more rain than could be wished, the fine days are beautiful.

160

I am sorry not to be able to get at my case all this time, but I shall be all the more glad of my things when I do get them. The worst of our long stay here is that we really are getting short of garments, boots especially; and I am sure you would laugh if you could see me patching mine about once a week with pieces of sheepskin, having previously borrowed an awl and persuaded Biddulph to make me a wax-end!

While I write there is a powerful odour of oil coming in at the window, as Biddulph is on the veranda brushing over some calico with boiled oil for a tent to take with him. A waterproof tent is very necessary in such a season as this, when it rains every other day. The Rockhampton papers contain accounts of another great flood in the Fitzroy; the road between Rockhampton and Marlborough had been flooded and the mailman had to spend a night in a tree.

Biddulph will have to go about 350 miles before he reaches Mr Devlin on the Flinders. He takes with him Alick, one of the blackboys—they are always called "boys", though the said Alick must be thirty-five at least. People who are going for a long journey almost always take a blackboy with them. They are most useful servants in the bush, get up the horses in the morning, light fires at night, and know by a sort of instinct if there are any wild blacks lurking in the neighbourhood of their camp. They are very faithful, too. I never heard of an instance of a traveller being murdered or robbed by his own blackboy.

We had the wild blacks on the run last week. They came down from the hills and robbed the shepherd's hut at the Two Mile station, carrying off everything he possessed; even his comb. Biddulph and the two station blacks Alick and Billy gave chase, and tracked the tribe to their camp among the hills, where they found the whole of the stolen property. They burnt the camp, and brought away all their weapons, as a lesson to them to keep off the run in future; but Biddulph would not allow the boys to shoot them as they were very anxious to do. They brought away some curiously carved boomerangs, and some most formidable-looking clubs made of a very heavy sort of wood, and with rough teeth carved on the top of them.

The blacks to the northward are said to be far more civilized and more ingenious than these tribes. They went out in their canoes and attacked a vessel in Rockingham Bay; and sometimes make a stand against the black police. The "far north" here is like the far west in America, and strange wild stories are brought down about it. They say that herds of the wild buffalo have been seen about the Gulf of Carpentaria. They are supposed to be Indian buffalo, and to have been left there by the Malays who used to visit the coast.

Then there are reports of a mysterious roaring which is heard in the neighbourhood of Rockingham Bay, and which is supposed by some to be an immense waterfall larger than Niagara, and by others to be a volcano in eruption. Mr Dalrymple, who has just explored the Rockingham Bay country and came here on his way back, told us that he thought it was a tremendous waterfall[3] about twenty miles off that he heard; but he was so short of provisions (they were nearly starved) that he dared not go in search of it.

A gentleman who has a cattle run up there, and who was staying here some time ago, told us that he had often heard the sound like great guns fired at intervals from among the mountains, and that many thought there must be a volcano somewhere among them. I suppose it will be brought to light some day if it is not all travellers' tales.

This wet season has been very unhealthy, especially on the low-lying stations. We have all been quite well, but several men on the sheep stations have been ill, and several have come in ill from other places. Biddulph was saying yesterday he thought he must build a hospital for sick travellers. Our stock of medicines is small. I think it consists of quinine, rhubarb, castor oil, laudanum and blue pills. They have taken all the salts; there are Holloway's pills in the store, and when the men have half poisoned themselves with them they come to know what they had better do next.

Our treatment is of a highly experimental character. Mr Hedgeland swears by blue pills. Annie believes in castor oil. I generally consider that laudanum will be soothing, and Biddulph recommends quinine as strengthening. Nobody has been poisoned yet, and three men who were really very ill have lately recovered on the station. One shepherd came in to say that he was certain nothing would cure him but brandy. Biddulph, however, took a different view of the case, and sent him an ounce of salts.

It is fortunate there is no public-house here where they can "cure" themselves with brandy. The nearest is at the Twenty Mile crossing on the Broken River. It was a terrible nuisance at Marlborough having a public-house on the station, and gave Biddulph more trouble than anything. Mr Robertson tells a story of Biddulph's once trying to effect a little gentle reasoning upon a tipsy shepherd who replied that he couldn't live without rum.

3 Apparently the Tully Falls.

162

"But you shouldn't get tipsy; you should take it in moderation," Biddulph remonstrated.

"Take it in moderation! I'd take it in a booket if I could," said the hopeful disciple, who was a Scotchman. So Biddulph was silenced.

Men often go away from here with a cheque for £60 or £70, a year's wages, perhaps, and stop at the Twenty Mile and spend every farthing of it. The publican takes the cheque, keeps the man drunk for weeks, and when he sees fit to turn him out gives him a few shillings, perhaps, to take him on; and tells him that is all that is left of his money.

Our clock has stopped, a great misfortune where it cannot be repaired. An unearthly sound proceeded from its inside the other evening at twenty minutes past seven, and there the hands stand; it has never gone since. Annie's watch is the only timepiece in the house—Biddulph's does not go. Mr Hedgeland's is gone home to be repaired; Julian took his into the wash-pool one day when he was washing sheep, and it immediately struck work; and Beckford does not possess one. I generally go by the sun. When the shadow of the lambs' pen reaches a certain point, it is time to give them milk; and when the sun is within a yard or so of the blue mountains, it is time to go out walking.

I had a nice letter from Captain Gray by the last mail, just like himself, pleasant and hearty. He says he is tired of the sea, and wants to know if he could manage a station, and thinks he shall buy one near Exmoor. He sent Annie a capital photograph of himself.

With kind love to the children, and the baby "Edith", as I suppose you will soon be calling her, and with much to Etta and yourself, believe me, my dear Mr Boyce,

Ever your affectionate sister,

RACHEL HENNING

EXMOOR,
APRIL 12TH 1864

My Dearest Etta,

I received quite a budget of letters by the mailman yesterday. Now I must tell you of Exmoor, which just now is less cheerful than it has ever been during the year and a half we have been here, for Biddulph is gone out to the Flinders at last, and, contrary to what was the case during his former long absences, there is no one left on the place except Mr Hedgeland.

Mr Taylor was to have come home long before Biddulph

163

started, but he has not appeared, and we are getting seriously uneasy as to what has become of him; and the possibility of his being lost in the bush does not tend to brighten matters, for there was no one so universally liked on the station as Mr Taylor.

He started with Mr Devlin for the Flinders River last January the 7th. Mr Devlin, who is the station superintendent, had general charge of the expedition, and Mr Taylor went in charge of the sheep, till Biddulph could find some suitable person to follow and take charge of them, when Mr Taylor was to return; for as he is the sheep overseer, he is wanted at Exmoor.

A few weeks after, Biddulph sent out a Mr Gilliat, who overtook the expedition about 150 miles from here. We heard of Mr Gilliat's having joined the camp, and of Mr Taylor's having started for home, and since that we have heard nothing of him, and can hear nothing. He ought to have been in more than a month ago. Biddulph waited for his return till he could wait no longer, and then started for the Flinders. He may hear something of him. But Biddulph went right through the bush, whereas Mr Taylor was directed to return a longer way, but one which would lead him by a line of stations, so that he would hardly have to camp out a night.

All we have heard is a vague report brought by a travelling Chinaman about the troopers having been out tracking him (Mr Taylor). The man spoke such bad English it was very difficult to make out what he meant, but as the native police are known to be up there, we are afraid that there may be some foundation for the report, and that he is lost, and they have sent to look for him. The delay must be owing either to that or to his having been laid up ill at one of the out-stations. There is something very wearing in the impossibility of hearing of anyone when once they are away in the bush. You can only look out evening after evening in hopes of their coming in, and fancy every time the dozen dogs set up a barking that they have arrived.

I do not suppose we shall hear of Biddulph till we see him again, which can hardly be for two months. There is no fear of his being lost, however, for he has a blackboy with him, who knows the country, having been out with Mr Devlin the first time; besides which, Biddulph is a very good bushman himself, which poor Mr Taylor is not. "A good bushman" means one who can find his way by the sun or the stars, or the rivers, or the lie of the country—through the trackless bush, where it looks all the same—a wilderness of gum-trees.

I believe it would be almost impossible for a black to be lost,

"... *a vague report brought by a travelling Chinaman.*"

put him down where you would, and some old white residents have nearly the same faculty—Mr Devlin, for instance. Biddulph is a very good hand for the time he has been out, though not at all like Mr Devlin.

Biddulph set off this day week, and a great scrimmage there was before his departure. He took with him seven packhorses, loaded with flour, tea and sugar, for Mr Devlin's party, who might be getting short of provisions before the drays could reach them. The saddles all wanted stuffing and lining, and the harness in general wanted mending, and any quantity of canvas bags wanted making, and as everything has to be done at home on a station, we were all busy enough, and I added lining saddles to my knowledge of fancy needlework.

Biddulph took young Julian with him also, though except making the party look larger I do not think he would be much good. They also had seven or eight riding-horses besides the packhorses, so they looked quite a formidable party. All three were well armed with carbines and revolvers, and they had plenty of provisions, also a very good tent for rainy weather. They started last Tuesday, April 5th; and Biddulph hopes to reach Mr Devlin and his sheep in about a fortnight. The distance is 350 miles; but, then, it is not on a road, but through the bush, where very often the ground is boggy and bad for packhorses. I shall be very glad to see Biddulph safe back. The long delay of Mr Taylor makes one doubtful of that western country altogether.

We are having lovely weather now. The rain seems gone at last, and we have cool mornings and evenings, and a nice breeze nearly all day, just like the weather we get in early summer in England. I am out of doors more than half the day—always in the early morning and evening, besides frequent excursions in the course of the day to see if the pet sheep are feeding in peace and safety; and when I find them I can seldom help sitting down in the shade, when they are pretty sure all to come and camp round me and nibble my shawl and put their heads down on my lap to have their noses stroked and their ears rubbed.

You would hardly believe how tame such timid animals get. I have one little black ewe that follows me like a dog, and will lie down at my feet for hours if I will let her. I have had the blight lately—not badly at all, like some people have it. My eyes never pained me, but I am afraid to draw or work much till they are well; so rambling about with the lambs and dogs is my great amusement.

We have not been riding since Biddulph went away. The last ride we took with him was to the Six Mile crossing under Tent Hill. I had not seen the river since the great flood, and I was surprised to see what a sweep the water had made. The bed of the river used to be full of trees and shrubs, and now everything has been swept away—only a few of the largest trees and some broken stems left in the middle of a waste of sand. In one place a log—the trunk of a moderate-sized tree—has been left in the fork of another tree, about forty feet from the ground. A lasting memorial of the height of the river. It must have been a grand sight when at its highest.

Mr Hedgeland has his hands rather full just now, there being no one else on the station. Biddulph went away fully expecting that Mr Taylor would be in in a day or two, and we still try to

166

expect him; though, as each evening comes, and he does not, our hopes get less and less, but it is too terrible to think of anyone we have known and liked, ever since we came here, meeting such an end as being lost in the bush.

To add to Mr Hedgeland's perplexities one of the shepherds took the opportunity of getting ill and then losing thirty of the best lambs. The cook has objected to scour the milk dishes, to Annie's great horror; and Billy the blackboy, who was left on the station to find lost sheep, cows and horses, has been away for two days, and is thought to have absconded. So on the whole tribulation has come upon us. However, things will work right again. A new shepherd has been found. My pet lambs have picked up and brought home four of the lost lambs; and perhaps Billy will come back.

It is a most lovely golden evening, and the mountains opposite are a beautiful rose colour. How I wish you could take a walk with me to the "Azalea Scrub", where I am just going. Down the hill to the shady flat below, over the station creek, then up a little rocky path through a patch of scrub and then out on a beautiful plain surrounded by wood, the plain running up into the wood in little bays of green. The wood is called the "Azalea Scrub" because the beautiful wild azalea grows there plentifully.

Excuse this dull dismal letter, but I am rather dull just now and have nothing to write about. My kind love to Mr Boyce and many thanks for his letter and yours.

Good-bye, my dearest Etta. Kisses to the darling children.

Ever your most affectionate sister,

RACHEL HENNING

EXMOOR,
MAY 1ST 1864

My Dearest Amy,

It seems a long time since I have written to you, but there is very little news to tell you just now. You will have heard from Annie that Biddulph left us on the fifth of last month; and since his departure the station has been less cheerful than it has ever been before, as only Mr Hedgeland is left here, which was not the case during Biddulph's former absences.

I cannot call it dull, for with this lovely weather and plenty of time to ramble about and enjoy it I do not think any place could be dull; but I shall be glad when Biddulph comes back, which he will probably do in about three weeks. He started with Alick, the blackboy, and young Julian, and a number of packhorses to take our provisions to their party with the sheep; but Julian knocked up about 150 miles from here; so, finding that provisions were to be had at a station further out, Biddulph left Julian and his packs at Mr Henry's and pushed on as fast as he could with Alick. Julian came back last week, bringing letters from Biddulph. He, Julian, has been laid up with fever and ague since, and has not been able to do anything—not that he is a boy that overworks himself at any time.

Biddulph intended Mr Taylor to be here during his absence, but the latter went out with the sheep, and on his return found the Suttor River so high that, thinking he would not be able to cross it for months, he went back and so joined the sheep, and now will not return till Biddulph does. Till we heard he had joined the sheep again we expected him every day, and were very much afraid he had got lost in the bush. I am very glad Biddulph has a blackboy with him in that wild country. I have heard so many instances of people being lost in the bush lately.

About a month ago a Mr Digby started on foot from Port Denison—he was coming up this way by the high road, but he unfortunately took a "short cut", lost himself and was out for fourteen days with nothing to eat but the gum which oozes out of the trees. I cannot think how he lived so long. He was found by some bushmen and brought to Mr Paterson's, a station about thirty miles from here. He has been there more than a fortnight, and every care has been taken of him, but they say he cannot recover, as he has been so weakened by want of food that he cannot keep down anything but liquids.

One of the shepherds who went out to the Flinders with Biddulph's sheep returned here a short time ago, and he told us that, having one day lost himself in the bush with his flock, he came upon the body of a man lying under a tree. The blacks had evidently found it, but instead of disturbing and robbing it they had laid a piece of bark over the head and another over the feet and left. He took the news on to the next station, Mr Henry's, and was told that a week or two before, a riderless horse with all the usual accoutrements of saddle, blankets, etc., had found its way in to the station; and by the books and clothes rolled up in the blankets it was evidently a gentleman's "swag".

The shepherd did not know whether they found out his name or not. It seems always to me a terrible end to be "lost in the bush". I had rather hear of anyone being killed by the blacks at once.

Annie received your letter on Friday, and read it under a bush on the Five Mile Plain, whither we had gone with Mr Hedge-

"He came upon the body of a man."

land. We met the postman on the plain, opened the Exmoor letter-bag and extracted the letters. When we arrived on the plain Mr Hedgeland went to the sheep station, but there and then we turned out our horses to feed, made a fire, boiled some quart-pot tea and encamped under the bush aforementioned, that being the only shade we could find. It was a cloudy day, luckily. We drank the tea and ate our sandwiches and I read our letters and then started home again.

As we forded the river on our way there we passed the three drays which are taking down the remainder of Biddulph's wool. One of them had got stuck in the sand, and it took twenty bullocks to pull it out again. It was such a picturesque sight— the river with Tent Hill frowning over it and the teams of bullocks crossing. I wished I could draw it.

Except for seeing you, I should not care much when we went

to Sydney, were we not in such a destitute condition for clothes, but my boots are a miracle of patching. I stitch on a fresh piece of sheepskin about every other day. Our undergarments have mostly departed this life, and our dresses are sorely dilapidated, as most of them were packed up and sent to Port Denison long ago in anticipation of going to Sydney.

We have not been riding much since Biddulph left, but I have been taking some nice walks. The climate and weather are perfection just now. There is one walk I have not been able to take since the floods; and last evening I constructed a bridge across the creek, which has hitherto been the barrier. I found some pieces of plank, and with the help of some stones I made a bridge to a rock, whence I can reach the other side, so I shall conduct the lambs that way this evening. I have eight now, their numbers having been increased lately by "Beauty" producing a lamb and by a poor little thing which was brought in from the Two Mile with its leg broken by a native dog.

We have lost the white kitten. She was killed by a snake— at least, I suppose so. She rushed in from the garden one night in a kind of fit, and died in about half an hour. We could find no mark but a slight swelling on one of her forepaws. The garden is rather a wilderness just now, but I cannot do much to it till I return from Sydney.

With best love to you all, believe me, very dearest Amy,

Ever your affectionate sister,

RACHEL HENNING

EXMOOR,
AUGUST 7TH 1864

My Dear Mr Boyce,

You inquire about Biddulph's new "purchase", but taking up country is not exactly a purchase, though it sometimes costs a good deal. By the new Land Act, whoever just puts his stock on a new piece of country and then puts in his tenders for it to Government has the right of occupying that country as a sheep run. Formerly, if anyone saw a piece of unoccupied country he liked he could send in tenders for it and claim it without putting a sheep upon it. Some men got a great deal of land this way, and it was to put a stop to land-jobbing that the new regulation was made.

Now the process is this—Biddulph sent out 7,000 sheep under the care of a superintendent with orders to occupy some land on the Flinders River which Mr Devlin had selected for him. Of course the sheep took a long time travelling. Biddulph overtook them just as they got to the ground, found it was occupied by another man, who had gone out faster with cattle, heard of some better country a hundred miles beyond, pushed his sheep out there and "took up" eight blocks, each containing fifty square miles of beautiful open downs, stretching along the bank of the river for nearly fifty miles.

Having planted his sheep there he made all speed back here, rode the five hundred miles in a very short time, spent a few days at home, and then went down to Rockhampton as fast as horses could carry him to catch the first steamer for Sydney and put in his tenders for the land. The reason of the hurry was that several people were after that piece of country, there being none so good about there, and if anyone else had put sheep or cattle on it, and then got in their tenders before Biddulph, they would have had the preference. It is certain, however, that no one came down as soon as he did, so he is safe enough.

This new run is not to supersede Exmoor, and I do not think he has any intention of moving. He has left a superintendent, a Mr Gilliat, to take care of the new station, and he will probably hold it till land becomes valuable out there—in consequence of squatters pushing out and taking up all the available country —and then sell it.

It is wonderful how runs increase in value as the districts become settled. When Biddulph first took up Exmoor it was the very outside run northwards, and when he dissolved partnership with the Tuckers a year after it was valued at £4,000.[4] Now it is quite an inside station, every bit of country is taken up for several hundred miles round it, and just before he went to Sydney Biddulph refused £25,000 for it. A man came up here from Adelaide with sheep, but could find no country to put them on without going hundreds of miles north, so I suppose he wanted Exmoor. The rent a squatter pays to the Government is £10 a block for the first five years, and it gradually increases afterwards.

But I do not intend to inflict upon you a dissertation on the Land Acts of Queensland, though of course every alteration in them is a source of great interest here. Perhaps you will like better to hear that we have just had twenty-four hours' rain, a blessing at this time of year which you must have lived in a dry climate to appreciate. The last rain fell in March or April, and the country was beginning to look very brown, though it is

4 Exmoor Run was apparently the unofficial name for a group of conterminous runs, the head station for the group being known as Exmoor.

wonderful how the grass continues to spring in this climate long after you would think there was not the smallest moisture in the ground.

The lambing season is just begun here, and Mr Taylor, the sheep overseer, was beginning to look very long-faced as to the prospects of any green grass for the young lambs, and to anticipate another dry lambing season, such as the year before last, when we only saved thirty per cent, and scarcely any other station did even that, but the day of the new moon the sky began to cloud up and continued cloudy for two or three days. How we watch for fear it should blow off again, as it has done several times before of an evening! Somebody was continually looking out and coming back with a report that "stars were visible", a piece of information which was greeted by a general groan and ejaculations of "What a bore!" or "It is all over with the lambs."

However, one afternoon it began to rain, poured steadily that night and more or less all next day. You could all but see the grass grow. The second day places where there were nothing but stones began to show green. The lambs are saved, though we can hardly expect such a lambing as last year—nearly 95 per cent— but it is a great matter for thankfulness, this rain.

Perhaps in another six weeks we may get another twenty-four hours of it to carry us on till Christmas, when the rainy season begins.

Biddulph will only spend about a week in Sydney and come home as quickly as he can. We expect him in a fortnight. I had a nice letter from him announcing his safe arrival at Rockhampton without meeting any bushrangers. They tried to set up the profession in Queensland as it flourishes so in New South Wales, but the squatters did not see it, and on the first attempt (viz., stopping the Marlborough mail), a pursuit was raised and never stopped till of the four men concerned two were shot and the other two captured, and there has been no bushranging since.

With much love to yourself and the darling children, believe me, my dear brother,

Ever yours affectionately,

RACHEL HENNING

EXMOOR,
AUGUST 8TH 1864

My Dearest Etta,

You seem surprised at our extensive housekeeping, but in

fact there is none here. It would be distracting if we had to keep house for the entire station. Every dray that comes brings its load of flour, tea, sugar and minor luxuries and necessaries, and everything is stowed away in the store, a large building at the back of the house, which is fitted up with a counter, weights, etc., like a shop. Mr Hedgeland is storekeeper at present, and he dispenses to the shepherds, bushmen, bullock-drivers and all employees their weekly rations of 8lb. flour, 2lb. sugar, ¼lb. tea and 16lb. beef nominally, though practically this latter article is unlimited.

The Irish family in the kitchen have so much a week of the same allowed them, though they are not kept strictly to any allowance, and everything extra that the station people want they pay for, such as pickles, vinegar, currants, sardines, jam, etc.

So you see we have nothing to do with them. There is a pantry in the house where all our things are kept, just as in your pantry at home. Tins of sugar, tapioca, rice, sago, etc., and these are filled from the store as wanted. Annie keeps house for us—that is, she makes puddings and pies and orders dinner just as you would for a small family at home.

Our things are quite separate. The remains of puddings, etc., are always put back in the pantry, unless given to the servants. When the milk is brought in, it is set in the same pantry. Annie skims it and makes the butter; if there is plenty, the servants are given some; if not, they do without. It is by no means a right as it is in England. If they want currants or anything of that kind they buy them out of the store. The store contains, also, boots and all kinds of men's clothes and nearly everything you can think of as necessary in the bush. Mr Hedgeland enters whatever he gives out or sells in a day-book, and I keep the station books, enter whatever the men buy with their wages in a debtor and creditor account, and make up weekly and monthly the entire consumption of the station. All that is sold and given out.

When we have six or eight shearers here besides the usual inhabitants the figures are very long. We kill our own beef. About once in ten days a beast is hunted in and slain. The best joints are reserved for the house, an immense roasting and spluttering takes place all over the station, and the rest is salted down into casks and kept in the meat store, a small room behind the other store. We have a smoking-house now, made of zinc, where the beef kept for the house is hung up and smoked with damp wood. An immense improvement on the cask beef.

I have given you quite a long description of our ménage, but there is not much news to tell you this month. We are looking for Biddulph coming home in about a fortnight, and very glad I shall be. The place is quite different when he is here. He is the pleasantest of people to live with, and none of the thousand and one vexations of a station ever put him out of temper.

They were talking of drafting sheep last night. One of the most provoking of employments, as the obstinacy and power of passive resistance in a sheep is something wonderful, and Mr Taylor said that Biddulph was the only man he ever saw who took it quietly and did not get in a rage.

Since I last wrote to you the station has been enlivened by an elopement. During the absence of Alick (the black boy who fought so valiantly on the Flinders), Billy, the other station blackboy, ran away with Biddy, the wife of the aforesaid Alick. Alick came back the next day, and his rage was great when he found out his loss, especially as they had taken all his property with them, and particularly 35s. which comprised his worldly wealth and which he kept tied up in an old sock.

He picked out a formidable "waddy" and set out in pursuit, vowing vengeance. In the meantime Billy and Biddy, finding running away not quite so pleasant as they had expected, came back the third day in a very penitent state of mind. The nights were very cold just then. They had had "nothing to eat but cold water", and Biddy said "I believe mine cry good deal, cry all day." Billy fled to the Two Mile station to be out of the way of Alick's wrath. Biddy was obliged to abide it, but he was persuaded not to give her the beating he promised, and which she certainly deserved, and in a few days they became good friends, especially as he recovered the precious 35s.

Since that Alick has been ill and Biddy has made her peace by carefully attending him. He caught cold and had a sort of chest attack, and used to lie in his hut and groan and cough and yell alternately. Biddy came down one morning. "I believe that fellow dead," she said. We went up to see after him and found him all right enough, only coughing. Annie called into the gunyah "Are you better, Alick?" "No," he shouted very loud. "I'm dead."

However, he did not die, and next day Mr Hedgeland prescribed a mustard plaster for his cough. So one was made, and then Mr Hedgeland took it up to Biddy and told her how to put it on, and to wash the place with a little warm water when it came off. About twenty minutes after, he went up to see after his patient, and he found Alick lying outside his hut groaning and shivering without a rag on him (it was a cold day).

Alick looked the picture of hopeless resignation. "What have

174

". . . groaning and shivering without a rag on him."

you been doing to Alick?" Mr Hedgeland asked. "I believe I washed that fellow all over," Biddy said with a doleful face. "And where is the mustard plaster?" "Pudding inside long of hut," she said, and there was the plaster carefully rolled up and put away in a corner, and if Mr Hedgeland had not gone up when he did I think it very probable she would have made him eat it as the second part of the prescription.

Of course, Alick caught a worse cold than ever, but he is better now, and consumes quantities of mutton broth and cornflour. I hope he will be well soon, for we are very short of horses. They have all betaken themselves to distant parts of the run, and no one can find them like a blackboy.

The new paddock is not progressing very fast. The man who has taken the contract always quarrels with those he employs, and generally has to work at it by himself. It will take in the first and second plains, and be bounded on one side by Blackwall, a range of steep precipices which no animal can climb. Where there is no natural boundary it is made of heavy posts with one crosspiece at the top and under that three rows of iron-wire fencing, so that it will be sheep-proof. On one side is a small paddock enclosing the house and woolshed. It will be a great blessing when it is up, for now there is perpetual search for horses and bullocks when they are wanted.

I hope the next mail will bring your August letters and good news of the children and all of you. With very much love,

Your ever affectionate sister,

RACHEL HENNING

EXMOOR,
SEPTEMBER 17TH 1864

My Dearest Etta,

Biddulph brought up the English letters with him. We were so delighted to see him back, for we were getting quite uneasy about him and began to fancy all sort of things which might have happened on the road.

He has been away just ten weeks. The delay was partly caused by the loss of three horses, between here and Rockhampton. He bought a buggy and pair of horses in Sydney, brought the whole turn-out safely up to Rockhampton by the steamer and was on his road, driving up here, when one night the horses were stolen, as he supposed, for if they had only strayed they could not fail to have been found in the three days that Biddulph stayed looking for them, and an innkeeper, close by there, has a very bad name for stealing horses and then hiding them till a large reward is offered for finding them and then producing them and claiming the money. Biddulph thinks that this is what has become of his beautiful pair of bays, though, of course, they may have been stolen altogether and ridden off to the diggings.

However it was, he could not wait any longer, for he was greatly wanted at Exmoor, so he took the buggy back to the nearest station and left it there and came on with the saddle-horses. He offered a large reward for finding the horses and has hopes of recovering them, but the disaster happened nearly two hundred miles from here. So I doubt if the buggy will ever be sent down for. I think it is more likely to be sold in Rockhampton.

It was very vexing and disappointing for Biddulph, for he had bought it entirely for us because he thought we should like it for driving out in, and very pleasant it would have been. The old dog-cart, in which we came up, is on its last legs. However, fate was against us in this instance.

Biddulph seems greatly to have enjoyed his visit to Sydney, for though his mornings were all taken up by business, he used to spend his afternoons in driving out the young ladies of his acquaintance and his evenings in visiting. His business pros-

". . . Driving out young ladies of acquaintance."

pered, too, for he got his licences for the new Flinders run without any difficulty, and is formally installed in possession.

He came home to hear bad news, however. We are visited with another drought. There has been no rain to speak of since March, and, of course, where there is no green grass there will be no lambs; their mothers cannot rear them. We are getting a very bad lambing and all our neighbours are in the same plight, except one man, who, having a run that is under water in the wet season, of course enjoys the benefit of it now.

On one station, about thirty miles from here, they are actually knocking the lambs on the head as fast as they come, to save the ewes. We are not so bad as that, but instead of 95 or 100 per cent, as we got last year, we shall probably not have 35 per cent. These dry seasons are very worrying for Biddulph, and a great loss.

We had quite a budget of letters brought up by Biddulph and one parcel. When he lost the horses, he brought it on with him on his packhorse, which I consider a great piece of brotherly kindness, for he had plenty to carry. He also brought us up a little kitten. He saw some very pretty ones at Waverley[5] and asked for one. It was so young it could not see when he took it. Of course there was no milk to be had, and he used to boil a bit of meal into broth for her and pour it into her mouth out of a pint-pot when he camped. She used to ride in Mr Alford's pocket, and she throve under the treatment, and travelled the 150 miles quite safely, and is now growing and improving upon any quantity of milk. She drinks it all day. She will be a very handsome cat, a very dark tabby.

This puts me in mind of Charles Henning. I was talking to Biddulph about him this morning, and he says that if he comes out he must do so entirely on his own responsibility, and that there is very little prospect for anyone out here now who has not a large capital to begin with—£8,000 or £10,000 at least.

Out of four seasons, two of them have been dry. About six weeks ago we had a fall of rain, and we all rejoiced and thought the grass would grow and the lambs be saved, but a succession of cold frosty nights came after the rain, and nipped off the young spring—and our hopes. The weather is glorious, but the country looks terribly dry and brown, and we cannot get anything to grow. Last year, at this time, we had lettuces and several sorts of vegetables, and now we have none. These dry seasons are very tiresome. However, it will rain by and by, and, meantime, we get on as well as we can.

5 Waverley station.

178

I should be sorry to leave Exmoor on many accounts, but I do not dislike the idea of further rambles and journeys in this wild country, and a settlement on the broad prairies of the Flinders. We may never go, but, as I said before, it is possible.

How I should like to be with you sometimes, but I think it will be a long time first, especially if we go out to the Flinders, as in that case Biddulph will not very likely marry for a long time, unless he were to fall in love before he goes, if go he does.

I do not think I am likely to return to England unless Biddulph were to marry, much as I wish to see you all again; and, fond as I am of home, I do greatly enjoy the lovely climate, good health and free outdoor life that we have here, and, though I like Aunt Vizard and love her, she would be a poor exchange for Biddulph, who is the very kindest of brothers and the pleasantest person in the world to live with.

I can be of some use to him, too. Annie keeps house and cooks, etc., but I keep all his books and accounts, copy his letters and invoices and am generally his clerk, and it is a department I much prefer to making puddings.

I was amused at Aunt's idea, in her last letter, that we should feel like Nodenic the Goth at the "unaccustomed face of man", the fact being that I never in my life saw so many strangers, and that, too, from all parts of the world—some fresh from England, some from Sydney, Adelaide, the Far North and all parts of Australia. A Mr Steward, who was lately here, had spent half his life in Madagascar; another had just come from India, another from California, etc., etc. We have had quite a houseful lately.

A Mr Huxham has been staying here some time to look after some cattle which he has on a run over the Broken River, and which he wants to sell. He is very pleasant and agreeable, and helps me look for my pet lambs. Mr Woodward has also been here again, and a friend of his, Mr Whitley, who is a great geologist and discourses learnedly of the curious fossils we find here. Also Mr Wiggins, the Pleuro-pneumonia Commissioner, a most comical old gentleman. He is very fat and exactly like pictures I have seen of Sir John Falstaff. He is very amusing, and seems to have read everything and comes out with the funniest quotations.

When Biddulph came up by the steamer this time he met with a Mr Hill, with whom he was very much pleased; he was a great botanist, geologist and a very agreeable man to boot. Biddulph asked him to come up here in his rambles, and I wish he would. I should like to know the names of the flowers we find here.

Biddulph showed him the poison plant that grows in the desert between here and the Flinders and which killed so many of our sheep. He named it directly and took some to analyse. Biddulph left some with several gentlemen in Sydney in hopes of getting it analysed. It must have some intensely poisonous principle in it akin to strychnine, they say. The sheep went quite mad after eating it. It is a pretty shrub with whitish leaves and a crimson pea-shaped blossom, not at all poisonous-looking.

Mr Devlin (formerly the station superintendent) has just started to mark a new road to Port Denison. The

". . . exactly like pictures I have seen of Sir John Falstaff."

present road makes a great round to avoid the ranges, and the distance is 110 miles. Mr Devlin thinks he can find a road through the coast range by keeping along a spur, which will be as good as the other and will shorten the distance thirty miles. If anyone can do it, he can, for he is a capital bushman, and it will shorten the journey to the port for the bullock-drays by five or six days making the journey three weeks instead of a month, as it is now.

Your most affectionate sister,

RACHEL HENNING

EXMOOR,
OCTOBER 11TH 1864

My Dearest Etta,

A good station manager needs a thorough knowledge of stock and of country, besides much tact and at the same time decision

180

in dealing with the very free and independent gentry whom we have to employ as shepherds, stockmen, bushmen, etc.

The difference in the *go* of the station when Biddulph is here and when he is absent is just that of trying to get along a rusty creaking vehicle on a rough road and the progress of the same machine on a smooth road and with all the screws and wheels oiled. Biddulph is a capital master. He never lets any of the men gain the least advantage over him and yet they all like him.

I am happy to say that Biddulph heard by the last mail that the pair of buggy-horses he lost on the Rockhampton road have turned up all safe, so perhaps we may get the buggy here yet, though if we move it may be sold. But we should want some sort of vehicle to drive out to the Flinders.

We had such a pleasant day's excursion yesterday. Annie and myself, with Biddulph and Mr Taylor, started about 11 for a spot on the Broken River, about five miles from here, where there are some fine rocks and capital fishing. A little way from the station we met Mr Hedgeland on his way home from Port Denison, where he has been to load a dray, which Biddulph is sending out to the Flinders.

Biddulph has a quantity of goods sent from Sydney and stored in one of the warehouses at the Port, and part of them had to be selected and a great many cases opened, so Mr Hedgeland went down to do it. He looked very sunburnt and grimy, and declined turning round and going with us, so we stopped to hear the news and then went on our way. We got to the rocks about one. I had never seen them before, and I never, in this part of the world, saw anything so fine as the tumbled masses of grey rock, the long reaches of blue water and the rocky wooded banks. I made two sketches, but they do not give any idea of the place. Nothing but a first-rate coloured drawing could do so.

As soon as the horses were unsaddled and turned out on some beautiful green grass we scrambled down the steep bank till we found a nice shady place under some rocks, by a large tree, and then Annie and I lighted a fire, while Biddulph and Mr Taylor went to catch some fish for dinner. They soon came back with some fine black bream. These Mr Taylor broiled on the embers, and very nice they were. We had brought some bread, a tin of jam, and with the universal "quart-pot tea" we made a capital dinner.

Then Biddulph and Mr Taylor got their horses and set off to ride a mile or two on the other side of the river to look at some green feed which was reported to be there, and on which they thought they could put a flock of sheep. Annie and I took the opportunity of their absence to get a beautiful bathe in the river. We avoided the deep holes for fear of alligators and chose a place where the water was running over rocks and so clear we could see the bottom. We enjoyed it so very much.

Then I proceeded to make frantic efforts to sketch the place while Annie fished; then Biddulph and Mr Taylor came back and fished till sundown. They caught some black bream and catfish, and when it began to get dark we packed up our traps, caught and saddled the horses and set out for home.

The next thing we did was to lose our way. There was some thick bush to go through before we reached the road, and we got talking and did not notice that our horses were following their own wills till we were suddenly stopped by a precipice, and, on investigation, there was the Broken River at our feet. We had got back to it instead of getting on to the road. It was very dark, for the sun had set and the moon not risen. However, we turned round and set off the other way. In a short time after a little more riding Mr Taylor and Biddulph, who were going first, to find the way, pulled up again. There was the Broken River once more, ahead of us. It winds very much here. "We'll keep out from it this time at any rate," Biddulph said, so on we went till we came to another steep bank. "This must be some gully," Biddulph said. Mr Taylor got a little way down the bank to examine. "By George," he said, "it's the Broken River again!" We all laughed, for it seemed as if we were bewitched and were condemned to wander up and down the Broken River for the rest of our natural lives.

It was extremely dark just then, and there was nothing for it but to ride slowly in the most probable direction till the moon rose, so that we would see the distant ranges of hills which would set us right at once. Presently up she came, but two days past the full. Then the Dart Ranges appeared on one side and the Tent Hill and Blackwall Range on another, and we knew our direction at once; and a quarter of an hour's ride brought us out on the plains again.

It seemed very absurd to be lost on the Broken River, five or six miles from home, especially as Biddulph is a very good bushman; but not having noticed the direction we took at first, it was almost impossible to find out where we were till there was light enough to see something beyond the stems of the trees.

We had a nice moonlight ride home, and got back about nine, to the great joy of the famished family, who I am afraid wanted their dinners.

The pet lambs were shorn this morning. Biddulph very kindly

promised the shearers a bottle of grog to shear them nicely and
not cut them, and accordingly they appeared coming down from
the woolshed about breakfast-time, very well shorn and only one
of them cut a little. But looking such little objects! They will
begin to recover their good looks in a month or so, and it must
be a great relief to them to have their fleeces off this hot weather.

Will you thank Mr Boyce very much for his letter to me. My
very kindest love to him and yourself and the children,

Ever, dearest Etta, your most affectionate sister,

RACHEL HENNING

EXMOOR,
NOVEMBER 27TH 1864

My Dear Mr Boyce,

I wrote to Etta by the last mail. It is very satisfactory that we
have lately had thunderstorms nearly every day and the grass is
growing as if by magic. In dear rainy old England you can hardly
imagine how glad we are when the first rain falls after a long
drought. How the green grass springs everywhere where before
there was nothing to be seen but stones and dust. I think the
East must be something like this. In these hot countries there
cannot be a more pleasant image than "rivers of water in a dry
place, the shadow of a great rock in a weary land".

How I should like to spend another Christmas with you all! I
wonder will it ever be. We shall be a small party this Christmas
at Exmoor, for Mr Taylor is already gone to the Flinders, Mr
Hedgeland will follow him in about a fortnight, and Alford is
going to the Port on his way to England as soon as he can find
his horse, which has either absconded or been stolen. There will
be only Biddulph here, with the exception of any visitors we
may have.

I was terribly afraid Biddulph would go out to the Flinders
himself. Biddulph is afraid they will be short of provisions on
Lara station before the horse-dray which accompanies the sheep
can reach them, so Mr Hedgeland is to take a small supply of
packhorses and travel out as fast as possible.

A great deal of stock is going out to the Flinders now. We have
just had a large party here branding cattle in our yards before
taking them out. They departed last Saturday, and I think they
must have been quite glad to get away, for nothing but misfortunes befell them during the last day or two.

Mr Woodward set the fashion. A beast charged him in the
yard, charged him again while he was climbing the fence, and

somehow knocked him over it, a fall of about seven feet. They all thought he had broken his neck, but he escaped with a good shake and some bad bruises.

The same day Mr Tooth, who is in charge of the cattle, cut his wrist right across the tendons and lost the use of his two middle fingers. His hand was terribly swelled and very painful, and we wanted him to go to the Port for advice, but he tied it up with cold-water bandages and it got better. He is gone out to the Flinders now, but I think it doubtful if he will recover the use of the two fingers.

The same evening Mr Alford went up to the forge, where a stranger's horse was being shod, and most foolishly jumped on its back. He is no rider, and the horse threw him at once and then he kicked him when down just on the temple. He had on a thick felt hat, which probably saved his life. The hat and leather lining were cut through and his temple cut to the bone, which was slightly splintered. Mr Woodward sewed up the cut and he kept cold-water cloths on it. His head was terribly swelled and he suffered much from headache for some days, but he, too, has recovered and walks about with his head plastered up and one eye very bloodshot from the effect of the blow.

As if this was not enough Julian went out the next day to drive in a wild cow from the bush and was foolish enough to get off his horse to drive her through a scrub, when she turned and charged him, threw him up in the air twice, and the second time he says he came down on her back. However that may be, he scrambled up a tree, and finally escaped from the scrimmage minus his hat and with his garments woefully torn. He left the cow watching his hat under the impression that his head was inside it.

Finally Mr Holdane, another of the cattle party, had three of his front teeth knocked out by the horse he was on suddenly throwing her head back when Holdane was stooping forward. I was quite glad when they and their evil fortune had departed. Biddulph might have been the next!

We have had quite a visitation of blacks lately—civilized blacks, that is. On Sunday evening Biddulph, Annie and I were taking a walk on the flat when we saw two or three blacks come straggling over the creek, and then two or three more, till we counted thirteen. They each had an old shirt by way of a garment and several were carrying possums which they had caught on their way. Biddulph went over to speak to them. "Good day, sare," they all said and grinned very much, and then told him they were runaway troopers from Rockingham Bay, where they seemed to think they had been very badly treated in being made to work—"too much carry log", one of them said. They were on their way to Wide Bay, their own country. Biddulph told them to go up to the station and he would give them some rations, and when we had finished our walk we went home and found them all clustered round the kitchen, Mr Alford and Mr Hedgeland talking to them, and Tom, the cook, in a tremendous fright. He knew their ways, he said. They were myalls (i.e., wild blacks) dressed up to take us in, and in the night they would all get up and attack the station. He did not condescend to account for the phenomenon of their all speaking English. And then he made a melancholy calculation that we had only about eight hours to live.

However, Biddulph gave them their rations, and they proceeded to camp behind the store, where they made the night hideous till a late hour by holding a corroboree with the station blacks. Tom announced his intention of sitting up all night in company with all the guns on the station, but I imagine he thought better of it when he got sleepy.

The next morning when they were peacefully eating their breakfasts up rode Mr Uhr, the officer of the native police in this district. He rode straight into the camp. "Bail up, you runaways," he said. There was not a chance for the blacks, as the mounted troopers had surrounded them on all sides before they found it out. They took it very philosophically, but I was quite sorry for the poor creatures; some of them were very lame and footsore, and three of them were gins. They must have walked nearly 400 miles from Rockingham Bay here. Mr Uhr said he only heard of it two days before; the whole police force of Rockingham Bay had absconded, leaving the settlers there in a great plight, surrounded by wild blacks.

Mr Uhr left two behind, as Biddulph wanted them on the station and they were not troopers but runaways from some station. A contribution of hats and trousers were made for these two, and they seem very well contented, and one of them has been out with Biddulph looking for horses today, while the other has been employing his energies in climbing gum-trees after "sugar-bags", or wild honeycombs. The rest were marched off to Port Denison.

Mr Uhr said he did not think they would be sent back to Rockingham Bay but would probably be put into Mr Marlow's troop—he is the commandant at Port Denison. I dare say they will bolt again before long.

Biddulph still intends selling Exmoor, but he has not heard

of a certain purchaser yet. There have been several inquiries after it, for it is called one of the best runs in the North. I shall be sorry for my own sake when he sells it, though glad for him, as he wishes to.

I hardly know now about our visit to Sydney. Biddulph will not be able to leave here till either Mr Taylor or Mr Hedgeland returns, and if the rivers are up that may not be for some time.

Yours very affectionately,

RACHEL HENNING

EXMOOR,
CHRISTMAS DAY 1864

My Dearest Etta,

A happy Christmas and New Year to you and yours. It is a time of year which makes one think of the home country and friends there, and when my thoughts do travel that way there is not much question as to where they go first.

I should like to be with you today to go to church with you (of course "you" includes Mr Boyce) in the morning and sit by the Christmas fire with you and the children in the evening.

What a different Christmas yours is from ours! I fancy snow on the ground and a hard frost, yet withal a bright sun as there ought to be on Christmas Day. The children wrapped up very warm going to church with you and having their attention sorely distracted by the holly-berries and evergreens with which it is dressed, and saying Christmas hymns and being regaled with figs by the fire when it is getting dusk.

On this side of the world it is rather a hot day, though there is not much sun. Thunderstorms are rolling about the hills, and very beautiful the mountains look appearing and disappearing among the misty clouds. The paddock round the house is emerald-green; the young grass has grown within this week since the rains set in. The gum-trees are in flower, and the passion-vine over the veranda is in fruit and the seeds are trying to come up in the garden but are nipped off by the fowls as soon as they show above the ground, so I have no hope of a flower garden this year.

The doors and all the windows are open, and I wish a little more wind would come through them. Biddulph is reading on the veranda and Annie ditto; and we three have the house to ourselves. We rather expected two or three of our neighbours to be here for Christmas, but the Bowen and Broken rivers are up and that has probably prevented their coming.

All our own people—i.e., those belonging to the house—are either at Lara or on the road there. The Flinders River station is a sort of Moloch and has swallowed up sheep, horses and men from Exmoor. Five thousand sheep are already there and 3,000 more are on their way. About twenty horses are gone and Mr Gilliat is out there taking charge of the station. Mr Taylor set out about six weeks ago with the additional sheep, and Mr Hedgeland started a week ago with a string of packhorses for the new settlement with the supply of flour, tea and sugar to last them till the drays arrive. Beckford is on the road with the wool-drays, and at present Biddulph is managing Exmoor single-handed.

I think he rather likes to have plenty to do, on the whole. This is not a very busy time on the station now that shearing is over, but he has to visit the out-stations every week, count the sheep and send rations to the shepherds. We still talk of going to Sydney some day, but I think, and rather hope, it will not be till after the rainy season, for, of course, Biddulph cannot leave home till either Mr Taylor or Mr Hedgeland returns to take charge of the station, and it is hard to say when that will be.

There has been some difficulty about finding a superintendent for Lara.[6] Biddulph is dissatisfied with Mr Gilliat and has written to recall him. He then offered the post to Mr Taylor before he went out with the sheep, but he declined it and said he would rather return to Exmoor if Biddulph could find someone else. But it is not easy to find a fit person, and finally Mr Hedgeland started last week with the understanding that he, Mr Hedgeland, was to stay till someone could be sent out. I do not think he liked the prospect of it much, but he will not have to stay, probably, for Biddulph has heard of a Mr Kennedy whom he thinks will do, and if so he will soon follow Mr Hedgeland.

I have little doubt that Biddulph will ultimately go out there himself, as I told you before, but Exmoor will have to be sold first and a great many arrangements to be made before we can journey out to the far west.

This is the second time I have written to you without any letters to answer. We quite expected an English mail, and I believe it was actually in the Port when the postman left, but the letters were not sorted. I was much disappointed at not hearing and at having to wait another fortnight, but for some months

[6] Lara was taken up by Biddulph in 1864. The property comprised eight blocks of twenty-five square miles each, and stretched from Alick's Creek to the junction of the Cloncurry River, a tributary of the Flinders.

the post is sure to be irregular now, for when once the rainy season has begun there is no saying when the rivers may be up.

Sometimes the Broken River, which is between us and Port Denison, is impassable for weeks. The postman was nearly drowned on his last trip up. Biddulph met him just at the creek below here, and wondered what dismal object it was riding up,

". . . hatless and bootless and trouserless attired only in a Crimean shirt."

hatless and bootless and trouserless and arrayed only in a Crimean shirt. Biddulph sent some garments down to him, and then he told his sorrowful tale; how in fording the Bowen it was not high enough for swimming, his horse had fallen over in a deep hole and he (the postman) contrived to scramble up in a tree while the horse and the mail-bags scrambled out, and how, not being able to swim, he stayed half an hour in the tree before he could make up his mind to cross the piece of water that was between him and the shore.

He did cross it at last, and luckily caught his horse, leaving his garments in the tree while his hat floated down the Bowen. He must have been very stupid and lost his nerve altogether to get into such a scrape, because the river is not at all deep yet.

The "desert lilies" are over and gone. They lasted a short time this year on account of the drought. None of the wild flowers have been very numerous for the same reason. Also the vegetable seeds have hitherto strongly objected to coming up in the garden. We had quantities of cucumbers and lettuces this time last year and now we have none. But we have a wild plant which makes a capital salad and which we very seldom dine without. It rejoices in the name of pigweed, and is a small plant with thick green leaves like the ice-plant and tastes slightly acid and slightly hot, something like watercress.

We have watercress growing in the creek, but it is not large enough to pick yet. There is another wild plant called fat hen, which is as good as spinach when boiled, so we get along with wild vegetables till the tame ones see fit to flourish.

There will be no lack of moisture for the next three months; the rains began about a week ago, and you can almost see the grass grow. There are thunderstorms nearly every day, and it is setting in for a wet evening at this moment. Christmas Day is almost always wet in Queensland; it comes just at the beginning of the rains. The great floods generally come about the end of January.

With love to you and Mr Boyce and the children,

Your affectionate sister,

RACHEL HENNING

EXMOOR,
JANUARY 23RD 1865

My Dearest Etta,

We have no servants just at present, as Tom and his wife are to leave by the first opportunity, and we have not yet replaced them. It seldom answers to have servants back when you have once parted with them. Emma was a good servant when she was here before, but since her return her principal occupation has been quarrelling with Tom.

We have just been edified by the sounds of a war of words, and what appears to be missiles flying in the kitchen; then I saw through the back window of the parlour Emma rushing out of the kitchen discharging some missile—I think a saucepan lid—at Tom as she went, and rushing up to the men's huts at the

"Emma rushing out of the kitchen discharging some missile. . . ."

top of the paddock with a tomahawk in her hand. Then we heard Tom bewailing himself in the kitchen, and saying if his poor old father could have known, etc.

Next Biddy, the black girl, made her appearance in the parlour grinning very much, and tomahawk in hand. She said,

"That fellow [meaning Emma] been running away with toma-hawk, and mine been running after and took away tomahawk, that fellow no good." A sentiment in which we heartily concurred. These quarrels are a source of great delight to the blacks, who stand in front of their camp and hold up their hands and roll about with laughter. But they are very disagreeable, and I shall be glad when the happy couple take their departure.

I am very much obliged to you for sending my watch. If it goes as well, or nearly as well, as yours, I shall be quite satisfied, and shall think it a valuable timepiece. I asked Emily to take care of it on its arrival in Sydney, and not to send it up here to be knocked about in our very doubtful post.

I suppose we shall go to Sydney when some of the people come in from the Flinders, and that will be probably at the end of March or beginning of April. I am in no hurry about it. Our return is so doubtful that I am in no haste to go away.

I have had some nice rides lately. There is a flock of sheep now at the Eight Mile, and we go out there with Biddulph when he takes the rations and counts the sheep. It is a beautiful ride there. The road is pretty the whole way, and then you turn off and cross the Bowen, and go through a little patch of thick wood till you come out on the plain where the station is. Such a pretty place. The little hut stands out against the dark forest, and in front are beautiful green downs, where the sheep feed.

It is rather hot going there, as we have to start pretty early and walk our horses the whole eight miles, or nearly so, as otherwise the packhorse would make a pudding of the flour, tea and sugar, and break the bottles of vinegar and lime juice. We generally leave the station about sundown, and the canter home in the cool twilight and starlight is delightful.

The last time we went out there we saw a man sitting down in a very lonely part of the road on the bank of the creek, and a grey horse in hobbles feeding beside him. He did not speak or look round as we passed, and next day a man came riding up post-haste to Exmoor station asking if we had seen anything of a man with a grey horse, as horse, saddle and bridle had been stolen from him (man Number Two). Biddulph directed him the road, and in three or four days he returned bringing the recovered horse with him.

He said he had overtaken the thief near Fort Cooper, and got back his property, but, being alone, he could not arrest the man, but was obliged to let him go. There is an immense deal of horse-stealing in this district, and the thieves reckon on immunity; the horse may be taken from them, but it is seldom people can or will take the trouble of going hundreds of miles to prosecute them.

I liked to hear about the children's garments very much. It must have been a great undertaking to turn a whole suit of tailor's clothes for Leighton, and you were very clever to succeed in it. I know nothing about tailoring. Annie's face would be a sight at any interference with Biddulph's clothes, but I have learned a good deal of dressmaking since I came out here, and no doubt the tailoring could be also acquired when necessary.

I wonder if you wear those very small hats, which they depict in the London news, and which Emily sent up to us as eligible articles for the bush. We wanted some new hats very much, and were rather grieved when we unpacked things that look like a good-sized saucer on the top of your head. I mended up my old one, and left the new one undisturbed in the box ever since. Annie wears hers on Sundays, but as her face is still longer than mine, I cannot be complimentary as to her appearance in it. For the rest, we are well off for clothes this summer and could even hold on through another winter if necessary, but I suppose we shall go to Sydney in the autumn.

Ever your affectionate sister,

RACHEL HENNING

EXMOOR,
FEBRUARY 18TH 1865

My Dearest Etta,

It is four years ago now since I left England. I wonder where four more years will see us. I hope I shall have seen you again before they are over, but it is impossible to say. The future is always uncertain, and just now it is remarkably so. Whether we shall return to Exmoor, whether go on to Lara, or what may happen in the next six months, I have not the least idea.

I do not think Annie will be married during this visit to Sydney. Biddulph's two stations, though very valuable, are very expensive. I believe the time for our going to Sydney is fixed at last, and I am sorry to say it is much earlier than we expected. Annie and I will go as far as Rockhampton with Biddulph, then leave him there and go on to Sydney alone. There is little chance of Mr Hedgeland being in from Lara by that time, and none of Mr Taylor, so Biddulph will have to get one of the Mr Lacks to take charge of the station during his absence.

I hate the thought of going so soon as far as I am concerned. Dust, and streets, and stuffy houses, and dull tea-parties make up the sum of my anticipations; but it cannot be helped. I shall like to see Amy and the children, that is the only thing.

We have the buggy up at last, and it will be very convenient for travelling to the Port in. It is a very pretty one—double-seated, runs on four very high, light wheels. The whole thing looks too light to be of any use, but it is the strongest of all carriages for a bush road, as it hops over gullies and holes where a heavier machine would break to pieces. Mr Kennedy, who is going out to take charge of Lara station, brought it up with him, but the pair of horses that Biddulph bought with it are most inveterate "planters", for Mr Kennedy lost them again on his way here, and drove up a pair of his own. The horses have been found once more, however, and are coming up by the postman. The old dog-cart in which we came here is quite worn out, and has been made into a water-cart.

We have changed servants again. Now we have a German lad in the kitchen, Carl by name. He does pretty well considering that he speaks but little English, but that is Annie's affair, as I never interfere in the housekeeping. Biddy the black girl washes at present. I cannot say that the things are the colour of driven snow, but, of course, it is only a temporary arrangement till we go to Sydney, and can look out for some servants. If you write to an agent you are almost sure to get bad ones sent up.

We are getting through the wet season very easily so far. We have had no floods, only a few heavy thunderstorms, but the Ides of March are not past yet, and I suppose we must have a flood or two before we have done with it. The country is beautifully green here, and we do not want more rain, but they want it on the western road.

Mr Taylor, who is taking out 3,000 additional sheep to Lara, has been for more than a month camped on the lake at the borders of the desert waiting for rain to fill the waterholes and enable him to cross it. Now there is fifty miles to go without water, and he will not risk it. One man lost his whole flock, 5,000, in trying to push through. They are all pitying the owner for his loss, but I pity the sheep far more.

We have seen a comet lately, or rather the tail of one, for the nucleus was below the horizon, and a very long tail it was, though not very bright. I wonder if it is gone to make its appearance in England.

Biddulph is rather busy, as usual, now that everybody is away from the station. He seems to turn his hand to any sort of bush work. He has sent both the bullock-drivers to the Port with the wool teams, and there was not a man on the station who could drive when some posts were wanted for the paddock fence, but he made nothing of yoking up a team and going out for two or three mornings till he had got in all the timber that was needed. He has been making wool bales and mending saddlery, and dressing sheep with the foot-rot, and, the last few days, breaking in a young horse. Nothing seems to come amiss to him.

I shall be very glad to see Amy again, supposing we are not captured by the bushrangers on the Bathurst road. They are getting fiercer and fiercer. At the last accounts the town of Goulburn was in a state of panic, daily expecting an attack and an assault on the banks. One of the leaders lately, Murray, I think, confided to a traveller whom he was easing of his goods that he was on the look-out for the Bishop of Sydney, who was coming up the road, and he meant to capture him and keep him till he—the bushranger—obtained a free pardon from the Government. Luckily the bishop took another road, so the plan did not succeed.

With very much love to you all, believe me, dearest Etta,

Ever your affectionate sister,

RACHEL HENNING

EXMOOR,
APRIL 18TH 1865

My Dearest Etta,

You will see that I have been troubling Mr Boyce with a commission again, and Annie ditto to you. Perhaps you will some day both take a trip to London to execute them for us. If you do accompany Mr Boyce, as I hope you will, do not "hold his hand". We want almost the best plain watch that he can get, and are prepared to pay accordingly. As you know, the watch is a present to Biddulph from Annie and me.

Biddulph left us yesterday for Port Denison, whither he has gone to load his drays, and start them for the Flinders River station. They are to take supplies for a year for the colony out there. I do not think we shall ever go out there to live. I hope Biddulph will sell it and keep Exmoor. He talks of doing so, and I should be so sorry to leave this place.

He set off quite in style yesterday, driving the buggy and pair, and with his big hairy dog "Tiger" running after him, and Jimmy, one of the blackboys, riding on horseback behind, the said Jimmy being gorgeous in new white trousers slightly too large for him, a scarlet Crimean shirt and scarlet cap. Biddulph bought scarlet for both the blackboys when he was last in Sydney. They are so fond of bright colours, and look best in them.

Nearly all the squatters take a blackboy with them when they are going a journey as a sort of groom. They are very useful to get up the horses of a morning, etc.

Biddulph has a great many things to bring up from the Port, and this is the reason he drove down instead of riding. Among other things we have bothered him with commissions to get us boots and winter petticoats, as we are sure to be here through the winter. I think Biddulph will be away about ten days. I hope he will not be more.

Old Mrs Lack is staying with us now. She is the mother of Mr Lack, who owns Blenheim, the next station to this. She was here for two or three days last year; now she has been here about a fortnight, and will stay a week longer. She is rather a nice old lady, very gentle and lady-like, though slightly meandering; but when you have lived a long time in the bush you get lazy, and do not like the trouble of entertaining anybody. Gentlemen visitors are different, as they entertain themselves or you.

Mrs Lack rode on horseback the first five miles of the way, and we drove over with Biddulph in the buggy and met her about eight miles from here, and I rode the horse home, as we thought she would be tired. She goes home next Friday, I believe. Mr Lack is coming over on Thursday evening to slay beef for us, and takes his mother back next day.

We are having a new fireplace built against when the cold weather comes, though at present there seems no chance of any cold. The hot weather has lasted longer than usual this year, and it is still hotter than any English summer in the middle of the day, but the mornings and evenings are cool and pleasant.

I have been telling Aunt that the first grave has been made at Exmoor, an event in the history of the station. A family travelling with two drays and horse-teams passed the house and camped over the creek one evening a few weeks ago, and a man came up after dark to ask for some medicine, etc., for his little girl who had been ill a fortnight—of diphtheria, I should think from his description. We gave him some milk and promised to come and see the child next day, but at daylight next morning he came over and told Biddulph the child had died in the night, and asked for some old cases to make a coffin.

Biddulph offered to have one made and send it over, but he preferred doing it himself. We asked if his wife would like us to come and see her, but he said she would rather not, which I did not wonder at. Biddulph also offered to come over and read

195

the service when they buried the child, but he said he did not care about it, so we could do nothing for them.

He had three children; this was the eldest, a little girl of five. There were several men with the drays, and they buried her in the morning, and then harnessed their horses and went on their way.

I went across the creek in the evening to where they had camped. It was very sorrowful to stand by the little lonely nameless grave among the gum-trees, and think what it must have been to the poor mother to drive away that morning and leave her little child among strangers. We did not even know their names. The grave is in a beautiful spot on a high bank shaded by trees, and the creek flowing beneath. It is fenced in most securely with whole trunks of trees so that it can never be disturbed. That is the first grave. I thought, who can tell whose the next will be?

The mailman is just come in, so I must not write any more now.

Your ever affectionate sister,

RACHEL HENNING

EXMOOR,
MAY 15TH 1865

My Dearest Etta,

Our last letters from home were full of Mrs Taunton's legacy to us. It must be an old story to you now, but it will not be so to us till we have received and perhaps spent the money. I hope that you and Mr Boyce did not consider our commission a very troublesome one, and that you will not spare a little expense (to us) in fulfilling it. If you get the watch I hope it will come out while we are in Sydney. Biddulph will probably join us there in December, as Annie will most likely be married then, and then we shall have the pleasure of presenting the gold watch to him.

Since I wrote to you last a bad accident has happened at one of the sheep stations. One of the shepherds at the Nine Mile, carrying his carbine in the careless way shepherds usually do, shot himself very badly in the leg with it. He was driving a sheep on with the stock, and the whole charge of shot entered his leg just above the knee and came out just below the hip.

Mr Taylor went out to see him when the news came in, though it was only a flesh wound and the bone not touched. However, the man wished to be sent to Port Denison, so an awning was rigged up for him over the spring-cart and grass

196

and blankets laid in it, and Peter, one of the bushmen, sent to drive him down as fast as he could bear it. We have not yet heard of his arrival. Biddulph raised a subscription for him on the station. All the men gave 10s. each and he got £9 altogether. Biddulph also wrote to his agents to send him on to the hospital at Rockhampton if he wished to go.

The Flinders party arrived from the Lara station on Sunday, April 30th. Mr Gilliat did not come on here, but Mr Taylor and Mr Hedgeland arrived in the afternoon with seventeen horses and a good deal of dust. The former had been away nearly six months, the latter not quite so long. They brought in a good account of the station, which is now left in charge of Mr Kennedy. It is a frightfully dry season everywhere, but the sheep are doing well and looking fat out there, and the horses came in in very good condition.

Last Tuesday we made another excursion to the Broken River, like the one I told you of in a former letter, only we were rather a larger party this time. Biddulph drove Annie and myself in the buggy, and Mr Hedgeland and Mr Taylor and the blacksmith rode on horseback. The blacksmith is very fond of fishing, and Biddulph always promised to take him next time he went to the river. We went a little further down the river than we did last time, and I think to a still prettier place where there were some enormous tea-trees growing in the dry sand close to the water and giving a lovely shade, made on purpose for picnics. When the horses were hobbled and turned out to feed, Biddulph and Mr Taylor set off to catch fish for dinner, the blacksmith likewise. Annie and Mr Hedgeland set about making a fire and unpacking the provisions, and I sat down to try and sketch one of the beautiful reaches of the river.

In due time the fish were caught, the fire was made and Mr Taylor scientifically broiled them on hot stones. The quart-pot tea was boiled, the beefsteak pie cut and highly approved of, the entire second half of it being neatly polished off by the blacksmith, to whom it was handed when we had done. Then a smoke —Mr Hedgeland and Mr Taylor are inveterate smokers, Biddulph a more moderate one—and a second departure was made for fishing while Mr Hedgeland set forth with his gun to look for wild duck, which, however, he did not find.

I finished my sketch and made another, and wished Mr Boyce had been there to do justice to the beautiful Broken River with its clear, deep pools and grey rocks and wooded banks and the blue Australian sky. One ought to be able to colour to make anything of this scenery.

197

We returned at dusk, as it is not pleasant to drive a buggy in the bush after dark—there are such very bad places to get over sometimes. We got home without losing ourselves this time after a very pleasant day.

Mr Taylor has since left Exmoor for good. Biddulph has sent nearly all the sheep out to the Flinders. There are only between seven or eight thousand left on Exmoor, and for that number he means to be his own overseer.

I think Biddulph had just started for the Port when I last wrote to you. He was away eight days and came back on April 26th. He brought us up some boots and some scarlet and black stuff for winter petticoats, though it if continues as hot as it is now we shall hardly want them.

A Mr Morisset, who is thinking of buying a half-share in the Flinders station, came up with him, and in that case he will go out there and take the management of it. The arrangements are not quite completed, but I shall be very glad, if he does, as it will take an immense deal of trouble off Biddulph's hands, and then he will never himself go out there to live, and I should not like to exchange beautiful Exmoor for those desolate prairies, however good they may be for sheep.

Mr Morisset is to give £5,000 for his share if he buys it. He is gone back to the Port now to make arrangements. Mr Hedgeland has been ill with fever and ague these two days, but he is better now. Last year a great many people had it, but there has been very little of it this year. The season has been too dry.

The fireplace is progressing, but not finished yet. The new servants arrived while Biddulph was away and seem likely to do. Mrs Reeve is rather a nice young woman and manages the washing very well; her husband has been a conjuror, of all things in the world, and practised in Port Denison. He has not done much work yet as he fell from a horse coming up and broke two or three ribs, but he seems quiet and civil, and has just cut down one of my favourite trees for firewood.

Kindest love to Mr Boyce and yourself and the darlings. It is no use to "wish I could see you."

Your most affectionate sister,

RACHEL HENNING

EXMOOR,
MAY 29TH 1865

My Dearest Etta,

This is not my usual fortnight for writing home, but I will

198

not let another mail pass without giving you a piece of information which will, I fear, seriously disarrange your hair if you have not a very tight elastic to your net, and cause Mr Boyce's hat to be lifted several inches above his head, if it is not a tolerably heavy one.

It is neither more nor less than that I have been engaged for the last six months to Mr Taylor, Biddulph's sheep overseer. Mr Taylor was just starting for a six months' trip to Flinders in charge of Biddulph's sheep; that is a bourne from whence it is highly uncertain whether any traveller ever returns, so I resolved to say nothing about it to anyone but Biddulph. Of course I thought it right to tell him.

Biddulph gave Mr Taylor a very nice horse and saddle as a sort of return for his exertions in getting the sheep out to Lara, and about a fortnight ago he went down to Mr Paterson's, our next neighbour below, to "spell" his horses before starting on a long journey southward. He has been up here once since to bring us our letters, and will be here again in about ten days or a fortnight, on his way to Rockhampton.

He has friends in the south, and hopes to get an overseership or managership somewhere down there. He may succeed, but so many are looking for situations now that it is extremely doubtful. Of course, everything depends on his getting one; and it was this very great uncertainty that made me wish to keep the whole thing to myself, except, as I said before, that I thought it right to tell Biddulph.

I must fairly confess that I would rather have said nothing till there was something decided to say, or, if there never was, to let it all die out in silence. However, silence seems a privilege not allowed. I have not written to Aunt, and shall not do so at present, and I shall be very glad if you and Mr Boyce will say nothing to anyone till you hear something more. Of course it is immeasurably foolish for anyone of my age to enter into an engagement like this, but I don't want to be told so on all sides at once. I would rather take it by instalments.

Of course you would like to know something about Mr Taylor; but what can I tell you? I cannot praise up anyone so near to me, and no one else is likely to do it. Biddulph does not like his being an overseer, though everybody cannot have stations; also, he does not like his age. He is, unfortunately, a boy of little over thirty, and I—well, the less said the better. It is bad enough, though not quite so bad as some.

I have known him ever since I came here, two and a half years now—we have known each other I should say—and pretty intimately, living in the same house nearly all that time. The only thing I will say of him is that I never met with anyone so thoroughly unselfish. The difficulty will be for him to get a situation, and it may turn out impossible. It cannot be helped, but you see, do you not, why I wish as little said as possible.

I have written to you so lately that I have no news to tell you. Besides, I am at the end of my paper, and I am afraid the above sheets will take some little time to digest.

Kindest love to Mr Boyce and yourself and the dear children.

Ever your affectionate sister,

RACHEL HENNING

EXMOOR,
JUNE 24TH 1865

My Dearest Etta,

I am afraid you were rather astounded by the announcement contained in my last letter that Mr Taylor and I are engaged, but you will have tolerably digested it by the time this one reaches you and have probably settled down resignedly with the original conclusion that "there is no fool like an old one", for I am now thirty-seven. Mr Taylor is still staying at Sonoma, about thirty miles from here. I expect he will be here in a few days on his way down south to seek his fortune.

I am afraid all this makes the prospect of seeing you again more hazy than ever, but where everything is so uncertain it is impossible to say, and it is just as likely as not that in a year or two the respectable Miss Henning may appear in the list of passengers by some homeward-bound ship. I do not like to think of the possibility of not seeing you and yours again; in fact, I am sure I shall come home sooner or later, perhaps, as an old lady with grey hair whom you will not recognize and the children will scream at.

You are just in the middle of summer now, and how lovely June is in England! I can fancy all the thorn-trees out on the downs and the children picking flowers in Leigh Woods and the bouquets in the shop windows and the flower-beds in the Zoological Gardens and the summer costumes on the green. It is fine and warm and sunshiny here, with just a cool breeze to remind us that it is winter.

We have had some rain, too; two days and two nights of steady downpour about three weeks ago, and the country is beginning to look quite green after it, though at this time of the year the grass does not grow at such a marvellous rate as it does in summer. It has greatly improved the prospects of the lambing, however, and I do hope we shall have a good one this year.

We are likely to have some agreeable neighbours on the next station, about thirty miles down the road. A Mr Lansborough and his family have just come there. He is brother to Mr Lansborough the explorer. Biddulph knew them at Raglan, their last station, and, like everyone, is loud in praise for Mrs Lansborough. The girls were children when he saw them, but Miss Lansborough is now seventeen and, I hear, very pretty.

They are too far off for us to see very much of them, but Biddulph is often going up and down the road. He is going to start for Port Denison on Monday next on some business. He is going to drive down in the buggy and will call on the Lansboroughs on his way, so we shall hear his report of them.

As usual, he will have any number of commissions. Annie is clamorous for onions and washing-soda, and I for boots and a crupper for my saddle. As far as anything in life, and especially in bush life, can be certain, I think we are pretty sure really to go to Sydney in September. Annie and I have made up our minds to go down with Biddulph to Rockhampton and on to Sydney.

I suppose Annie will come back as Mrs Hedgeland, but I do not think their plans are quite settled. Some bushmen are at present employed in cutting slabs for their future residence, so that looks like business; but I dare say Annie has told you all about it.

We seem fated to have quarrelsome servants. Our former ones, Tom and Emma, used to wage war which generally ended by Emma running away into the bush. Our present ones reverse the matter, and on Tuesday morning the husband suddenly appeared in the parlour and mentioned that he could not live with his wife any longer, she had such a temper, and he was going to leave the house instantly. So off he went. Biddulph was out at the time. Next morning at breakfast Sarah was missing, having started off at daylight to look for him, and we were bewailing the prospect of an interlude with black Biddy washing and the blacksmith cooking, but in the evening Sarah returned, having walked about twenty miles and then thought better of it. She mentioned that her husband had often run away before, but generally came back in a few days.

Accordingly, yesterday evening Alick met him lurking about in the bush, and he sent a message to Sarah to meet him in the woolshed at dark. He was afraid to come home lest Biddulph should exercise his right of taking him up and giving him three months in jail as a runaway servant. Biddulph was not likely to take that trouble, and this morning he came back, penitent, having had very little to eat and having lost his way in the bush.

Biddulph scolded him for his folly, and now I hope they will

"Biddulph scolded him for his folly."

keep the peace. I suppose both were in fault as usual in such cases.

I have been busy several mornings pruning the passion-vines which grow over the veranda. It took me some time; they were grown in such a mat, but they look all the better and will bear all the better for it. The passion-fruit is very nice. It looks like a large purple plum when ripe, but has a sort of hard shell and you eat the inside. The vines are different from the English, with large evergreen leaves and a smaller blossom.

They are bringing in lunch, and I am at the end of my paper. Kindest love to yourself and Mr Boyce and the darling children. I hope we shall get some later news of you before next mail. It seems so stupid to write, with no letters to answer.

Believe me, ever and always your affectionate sister,

RACHEL HENNING

EXMOOR,
JULY 22ND 1865

My Dearest Etta,

I received your letter of March 25th by the last mail (July 6th); there is another English mail in now, but we shall not get the letters for another fortnight, I am afraid. We are having such a cold winter here. At least we consider it cold. We have had quite sharp white frosts early in the morning and then a brilliant sunny day but with a sting in the air, as dear old Mr Ball used to say. One morning the pump was actually frozen!

It is warmer again now, and I hope we have done with the frosts. Strangely enough, I am perfectly well when the thermometer stands at 90 in the shade, but I have never been free from colds since the winter began. I am probably the only person in Queensland who wishes the summer back again. One morning it was so cold that we were fairly driven out of doors. There was a sharp south-west wind blowing hard, and a very creditable imitation it is, for a colony, of an English north-easter. It came into the house at every point, made the fire smoke and chilled the marrow of our bones.

So as there were rations to go to the Ten Mile we got our horses and packed up some dinner and started with Mr Hedge-land. The wind was behind us, fortunately, and a good canter soon warmed us. Of course the sun was shining; it always does shine here. When we got to the Ten Mile we found a sunny sheltered spot on the bank of the Broken River where we made a fire and had our dinner, and said what a beautiful day it had turned out; then I rambled down into the bed of the river and looked into the deep pools in hopes of seeing an alligator, as their tracks have been seen there and they have sometimes taken a shepherd's dog; but they did not show up, and I only found some pretty little white water-lilies instead.

When the sheep were counted we set off towards home about sundown. The wind had gone down, but it was rather a cold, frosty evening. However, there was a good fire when we came back, and we had a very pleasant day.

Biddulph went down to the Port the week before last to arrange about the sale of Lara, which he did satisfactorily, having sold a half-share in it to Mr Morisset for £5,000—£3,000 in cash and the rest in bills. Mr Morisset is going out there almost immediately to take charge of the station, and it will be a great save of worry and anxiety to Biddulph.

It is very troublesome to manage a station so far off and difficult to find a good superintendent. Biddulph offered the post to Mr Taylor at two different times, but he objected to going so far from Exmoor. Biddulph will sell the other half of Lara if he can get a good offer for it, I think. Of course he has given up all idea of selling Exmoor and is improving it instead. It would certainly be a thousand pities to leave this beautiful country and comfortable house and station just as everything is getting into nice order. I am very fond of the place and should be very sorry to leave it.

I do not at all look forward to our trip to Sydney. I think it will be a great expense and a great bore, but I suppose a change is good for one after three years in the tropics, and I certainly want some garments, and I expect I shall put on and wear new dresses with great satisfaction. I think the wide waistbands they are said to wear now must be hideous. Have you altered the way of wearing your hair yet? Emily writes word that nets are quite gone out and that most people cut their hair off pretty short and then friz it out with their hands! I think I see myself!

Emily does not mention whether she has adopted this elegant style. She also says they make their own bonnets in Sydney. I should rather like to see a bonnet again, though not to make one. Except my old sunbonnet I have not beheld one for three years. We shall be taken for aborigines, I expect, when we present ourselves in the town.

Biddulph saw our new neighbours when he went to the Port. I do not suppose we shall see much of them, as they live thirty miles off. Another of the neighbouring squatters, Mr Selheim, is just married to a sister of Mr Morrisset's, Biddulph's new partner. She is very handsome, I believe, but they live a long way from us.

Your most affectionate sister,

RACHEL HENNING

204

My Dear Mr Boyce,

Many thanks for your letter of March 24th. I have just been reading it through again, and thinking how kind it is of you to sit down and write me such nice long, talking letters. They are not thrown away, I assure you, if they are intended to give pleasure in this far country.

Next month (August) you will probably receive my letter to you and Etta, giving you a good reason why I am not likely to come home just at present. There is nothing I should like better, and at one time I did turn over in my mind whether I would not, after Annie was married, just fly home for a visit while Deighton (Mr Taylor) was making researches after a position, but the expense would be too great. I do not think it would be right to spend two or three hundred pounds now, and then there would be a terrible parting again, so I gave up all idea of it, though it was very tempting. I can only hope that something may turn up in the far future to enable me to see you again, for I never even venture to look the thought in the face that it may never be in this world.

What you say about the Flinders is very true. It would have been dullish there, though I should not have objected to going there, and I should have liked the journey out; but, as I have been telling Etta, there is now no fear of that change. Biddulph has just sold a half-share of the Flinders station for £5,000, and he some time ago withdrew Exmoor from the market. He was disgusted with the dry season last year, but this year we are having a very good season. The sheep are as fat as sheep can be, and both yesterday and today we have had a steady pouring rain, succeeding the frost, which will just make young grass grow in time for the lambing, which commences in about a fortnight.

You were asking me about the value of runs in your letter. A block of land is supposed to contain twenty-five square miles, i.e., it measures five miles each way. In general, there is about half as much again in a block, as, of course, the squatters go to the utmost limit in taking up country, and the Government allow so much for "unavailable land"; that is, scrubs and dense forest where sheep cannot feed. There are eight blocks on Exmoor, and Biddulph offered it for £20,000, so you see the value of land is very small here compared to what it is in England. The rent paid to Government for runs is 10s. per square mile the first four years, and £1 to £2 per square mile the next five years.

Lara is a larger run than Exmoor, but, being outside and in an unsettled district, he offered it for £10,000, which is less than its value, but it has been an incessant worry to him; it is so far off. I think he will sell the other half as soon as he can, and settle down on beautiful Exmoor.

How I wish you could all come out here and see us! How I should like to show you my favourite walks, and see you draw the brilliant colouring of the woods and mountains. That reminds me of your kind present of drawings and books and telescope sent us with my watch. The parcel is safe in the hands of Miss Tucker, and in about two months I hope it will be in mine. I would not have it sent on here on account of the perils of the way. Don't you envy me? I shall have two boxes from home to open when I get to Sydney!

I do not think there is anything so beautiful out here as the Downs, and the Avon, and the Leigh Woods and rocks, but this country has a wild, uncivilized grandeur of its own. We have been taking a good many drives lately. You would be astonished in England at the precipices, almost, which we composedly ride up and down in the buggy. We have a pair of horses now that pull like steam-engines, and I believe would take a buggy up Spring Hill.

Biddulph has given me a new horse lately. A very pretty creature she is, bright bay with black mane and tail, stands rather high with a very pretty thoroughbred-looking head. She is quite quiet, and at the same time spirited, and very fast. She will not let anything pass her, but she has not run away with me yet. "Her name is Cora and she lives at Exmoor."

We have got the April telegrams, and very lamentable they are as to the American War. We are all so sorry that the Confederates are beaten. They have made the most gallant struggle of modern times, except perhaps England versus Europe in Napoleon's time, and it seems such a shame they should be just overpowered by numbers. But I can't help them, and I have got to the end of my paper.

With kindest love to yourself and Etta, believe me, my dear brother,

Ever yours affectionately,

RACHEL HENNING

My Dear Mr Boyce,

I have received two letters from you since I wrote last month, one dated April 24th, and the other dated May 18th, both of which are lying on my desk. I see in the former one you ask me something about the value of stations, which I think I partly answered in my last letter. It was quite true what I told you, that two years ago (1863) Biddulph refused £25,000 for Exmoor, with 10,000 sheep on it. A man who came up from Melbourne offered it him.

There had just been a splendid lambing season, and the northern stations were high in the market. Then came the drought of 1864, and Biddulph, in disgust at the brown appearance of everything and the disappearance of the lambs, advertised Exmoor for sale, and fixed £20,000 as the reserve price. He had, however, sent out 3,000 more sheep to Lara, so only 7,000 were left. That was when we thought of going out to Lara to live. However, it soon appeared that the dry season extended over the entire north, and instead of being worse off than most of our neighbours. At the same time, Lara was offered for £10,000 with 8,000 sheep on it.

This seems very disproportionate to Exmoor, but an "outside" station, five hundred miles from its port, and with no buildings but a few huts, is worth far less than an "inside" one with all the improvements ready—house, store, woolshed, stockyard and men's huts, and only one hundred miles from the Port. A few months ago Biddulph sold a half-share of Lara for £5,000. As I told you, it was very cheap, but it was an awful bore to look after such a distant station, and he would be glad to sell the remaining half for £5,000 more. The purchaser is gone out to take charge, so I hope Biddulph will not have much more trouble with it.

Exmoor has long been withdrawn from the market, and I do not think Biddulph has any idea of selling it. He seems quite settled on it as a residence, and a very pleasant one it is. The present fine season will, however, send up the value of these stations again. There has been rain all through the winter at intervals, and there is plenty of grass for sheep, so we are expecting a 95 per cent. lambing, instead of the 30 per cent. of last year.

There is one comfort as to the climate. Morrell (the man who lived seventeen years among the blacks) says that he has known far worse floods than those of 1863, but never such a drought as 1864. This is small consolation for the low-lying stations, but much for us. Floods do us no harm, but droughts do. Another thing in favour of the northern squatters is that wages are coming down. When we first came here the shepherds all got 25s., 30s. and even 35s. per week, and you had to put up with perhaps impertinence besides for fear of having a flock of 1,500 sheep driven into the station and left on your hands.

Now, owing to the failure of the Peak Downs diggings and the tide of emigrants, the masters have their turn. Biddulph never gives more than 20s. a week, and dismisses every man who does not please him. One old shepherd who has been here ever since the station was formed gets 25s., but then he takes the heaviest flock of all, 2,200 weaners. This season, too, the Bowen squatters have combined to put down the shearing wages. In past years they were 5s. 3d., 5s., 4s. 9d. a score of sheep. Mr Selheim, of Strathmore, always shears the earliest, and this year he refused to give more than 4s., and sent to all his neighbours to support him. The gang of shearers stood out for 4s. 6d. and left him, but were astonished to find that the next station was not more liberal, nor the next. Finally they returned to Mr Selheim and took what he offered.

Biddulph thinks it better to shear late, and never begins till October. When a station is in working order, the improvements, etc., done, the price of the wool is supposed to pay all the expenses, and the increase of the sheep is the squatter's profit. This is the regular formula, of course. Therefore, a bad lambing destroys his profit.

Kindest love to yourself and Etta, my dear brother,

Ever yours affectionately,

RACHEL HENNING

S.S. "RANGATIRA",
OCTOBER 17TH 1865

My Dearest Etta,

Once more I write to you from on board one of what Annie calls "those dreadful steamers", though this time she really has not much to complain of, as we are having a splendid passage.

But to take up my parable from the beginning. I think I told you in my last letter that, seeing that Annie had no other chance of getting to Sydney in time to have two or three months to prepare her garments and see her friends before her marriage, I one morning in a misguided fit of philanthropy undertook to go with her. You see the difficulty was that, lambing being hardly over, and shearing just beginning, Biddulph could not possibly spare a week or ten days to take her to the Port, and Mrs Grundy's feelings would have been hurt if she had gone with Mr Hedgeland unless I was there also.

You will hardly believe how sorry I was to leave Exmoor. However, I could not draw back, for Annie was rejoiced to go. So I took a farewell of my favourite walks in the scrub, put collars with conspicuous red streamers on the pet sheep and exhorted everyone on the station, from Biddulph to the black-boys, on the subject of their welfare, took an affectionate leave of my great kangaroo-dog and white cat, and about ten o'clock on the eighth we left the dear old station where I certainly have spent three very happy years.

Biddulph drove us in the buggy to Mr Paterson's, the first stage of the journey. Mr Hedgeland rode, driving before him our saddle-horses and an extra pair for the buggy. Biddulph likes to drive very fast, and therefore always changes horses in the middle of the day.

We stopped at the river about twenty miles from home, turned out all the horses to drink and feed, lighted a fire, boiled some coffee and had lunch and enjoyed ourselves very much for about two hours, then we started again, and after a beautiful drive reached Mr Paterson's about sundown.

There is an immense party of them at Sonoma station. Mr Paterson, Mr and Mrs Lansborough, three Miss Lansboroughs and some small fry, and though they were very kind I have not spent such an uncomfortable evening for three years. Didn't I wish myself back with the lambs and the dogs when we were all sitting up in a great circle trying to make talk! I thought bed-time would never come, but it did at last, and we also got away next morning, Biddulph driving us half that day's stage.

We went through more beautiful country, and through plains so covered with flowers that they looked like the Flowery Prairie we read of. We stopped at a bush inn about twenty miles on the road, where we had lunch and put on our riding-habits and packed our property on a stout pack-horse, then we said good-bye to dear Biddulph, and he started on his return to Sonoma, which he would reach that evening, and get back to Exmoor, next day, so as to be only from home three days.

I was so sorry to see him drive away; it seemed as if we were really away from home. However, we mounted our horses and started on our journey and about dark got to the Bogie River, about twenty miles, and put up at a very good inn for the bush.

We met the postman there, got the mailbag and took out our letters. One from you of July 25th and from Mr Boyce of July 26th from London.

Next morning we set off again early, and rode through very dull country, except the Bogie Range, where there is some very fine scenery, five or six miles through beautiful wooded mountains. We camped as usual by a creek in the middle of the day, under the shade of some gigantic aloes. They do not grow about Exmoor—curious tropical-looking plants they are. We turned out the horses to feed and boiled the unfailing tea. You cannot think how pleasant these campings are on a journey, and the horses seem to enjoy their dinner just as much as you do.

We got to the Don that evening, thirty-five miles, where there is the best inn on the road. From thence it is only about fifteen miles to Port Denison, so we got in quite early. When we got within a few miles of the town there was an immense deal of racing and chasing of horses and buggies, and it turned out that the Governor was expected to land the next day. We got very good rooms at Wills', the best hotel in the town, with a pleasant sitting-room opening into the balcony. We got some dinner and then, having made ourselves look as civilized as might be under the circumstances, we set off to do some shopping and reconnoitre the town with Mr Hedgeland.

Of course the town itself is nothing, but the bay is most beautiful. Landlocked all round except one narrow channel, the clearest and bluest of water, the green mangrove swamps in some places growing actually in the sea. We sat down on the beach and watched the tide come in. It was so pleasant to see the sea again.

In the evening several people called who knew Biddulph, and we were asked to meet the Governor at a sort of public lunch at Mr Macleod's, and on board the *Diamantina*, to see the regatta, and to a ball which was to be given in the evening, but we declined all these civilities. I think Annie would have liked to go, but she had no dress. I could have got a dress, as your case was at Biddulph's agents at Port Denison, but I cannot think of any earthly inducement that would make me voluntarily present myself among 150 or 200 people.

The steamer was to have sailed Thursday, but was delayed on account of the Governor's visit, so we saw all the sights that could be seen from the balcony of Wills', for we did not go out. There was a triumphal arch right across the street, which, by the way, my mare strongly objected to passing when we came in the day before. She is very easily startled, and as unused to streets as her mistress is now.

"We set off to reconnoitre the town with Mr Hedgeland."

The Governor landed at ten, heard several dull speeches at the pier, and then a very irregular procession conducted him into the town, where just in front of our windows he proceeded to plant the first telegraph post; then he went to the luncheon on board the *Diamantina* for the regatta, and then to the ball.

It was a very hot day, and how tired he must have been of it all! The only part I should have liked would have been the regatta, but Annie objected to going on board a steamer before it was necessary as strongly as I did going to the lunch and ball.

The *Rangatira* did not sail till daybreak on Saturday, but we

211

went on board on Friday night. She was lying nearly a mile and a half from the jetty. Mr Hedgeland went on board with us, but returned again in the boat. I don't know what Annie thought, but I would have given the world to go home with him—to ride pretty Cora over those beautiful plains back again, and see the old vine-covered veranda, and Biddulph, and the lambs, and the old easy life instead of that tiresome Sydney.

However, there was nothing for it but to make the best of the the closest and smallest "ladies' cabin" I have seen, though the *Rangatira* is a fine large boat. By a quick dive therein before any other women could find the dark stairs, I secured the two top berths under the portholes for myself and Annie. No light matter when you have a week's voyage before you. The weather has been beautiful ever since we sailed, the sea calm and the north-east trade-wind to keep the ship steady.

Annie dreaded the voyage very much, but she has not been seasick, only sometimes squalmish and uncomfortable, and has generally been able to come into meals. There is a lady (?) also in the cabin with a very pretty but most squalling baby and an enormous good-tempered and untidy Irish girl as a nurse, and an unmitigated nuisance the trio are, especially the baby. Decidedly people ought not to bring such articles to sea or else to take a private cabin if possible.

A Mr Gilliat is on board whom we knew at Exmoor, and who at one time had charge of the Flinders station for Biddulph. He is a pleasant gentlemanly man, and I like the stout, comfortable-looking captain, but I cannot say much for the other passengers.

The passage from Port Denison to Gladstone is most beautiful. They keep inside and among the islands, and I think it must be like the Grecian Archipelago, the bluest of seas and islands large and small in every direction from fifteen miles long to mere rocks, all more or less mountainous, some of them wooded ranges, with little strips of yellow beach, some rounded green hills with trees growing only in the hollows and gullies and tempting little bays on the shores. Others have precipices rising sharp from the water's edge. I believe they are nearly all inhabited by blacks. On one rocky point we saw a mob of them spearing fish.

We anchored off Gladstone on Monday morning, and a very pretty-looking place it is from the sea, for we did not land. We only stayed a few hours and then steamed off again, and after a few more islands went out to sea out of sight of land, except now and then a misty headland came in sight. They say we shall reach Sydney Thursday evening or Friday morning, and much

Annie will rejoice. For myself I rather like being on the sea.

October 18th. Your birthday, my dearest Etta, and I wish you many happy returns of it. I wonder if we shall ever spend it together again? I hope so, but it looks very uncertain just at present. We are bewailing a head-wind today, which makes the steamer roll, and as Amy said of the great sea-horse, "impedes our course". I am writing in the saloon, which is at present a sort of temple of Aeolus. Annie is reposing on a sofa rather disgusted at the proceedings of the ship, and most of the other people are on deck, except one man who is coughing over a strong dose of brandy, wherewith he is trying to fortify his sinking nerves or stomach.

I have just been reading your letter of July 26th. How I should like to hear Leighton read the "Queen of the May"! I can hardly fancy those babies as they were when I left growing up to understand and like Tennyson. In spite of all efforts I still fancy them as they were four years ago. Now, I will put this away till we reach Sydney tomorrow or next day, when I hope to get your August letters, which must have arrived by this time. We telegraphed from Gladstone, and I only hope we have been in time to prevent our whole correspondence from being forwarded to Exmoor. If it is we shall not get it back for six or eight weeks.

October 21st, Sydney. I boasted too soon of our calm passage, for on the afternoon of the 18th a southerly gale got up and lasted us all the next day, tumbled us about to the great discomfort of the seasick and delayed us at least a day. However, we got to Sydney about eleven on Friday morning, found Mr Hirst, Captain Treloar and Mr Ebsworth waiting for us on the wharf, and drove out to Mr Hirst's house, where we found Caroline and Emily, and very kind they were and glad to see us. Our first inquiring was for letters, you may be sure, and our telegram had been just in time to save them from being shipped off to Port Denison.

You will imagine I read your letter with great interest in answer to the astounding announcement I made to you. I have no doubt Biddulph told you Mr Taylor's father was a lieutenant in the Navy, his mother the daughter of a clergyman, the rector of Woolsingham, in Durham. She must have had some wonderful talent for mathematics, for when her husband left the sea (he has been dead for years) she established a school for preparing midshipmen to pass the examination in navigation and mathematics, and published the Nautical Almanac. Mr Scott, that young sailor who was staying with us some time ago, had studied with her. In connection with these she established a shop for the manufacture and sale of all sorts of nautical instruments. They had a most extensive business at one time and furnished half the ships leaving London with instruments.

Mr Taylor used to go down the Channel sometimes with new ships to adjust them to their instruments, as it is called, and this way became half a sailor himself. There is a good deal of the sailor about him. Mrs Taylor has a pension from the Government now. Mr Taylor was at a classical school, as his mother intended him for the church, but he did not like that, and wanted to make music his profession.

The whole family are wild after music. He studied the violin for two years, then worked at the instrument trade and adjusting, and finally came to Australia, where for about six months he was on a station of Mr Towns's; ever since, namely for five years, he has been with Biddulph. The consequence of all this is that he has a most curious collection of knowledge of things Biddulph never dreamed of, though he doesn't like Tennyson and Biddulph does.

From his trade he knows a great deal about chemistry and metals and astronomy. I think our acquaintance began with my learning the names of the Southern Constellations. He sings beautifully, as I think I told you before, and when Biddulph wanted to sell Exmoor, and wished for a map of the run, he set off and climbed the hills and took the different bearings and measured distances and mapped it out without any difficulty.

You may depend upon it, I should never like anyone who was without intellectual taste or knowledge, although I don't mind the line of their intellect being different from that of mine.

Next to the letters on which I have, I am sure, commented *ad nauseum*, I inquired for your parcel, and it was duly handed over by Emily and unpacked with great delight by me. I disinterred first the watch, which I have not yet been able to get opened, but which I shall be very glad of when I get it, and next *Enoch Arden*, for which I am very much obliged to you, my dearest Etta. I have read the poem some time ago, but only once, and that is very different from having it myself. I like it much, and some of the shorter pieces better still.

Annie is very much pleased with Jean Ingelow's poems. They were lent us once for a short time, and we liked them greatly. She tells me to thank you, and she will write herself next week, but she is only this moment come in from a shopping expedition. She has had her hair made more fashionable, arranged in curls in front and a plait behind, as of old days, and looks quite nice. Our nets and rolls are quite old-fashioned, but I have not changed yet.

Tell dear little Constance I am very much obliged for her kettle-holder. I think it is very nicely worked, and we will use it at Exmoor, where we always have a kettle for tea. I have not yet got my box of dresses up from the wharf, so as the post closes this evening, I shall not be able to tell you about them in this letter as I hoped, but it is quite long enough as it is. Good-bye, my dearest Etta, and believe me,

Ever your most affectionate sister,

RACHEL HENNING

SYDNEY,
DECEMBER 19TH 1865

My Dearest Etta,

Biddulph and Mr Hedgeland are expected down on Thursday evening or Friday morning, according to the sort of passage the *Rangatira* has. They are later than we expected owing to Biddulph not being able to get the sheep shorn till late.

Mr Taylor is only down here for a short time. He comes to see me every day. He came down from Maryborough (a port about 500 miles north) to see me, intending only to stay a week, but he has heard of a situation here, and is staying on to see about it. It is uncertain yet whether he will get it or not. I do not mean a situation in Sydney but a berth as overseer of a New South Wales sheep station. He will probably leave here after Christmas, as he will know by that time.

Meanwhile it has been very pleasant to see him again for a week or two, and the Hirsts and Tuckers have been very kind in asking him to their houses. We have spent the greater part of this morning in Sydney getting our photographs taken to send home to Mrs Taylor.

Everybody in Sydney knows of my engagement now—all that know me, that is, for of course when Mr Taylor had come so far to see me I could no longer keep it a secret, though I had much rather have done so while everything is so uncertain. I hate being talked about.

I shall think of you on Christmas Day, and wish we could spend it together once more. Annie is making extensive preparations now for her wedding; she has bought a great many dresses, some of them very pretty. The last was a ribbed silk of the same kind as my brown one, only that brilliant new blue, and it cost

215

seven guineas instead of four, which I should have sorely demurred at. She has bought some beautiful muslins and two of those thin grenadines. They are very pretty but very expensive. Also a Scotch plaid winter dress and a variety of prints and ginghams for mornings. She has got beautiful undergarments, almost too good for the bush. Such quantities of embroidery as as would have made our hair stand on end in the old days, and petticoats with no end of tucks and insertions let in between. Also a velvet jacket and shawls and mantles for outside wear.

Her wedding dress is to be white muslin, as white silk would be utterly useless in the bush. There are to be eight bridesmaids, four in pink and four in blue. Emily Tucker is her Prime Minister and adviser, for just now my own time is pretty well taken up. So all I do is to wear what I am told when the time comes. The wedding is to be from the Tuckers' house at Double Bay.

The English mail is telegraphed at last. Perhaps there will be a supplementary mail again sent. I must not write more, as Mr Taylor, Caroline Hirst, Miss Ebsworth and myself are going for a drive to the South Head to spend an hour or two there rambling about among the rocks.

My kindest love to you all,

Your most affectionate sister,

RACHEL HENNING

III

MR AND MRS TAYLOR

[*As Rachel anticipated and revealed in her correspondence with her sister Etta—"Of course it is immeasurably foolish for anyone of my age to enter into an engagement like this, but I don't want to be told so on all sides at once"—there was some family opposition to her marriage with Deighton Taylor, partly because he was several years her junior, and partly because of doubts about his security of employment at that time. However, following the marriage in Sydney of Annie and George Hedgeland on 24th January 1866, Rachel and Deighton Taylor were*

216

*quietly wed on 3rd March of the same year, Biddulph Henning
giving the bride away. Shortly after the wedding Rachel and
Deighton went to live at what is now known as Bulahdelah, on
the Myall River, near Stroud, N.S.W., where Deighton managed
a timber logging business for Mr Somerville, who became Lord
Somerville shortly afterwards.*]

MYALL RIVER,
PORT STEPHENS, N.S.W.
MAY 16TH 1866

My Dearest Etta,

I think I last wrote to you just as I had received notice to
quit Sydney for the Myall. I think I was never more glad than I
was to get Mr Taylor's letter, which I did on the Saturday on
which I posted your last. I packed all day on Monday, April
23rd, and at eleven o'clock that night Mr Hirst put me on board
the Hunter River steamer, and at twelve we sailed. It was a very
calm night, and I went to bed and to sleep, and only woke when
we stopped to land passengers at Newcastle about six o'clock.

Thence we steamed for three hours up the Hunter River, and
a noble river it is. Steamers of 300 tons go up it. At nine o'clock
we got to Raymond Terrace, where I found Mr Taylor waiting
for me on the pier. We went to the inn and had some breakfast
and a long talk over our adventures during the five weeks that
we had been separated, and then we mounted our horses and
took an easy ride to Limeburners' Creek, a distance of sixteen
miles. There is a very comfortable little inn there, and we got
there to dinner and took a ramble in the bush in the evening.
I was so glad to be in the green bush again after those weary
Sydney streets.

Next day we rode to Stroud, the capital of these parts, but
what would be a small village in England. There is an excellent
inn there, and a mail road goes from Raymond Terrace to
Stroud. Our third day's journey was from Stroud to the Myall,
a distance of twenty-two miles. There is no road, only a bush
track, and a very beautiful ride it was, especially over the range
that we had to cross. I do not know how the horses liked it, as it
was almost climbing for them in some places, but I wish you
could have seen the steep green slopes and rocky peaks and deep
gullies and creeks that we rode among.

We stopped for dinner by one of the creeks and made some
quart-pot tea, then rode on again, and about sundown came to
the Myall, which we crossed in a punt, and then ten minutes'

riding brought us to the house. A very pretty little house I thought it as I first saw it through the trees, with the evening sun shining upon it, and the garden gay with chrysanthemums and roses. The house stands on the side of a small hill looking down upon the river. There is a veranda in front, and beyond that a trellis so as to form a sort of double veranda.

There are four rooms inside. The sitting-room where I am now writing is remarkably bright and pleasant. On my right is a large fireplace wherein a wood fire is burning, for though the sun is still hot the mornings and evenings are cold up here. On each side of the fireplace is a window, a real glass window with nine large panes in it. These windows look into the garden on the side of the house, and beyond the garden paling into the forest and the path from the village that winds down between the trees. In front of me is another window looking into the veranda, and from it I can see as I sit a rose-tree covered with blossom, and then down the paddocks to the river, lying dark and still under the trees on the opposite bank. The blacks have an encampment there now, and I can see them moving about their boats, which are moored to the bank.

Next the window is a very nice cedar bookcase made by Mr Taylor wherein are arranged all my books. They have not seen the light before since they left Bristol. The cedar table at which I am writing and a side-table that is under the window are also of Mr Taylor's manufacture. The rest of the furniture consists of a mahogany chiffonier, some mahogany cane-seated chairs, an American chair (mine), a hearth-rug, some strips of India matting, a green damask tablecloth, and buff blinds to the windows. These last are my making, and I am rather proud of the way they roll up with a lath. My bedroom opens out of the sitting-room and is very comfortable, a window on to the veranda; the rest of the house consists of a passage and two rooms, one of which is fitted with shelves and a dresser as my store-room, the other has a large fireplace, but is not furnished except by our boxes and cases.

The kitchen is as usual detached and at the back of the house, and is inhabited by the bullock-driver and his wife; the latter, Mrs Murphy by name, is our servant. I expected to have had some trouble with her, as she had been used to a bachelor establishment, but she is very civil and obliging and we get on very well. I let her take very much her own way and she does all the cooking and housework, everything except Mr Taylor's and my washing, and that I put out.

I have nothing to do myself except a little dusting and making puddings when I have anything to make them of. There is nothing to complain of in that line, however. Some one of the settlers round kills beef once in a week or ten days, so we do not often eat salt meat; then we have about sixty fowls, and some of them are slain occasionally. They also lay quantities of eggs. Milk and butter we get from a farm close by. The first at 2d. a quart, the latter 1s. 3d. a pound. Potatoes are cheap, and we have them at all meals, and there are plenty of vegetables in the garden. Mrs Murphy makes excellent bread, and we often have fish which Mr Taylor and Mr Somerville catch in the river.

Mr Somerville is one of the owners of the concern. He talks of going to England, but I dare say he will be here some months at least. He has a den of his own on the other side of the store, but has his meals with us and sits with us of an evening. He is about Mr Taylor's age, pleasant and gentlemanly and exceedingly fond of poetry, especially Tennyson. He reads it aloud better than anyone I ever heard. He and Mr Taylor are great friends and get on very well together.

There is a storekeeper on the place who lives over the store and attends to it, but Mr Taylor makes up the books. There are three men employed about the place. The bullock-driver, the punt-man and a "generally useful" man. There are two great awkward-looking timber punts which take the timber down the river at the rate of a mile an hour. We have also four other boats on the place, and I often have a row on the river with Mr Taylor. We have a nice little garden which is being rapidly improved and enlarged, and a six-foot paling fence has just been put round it, which I hope will keep out the fowls, and yesterday Mr Taylor and Mr Somerville were busy all day planting some new flower-beds which have been cut out and measuring and marking out some new ones. I am getting very lazy in that way, and only sat on the grass and gave advice and watered the flowers when planted.

Things grow like magic here. Every stick that is stuck in seems to take root. I hope we shall have a nice garden in the spring. It is too late now for anything but roses and chrysanthemums, and they will soon be over. We are about half a mile from the village. It is such a pretty walk there through the bush. The natives call it the town of Bulladilla, but you look in vain for anything like even a village street. You see only little wooden houses dotted promiscuously about in twos and threes among the great trees. There is, however, a weekly post there from Stroud, and also a village school and a service every Sunday afternoon conducted by the schoolmaster. Mr Taylor and I

"I often have a row on the river with Mr Taylor."

generally go, but I cannot say there is a very large congregation. Mr Olive, the schoolmaster, reads the evening prayers and a short sermon. He drops his "h's" sorely, but otherwise he does not read badly, and it is rather a nice little service The singing is most wonderful. They uplift tunes that I have never heard since the days of papa's old cottage readings at Stogumba, and sometimes they have words which I never heard before nor I should think did anyone else.

There is a week-day school at the village which I go and see sometimes, and look as wise as I can over the boy's copy-books and the girl's crochet, not thinking it necessary to mention that I never could learn crochet myself. Last Sunday Mr Taylor and I rowed up to the village in the boat, then landed and went to church, and afterwards came down to the river again, where we found Mr Somerville waiting for us with the boat, and then we took a beautiful row up the river much further than I had ever been before.

I wish you could see the Myall. It is quite unlike the deep, dry rocky river-beds of the North, but very beautiful in its own way, not very wide but very deep, so that the great timber punts can go up and down it, and the banks shut in by dense forest so that you cannot see any light through, the beautiful vines hanging from the trees and dipping into the water. Then you turn a corner and come upon a bright little clearing with a settler's wooden house and patch of maize and perhaps an orange orchard or a vineyard. Further on the forest shuts you in again.

The whole country is covered with dense forest, giant trees and thick under-wood and vines and creepers. Here and there there is a settler's clearing for some distance round, as, for instance, there are open paddocks down to the river; then, backing up our house and the village, is "Bulladilla", a great rocky mountain with steep sides clothed with forest and a range of perpendicular cliffs at the top which always catch the last rays of the sun long after they have left us, and very beautiful old Bulladilla looks then.

There are plenty of bush tracks, and Mr Taylor and I often have an evening walk in them or by the river, or when he is busy I wander by myself with only the dogs of the establishment for company. Of course I struck up an instantaneous friendship with two cats, two terriers, a kangaroo hound and a cattle-dog, and I am at present rearing a brood of chickens under a wire dish-cover!

I wish you could look in at my new home. I think you would arrive at the conclusion that it is not such an unhappy one after all. I am only taken too much care of, and I never was in better health, if that will only last. I am getting quite plump, and Sydney "grinding" had worn me to nothing when I came here.

My kindest love to Mr Boyce, yourself and the children. Ever, my dearest Etta,

Your most affectionate sister,

RACHEL TAYLOR

MYALL RIVER,
JUNE 19TH 1866

My Dearest Etta,

I received your letter of March 24th a few days ago. Amy forwarded it to me from Bathurst, and I was very glad to get it, for I was afraid you had written to me at Exmoor.

You will have known long before this that you were right in thinking that I did not return there. We are very well off at present, for Mr Taylor gets £100 a year for salary and we are found in everything—house, servants, food, even such things as kerosene oil and milk and butter. The only expenses we are at is the washing, which I put out, and extras in the way of currants and raisins and other groceries; a case of which I had up from Sydney.

Of course Mr Taylor's salary more than covers all our expenditure, and my own income is lying by against a rainy day or his being out of a situation again. The place not being our own, of course, this is quite possible, and I often think we are too well off and too comfortable for it to last, and that we shall have to "move on" at the end of the year. However, "sufficient unto the day", and perhaps something else will turn up.

For the rest, I doubt if there is anyone else in the world who would have made me so happy or whom I could have made thoroughly happy. You know I am not the most patient of tempers, and I might very possibly have quarrelled and skirmished with anyone of less unvarying kindness and good temper. As it is, we have never had a word or thought of difference.

I should not have written so much about myself had not so much been written to you against my proceedings, but Biddulph's objections all resolve themselves into the general proposition of "not good enough", and, as you know, that is an hallucination very common to brothers and sisters. I hardly know any girl in the world I should think good enough for Biddulph, so that does not go for much; however, enough of this.

It is rather a forlorn hope my writing at all by this mail, for tonight it is raining as I believe it only rains in Australia. The river is rising fast, and unless it ceases before morning the creeks will be up between this and Stroud and the mailman will not be able to go. If he goes on the right day the letters will just catch the English mail, but a day's delay will lose it.

I shall be very sorry if you miss hearing from me by a mail. I would have written last week if I could have foreseen this weather. We have had one flood since I wrote last. It rained incessantly for five days and the river rose steadily till one morning we looked out and saw it all over the flat, and our boats, which are generally kept moored to some oaks at the bottom of the paddock, appeared in the middle of the stream, oak-trees and all. One disappeared altogether, and Mr Taylor and Mr Somerville rowed about some time looking for it, but when the

222

river subsided she was found sunk at her moorings and safe under the oaks.

There was a great skirmish at the beginning of the rain to save some timber (about 6,000 sleepers) which had been brought down close to the waters' edge ready for stowing in the punt, and, of course, when the river rose it was in danger of being washed away.

Mr Somerville, Mr Taylor and all the men on the place worked all day in the pouring rain and up to their knees in water to get the sleepers into the punt before the river rose higher. They succeeded in saving them all, though they were only just in time.

Several settlers lost a great deal of timber. A flood is rather a fine sight when seen from a hill like this, where you are quite safe from the waters as we are, but it must be very unpleasant for those who live at the river's edge and have to be taken out of their houses in a boat, as once happened to Mrs Murphy, the woman in the kitchen.

There is not much news to tell you on the Myall. We have been gardening a great deal lately, and I think we shall have a very pretty garden in the spring. We are making a large flower garden at the side of the house. Mr Taylor arranged and drew the beds, and they have been trenched three feet deep, so things ought to do well. We have had contributions of plants from all quarters. Mr Somerville brought back a quantity of seeds and roots from Sydney besides a whole sheaf of cuttings.

I had a nice long letter from Biddulph and another from Annie a few days ago, but I expect you get Exmoor news direct. With love,

Your very affectionate sister,

RACHEL TAYLOR

MYALL RIVER,
JULY 18TH 1866

My Dearest Etta,

I did not hear from you by the last (April) mail, and I suppose you wrote to Exmoor to congratulate Annie on the news of her marriage, which must have reached you by that time. I dare say there will be a letter for me by this month's mail, but there is no chance of its being here in time to answer, for the mailman was stopped by the floods, and we have no letters at all this week. Since I last wrote to you we have had another flood still higher than the first. It was a grand sight to see the whole flat covered with water like a great lake, and the water gleaming far away among the trees. The flood does us no harm except by stopping the men from drawing the timber, but I am afraid that if the heavy rains have been general, as I hear they have, Tregenna will have had heavy losses again.

We are still busy with the garden here, but it is almost finished now. Some beds are being cut out in front of the veranda, one of which is to contain roses and the other scarlet geraniums, and a path has been cleared from the veranda down the hill to the gate in the garden fence. It is to be planted on each side with vines trained on a trellis.

You should have seen some of the boulders that were dug out of the beds and path. The whole strength of the place was called upon to get them out of the holes and roll them down the hill and out at the gate. It is a great improvement, and now that they are gone I have been planting a large strawberry-bed, so I hope we shall have some strawberries in the spring, and we have had various presents of new flowers, roses and fuchsias and hollyhocks.

We made such a pleasant expedition one day in search of plants. We rowed up the river for about four miles—that is, Mr Taylor and Mr Somerville rowed and I did nothing harder than steering the boat among the snags and submerged trees. Then we landed and walked about a mile through the bush, Mr Taylor carrying a bag and Mr Somerville a spade, till we came to an old deserted clearing where were the units of a house and the remains of a very good garden.

I never saw two finer lemon-trees than there were there. There was also a whole jungle of a handsome yellow mimosa in full flower. I suppose it had once been a hedge. It was such a pretty, lonely place; the garden was all overgrown with grass and wild raspberries, but you could just trace the paths.

We went principally to search for vine-roots, but we could not discover any. We, however, carried off plenty of young lemon plants and some rose-trees and mimosa and some creepers, walked back to the boat and got home just as it was getting dark. I made booty of a great bunch of lemon blossom and mimosa flowers and scarlet raspberries, which I "set up" in a large red Bohemian vase which Mrs Ebsworth gave me as a wedding present.

I do not remember if I told you how kind people were in that respect. Mrs Hirst gave me a very pretty green and drab table-cloth, which at present adorns the table, and in the centre stands the red vase before-mentioned upon a crimson and white mat

224

knitted by Emily Tucker. The luncheon or dinner table looks quite smart with all the things that were given me. A very handsome cruet stand from Biddulph stands in the centre, the teapot, sugar basin and cream jug were Annie's gift, and the jam or honey always appears in a pretty ground-glass dish which Emily Tucker gave us. Mrs Tucker gave us a set of dinner mats made of strips of white and dark wood fixed on a lining so that they roll up. You know the sort.

Although we spent so little about furnishing, the place looks very snug and comfortable. The sofa Mr Taylor made is a great success. I almost always sit there to work, and it is adorned with an antimacassar I sent for to Sydney, a black net darned with flowers; at least it is a woven one in imitation of those darned ones you used to make.

Since I last wrote we have had a visit from the clergyman of Stroud. I believe this is his parish also, but as it is twenty miles from Stroud, he only comes here about once in three months. We heard he was coming on the Saturday, but we did not the least expect a visit from him, as he was not on good terms with Mr Taylor; but while Mr Taylor and I were dressing for dinner on Saturday evening the voice of Murphy (the man who lives in the kitchen) was heard in the passage: "Mr Taylor, here's the parson a-coming down the hill," and a very short time after Mrs Murphy was heard outside our door: "Mrs Taylor, here's the parson coming to the gate." Luckily I was dressed (in that blue mohair you sent me and which I am wearing out in the evenings) just in time to let in the cause of all the excitement.

The sitting-room opens straight into the veranda, and I admitted the clergyman and the schoolmaster. Our dinner was on the table and the boiled beef and dumplings and apple pie were all getting cold before our eyes. We asked Mr Simms, the clergyman, to dine with us, but he said he had dined, and at last he went.

Mr Taylor and I went to church the next morning. The little schoolroom was very much crowded when we got there, and, seeing two ominous-looking chairs at the top of the room, I made a dive for a haven of refuge on a bench by the side of a fat woman about half-way down the room, but I only made matters worse, for I saw Mr Simms beckoning to a chair which appeared to be nearly in his pocket, while the schoolmaster pulled Mr Taylor by the coat-tails, so we had to go up, and, having been comfortably placed facing the whole congregation, I had some difficulty in keeping my crinoline out of the way of Mr Simms's surplice.

Mr Taylor continued to edge his chair back into the fireplace, and as there was a steep step I fully expected to see him go over on his back and be despised by the congregation. However, the service proceeded, and we had a good moral sermon, but it was nothing more. There was service again in the afternoon, and the next day Mr Simms returned to Stroud for another three months.

Mr Somerville was absent in Stroud all the time, but he would not have gone to hear Mr Simms, as he was more angry than Mr Taylor was at the offence given, which was this. Mr Taylor had a letter which he particularly wished to send before the usual weekly post-time (it was to me), and Mr Somerville had also an important letter to go, so Mr Taylor journeyed over into the village to ask Mr Simms to post them in Stroud as he rode back. He passes the post-office. Whereupon he replied that he had been pastor of this parish for eleven years and such a request was never made him before, and on a Sunday evening, too! As he started early on Monday, it could not well have been made at any other time. Mr Taylor said he was very sorry he had asked him and went home, but of course they were not greatly pleased at the want of courtesy.

We have just been out in the kitchen to see an enormous kangaroo tail which Murphy brought home. Spring, a very fine kangaroo dog we have here, killed the owner of the tail, an old-man kangaroo about five feet high, today in a waterhole, but he paid for his exploit, poor fellow, for the whole of his shoulder was laid open by a stroke from the kangaroo's hind claw. He is a very powerful dog, but he has several times been nearly killed in his wars with the kangaroos. We shall make soup of the tail tomorrow.

Some bad news came today of the loss of the *Cawarra*, a large Brisbane steamer, with the loss, it is said, of a hundred lives, but I think this must be an exaggeration, as the coasting boats are not likely to carry so many. Fifty would probably be nearer the mark, but that is bad enough. We had one awful night last week during the flood in the river. I have seldom heard such wind or such rain, besides thunder, and we were saying, Mr Taylor and I, what a terrible night it must be at sea and how glad we were that none of our friends were out in it, and it was that night the *Cawarra* was wrecked. She was running into the port of Newcastle for shelter and got on the oyster rocks.

I hope, my dearest Etta, I shall have some letters to answer next time I write, but I cannot expect to hear by every mail now that Annie, Amy and I are scattered over the face of Australia.

226

My kind love to Mr Boyce. I hope he will not discontinue his correspondence with me. I used to look forward to his letters.

Your most affectionate sister,

RACHEL TAYLOR

MYALL RIVER,
OCTOBER 17TH 1866

My Dearest Etta,

I have again received the English letters in time to answer, and it is much pleasanter to be able to write at once while your letters and news are just fresh in my mind than it is to wait a month for an opportunity of answering them.

Thanks for your note of August 25th. You are quite right in the opening sentence: that I have "fallen on my feet in the choice of a husband". I do not think anyone else in the world could have made me so happy, and it is something worth living for, to be able to make him thoroughly happy also. I do not think with Amy that Annie is so much to be pitied. To be without a servant for a short time is a very common episode in the bush, and, though tiresome enough for the time, is soon over and forgotten.

I was very happy at Exmoor, and so, I have no doubt, is Annie.[1]

I must not forget that tomorrow is your birthday. Many happy returns of it, dear. I am afraid it is not very likely that we shall spend another together, but it is possible in the changes and chances of life. How I should like to look in on you in your new house and see what the children are now! Do what I will, I cannot fancy them growing up. I should like you too, to have a look at my bush home and see the lights and shadows on the trees, and grass, and the river sparkling in the sun and a fresh breeze, as I see them every time I raise my eyes from my writing.

Last evening we scrambled up one of the lower peaks of Bulladillah, the mountain that rises behind our house, to look for rock-lilies and see the view. It was very steep, but, being pulled in front by Mr Somerville's stick and propelled behind by Mr Taylor, I continued to get to the top, a sort of labyrinth of splintered peaks and crags.

The view was magnificent—miles of hill and valley covered with forest, the river winding along, then the blue lakes, and beyond all the sea. The white waves breaking on the Port

[1] Annie had returned to Exmoor with her husband, George Hedgeland.

"... *pulled in front by Mr Somerville's stick and propelled behind by Mr Taylor.*"

Stephens Heads. I got plenty of rock-lilies and a large hole in my boots from the sharp rocks, and came down safely and dined upon beefsteak pie, which I manufactured before we went.

We talk of taking a rope with us and climbing the real peak of Bulladillah, but whether we shall accomplish that feat this summer I do not know. We also talk of a boating excursion to explore the Myall Lakes and shoot black swans, and this I hope we shall manage.

The weather is beautiful now, neither too hot nor too cold. We have not left off fires yet in the mornings and evenings. I am afraid I shall not be extravagant enough to send for another box of dresses just yet. Our great ambition is to get a piano when we can afford it. Mr Taylor is exceedingly musical, and I could pick it up again with a little pains.

Ever your most affectionate sister,

RACHEL TAYLOR

MYALL RIVER,
NOVEMBER 26TH 1866

My Dearest Annie,

Thank you for your nice long letter of October 30th. The stopping of the Brisbane mail is very tiresome for you. One is glad to get letters and papers regularly in the bush. Thank you for all the Exmoor news. I was very glad to hear that Biddulph has got an overseer to suit him.

It is a great improvement getting men at £40 a year; that is, if they are good for anything. I hope you have got a married couple by this time—it is such a nuisance to have any difficulty about washing. Wages are cheap here. Murphy, the bullock-driver, and his wife, who is house-servant, only get £45 a year between them.

I like Mrs Murphy very much, and we have always got on very well together, but as you will see by my letter to Biddulph we shall be leaving here in a month or two; the place is to be sold or let as soon as it can be, and in the meantime Mr Somerville is only going to keep one man just to look after it. It doesn't pay in the least, and I am afraid he has lost a good deal by it.

I like the place exceedingly, and so does Mr Taylor, and we shall both be very sorry to leave it in many respects; and no one can be kinder than Mr Somerville has been. Still, I like the idea of having a home entirely my own, and though we have taken great pleasure in the garden here, it has always been under the idea that we might have to leave it, and it would be a greater pleasure to cultivate a garden that was all our own.

We do not want to leave this part of the country if we can get some land here. I like the climate, and the scenery is the prettiest I have seen after Illawarra. Mr Taylor is going into Stroud next week to make inquiries about land, etc., and I hope to be able to tell you more about our proceedings in my next letter.

The *Bullah-deelah* (as the punt is grandly named) met with a bad accident a few days ago. She was loaded with first a tier of heavy girders (that is, whole trunks of trees, just squared on the four sides, some of them measuring fifteen by fifteen and thirty feet long); then some thousand palings, and finally fifty bags of maize; and she was lying at our wharf with provisions and everything on board just ready to start for the Tea Gardens.

Murphy, the man, inspected her at nine o'clock, and Mr Taylor and myself took a moonlight walk at ten o'clock to see that she was all right and not making any water. She was all right, and everybody seemed to be quite happy, when about six in the morning a man came running up to say he had just seen the punt sink! Sure enough, she had gone down in twenty-two feet of water. This river does not shelve, but is deep close to the bank.

The maize was the first thought, as it would soon spoil, but they fixed hooks on to long poles, and in the course of the morning fished up the whole fifty bags. It was not long enough in the water to be hurt, but the drying was dreadful work. It was spread in the loft, in the spare room, in the pantry, in the veranda; in fact, go where you will, you walk upon maize. It is nearly dry now, and will soon be bagged up again.

The palings floated about and were soon collected and stacked, but the punt and the girders still remain at the bottom of the Myall, and cannot be got up till next week, when two other punts are coming to try and lift her. There would be no difficulty were she empty, but the girders are such an enormous weight. Nobody can make out why the punt sank, as she had been making no water all the day before. There are strong suspicions of somebody having scuttled her, but it is almost impossible to prove it.

I think the little chestnut mare will turn out very well. I rode her twice, and she seems very fast. Murphy brought her in a few days ago with a weakly looking foal, which Mr Taylor shot immediately. I was afraid she would fret over it, but after standing by it one night she went to feed with the other horses. Murphy dragged the foal away in the morning, and she does not appear to have thought of it since. I hope she will now get into good condition; she is a pretty, well-bred-looking thing if she was not so poor.

Mr Somerville brought back with him from Sydney Aytoun's *Lays of the Scottish Cavaliers*. I never saw them before. They are extremely spirited. He brought up a book both for me and Mr Taylor, very kindly. I never saw anyone so fond of poetry. I still take in the *Cornhill Magazine*. There is rather a good story in it by Anthony Trollope called "The Claverings", and a pretty tale by Miss Thackeray, "The Village on the Cliff". We also take in the *Home News*. Mr Somerville takes the *Sydney Herald*, but I do not often read it. I like to look at the Port Denison papers, which come here for Mr Gilliat.

Thank you for your receipt for making a cake. I did not know exactly the quantities, but I have succeeded much better lately. I think, as you say, a great deal is in the baking, and Mrs Murphy, after failing two or three times, has got into the way of it now.

No cookery book tells you exactly how to do things; for instance, when I wanted to know the quantity of peas for making a tureen of soup, I found the advice "Take peas". I constantly make cornflour blancmange, and very nice it is. I once tried custards, but failed signally. Nothing would induce the stuff to thicken, and at last it boiled! So I added some sago and made a pudding. Plum pudding, roley puddings made of gramah-jam, beefsteak pies and puddings I am quite clever at. I also make tarts of wild raspberries and dried apples. It is a pleasure to make things for Deighton, he always likes them and thinks them so good.

Good-bye now, my dear Annie. With kindest regards to Mr Hedgeland and love to yourself.

Your ever affectionate sister,

RACHEL TAYLOR

MYALL RIVER,
FEBRUARY 17TH 1867

My Dear Mr Boyce,

As is often the case, we have to write our English letters before receiving the last mail. What you suggest about buying this place if Mr Somerville sold it occurred to us also, and Biddulph consented to let me use Aunt Vizard's legacy for the purpose, which, with what we have saved here and Uncle John's money, would have nearly paid for it, but on further consideration Mr Taylor and I thought it would be a considerable risk and would not pay, so much outlay is required.

A bullock-driver and two punt-men at least have to be kept, and the men who split and saw the timber have to be paid, and then timber has lately been so low in Sydney that you probably lose after all your trouble. The trade is overdone there. Everyone is sending down timber, and two steam sawmills are being erected which will probably take all the trade.

So we thought our present plan far the best, as if we do not gain much neither can we lose, and we shall be independent of the whole tribe of sawyers, splitters, timber merchants at Sydney, etc.

We are going to buy about 150 acres of land, put up a comfortable wooden house upon it, fence it all in with a sheep-proof fence and by and by, when everything is ready for them, buy about a hundred sheep and run them on the land in a fenced paddock where they can do as they like. They ought to thrive as well as pet sheep, and what looking after they require Mr Taylor will give them himself, so they will not cost anything after the first outlay. The same land would maintain our riding horses and a cow, and I think we shall do very well.

The fact is that our income (£205) is quite enough to live on most comfortably in the bush, but the sheep will give Mr Taylor an employment that he likes, and their wool, and selling the increase in Stroud or Sydney, may give us some £20 a year more.

We have taken a fancy to this part of the country to settle in. I do not mean the Myall; the land here would never do for sheep, but about Stroud, which is twenty miles from here. The land there belongs to the Australian Agricultural Company and they are very slow in their proceedings. We wanted a piece of land near Stroud, but after waiting nearly a month for an answer from the manager we found that they wanted too much for it as being close to the town. Mr Taylor and I are going to ride in again this week to see some land about six miles from the town, which I hope will suit us, and perhaps it will be better to live at that distance than close to a gossiping village.

If the land does, and we can come to terms with the co., I suppose we shall conclude the matter. Biddulph let me keep £150 of Aunt Vizard's money. The rest was invested in Treasury Bills, as I think I told you.

I am afraid I have tired you with this long history of our plans and intentions, but we are very full of it just now, and do nothing but draw plans of houses and gardens. Mr Taylor has been drawing an elaborate plan for laying out the garden besides elevations of the intended house from every possible point of view.

It seems quite a pity to leave this place; it is very pretty now The trellis is covered with creepers, and through the green arches the river looks beautiful, sparkling in the sun. We can make our house as pretty in a short time; things grow so rapidly in this climate, but we shall miss the beautiful Myall River. This part would never have done for sheep, though; the ridges

232

are coarse and weedy, and the flats are periodically flooded by the river.

The country is looking most beautiful now. After a long drought we have had heavy rains, and the whole bush is green. We have been out for a walk this evening, and you never saw anything more beautiful than the golden sunset light on the green slopes and the tree-stems in the bush, and the rocks on the summit of Bulladillah catch the last of it and turn from gold to orange and crimson. I wish you could see it.

You will perhaps hear from Biddulph that he is again down in Sydney. He has made a very good sale of Dartmoor, a run adjoining Exmoor, and he came down about that and also to settle the last of the Lara business with Mr Morisset. He told me he could not come up here this time. I should have much liked to take a trip to Sydney to see him, but I could not well leave home just as this land affair has to be settled and as Mr Taylor and I must go down while our house is building to get a number of things we want for it. I do not think I ought to go to the double expense when we have so much to pay for.

I hope to get your December letters this week, and if there is anything to answer immediately I will write next week via Panama.

And now with kind love, believe me, my dear Mr Boyce,

Your affectionate sister,

RACHEL TAYLOR

MYALL RIVER,
FEBRUARY 18TH 1867

My Dearest Etta,

I must only write a short letter this time as I have already written a long one to Mr Boyce, and the December mail is not yet arrived. There is not much news from this part of Australia, and you will probably have heard from Annie and Amy their news. How that a little Hedgeland is expected in July and a sixth little Sloman is just arrived. I have written to congratulate both.

I have just returned from an expedition up the river in quest of fruit. We paid another visit to the vineyard, ate rather more than we did before, and brought home with us about eight pounds of grapes. Whereof I see only one or two bunches remaining on a plate. We also got some peaches.

I have been doing a great deal in the preserving line lately. Last week we sent the storekeeper with a packhorse up the river and he got fifty dozen peaches for about 7s. I made about thirty-five dozen into jam, and the rest we kept for pies and eating. All hands helped at the jam. Mr Somerville and Mr Taylor peeled the peaches while I cut them up. Then Mr Taylor and I alternately stirred the jam while Mr Somerville cracked the stones that we might put in the kernels.

"Mr Somerville cracked the stones."

I have also been making some passionfruit jelly, and exceedingly nice it is. Better than redcurrent. It is a bright amber colour and looks very pretty in the glasses. The quinces will soon be ripe, and then I must make some marmalade. Both Mr Taylor and Mr Somerville are very fond of preserves.

It is very disappointing that I cannot see dear Biddulph. He does not write in very good spirits. I do so wish he could find a nice wife, but he is too fastidious ever to do so in Australia, I am afraid. I am sure he would be much happier.

Fancy, in a fortnight (March 3rd) I shall have been married a year! I can hardly imagine it myself; the time has flown so. I wonder if they would send us out the sketch of Dunmoore? We could most conscientiously claim it, but no thanks to me.

I often hear from Sydney. Emily rambles about as ever, Caroline is "daily" expecting Number 10. Lizzie Chapman, ditto. We shall go down there in a month or two to buy windows and doors and wallpapers. We nourish distant hopes of a piano, but that will not be yet, but I don't think anything would give us both greater pleasure.

I must not write more now. Will you forward the enclosed to Mrs West? I am not sure of her address.

Kindest love to the children and yourself, dearest Etta, believe me,

Your very affectionate sister,

RACHEL TAYLOR

MYALL RIVER,
MARCH 20TH 1867

My Dearest Etta,

We have to write again without any letter from you to reply to. The English news is telegraphed, but we shall not get the letters till the next mail. I wrote to Mr Boyce via Panama and sent him the receipt for the legacy.

I see by the telegraphs that you have had a most severe winter since the mild Christmas. I wish I could send you a little of our sunshine. England is a far better country than this in many respects, but there is nothing like the bright warm Australian climate for comfort and also, I think, for cheerfulness. It is difficult to be out of spirits when the warm sun is shining.

We have at last got the land question settled. About a fortnight ago Mr Taylor and I went into Stroud and took up our quarters at the usual little inn. Next day we rode out to see the country he had heard of, and we both liked it very much. It is very pretty, green undulating ridges, lightly timbered and well grassed—just the thing for sheep. Sloping down to a creek and backed behind by high wooded ranges.

We rode and walked about there nearly all day, looking out for the best piece. At last we fixed upon a part that had been an old sheepyard of the A.A. Co.'s and where in consequence the grass was very thick and good. Next day Mr Taylor went out there with the company's surveyor and got 150 acres measured off, and before we left Stroud it was bought and paid for.

Then we made an agreement with a carpenter to put up the house for us; that celebrated house which we have been so long planning. He agreed to do it more cheaply than we expected, which was very satisfactory. The house and kitchen, complete with doors, windows, floors, water-pipes, boarded ceiling to the parlour, etc., will cost £115.

The kitchen and servants' room is in a detached building, as is always the case in this country. The doors and window-frames are to be of cedar. The house is twenty-four feet by thirty feet, with a veranda eight feet wide on three sides of it. It is to be finished in three months, then there is the kitchen and various out-buildings to be put up afterwards, so I do not suppose we shall get into it before the end of June or beginning of July.

The place we have bought is called "The Peach Trees"—I believe because some shepherd planted some peach-trees at the old station I mentioned before. There are certainly none there now, but I hope there will be, as we intend to have a very nice garden. It is about eight miles from Stroud, but a good road all the way, so the distance will not matter; it will be a pleasant ride once or twice a week to get our letters, etc.

While we were in Stroud we looked at a very comfortable house there which will do for us to live in while our house is being built. I suppose we shall move into Stroud in three weeks or a month; as soon as the stuff is split ready for building our house. We shall be obliged to go in then because Mr Taylor will be then able to ride out to The Peach Trees every day or two to superintend the putting up of the house, whereas it is too far to go from here.

I would rather remain here otherwise till it is time to get into our house, for though Stroud is so pretty I do not like living in a small town; besides, I know the people will come and call on us, and over and above my original dislike of strangers we have very little furniture. A great deal that we have used here was Mr Somerville's. He furnished our own bedroom comfortably, but a table, chiffonier and three sets of curtains and blinds are all the parlour furniture we have. I forgot to mention lots of books and a hearth-rug. Mr. Taylor made a sofa and book-stand when we came here, but these we leave for Mr Somerville.

236

I wanted to have gone down to Sydney before we go to Stroud to get some chairs and other things, but when we have paid for the land and house we are afraid of running short of cash, so we are going to make the bedroom chairs do for the present.

The new mare (Persephone, as Mr Somerville named her) is as free as possible and very fast. She pulls almost too much. I sent for a new bridle chiefly for her, because I do not like riding her without a curb. Mr Taylor still has his old Exmoor favourite, Charley, and Cora will do to carry a pack-saddle when we want to fetch things from Stroud.

The first anniversary of our wedding day passed while we were in Stroud seeing about the land, etc., and we were rather glad to spend it quietly there by ourselves at the pleasant little inn. It was Sunday, March 3rd, and a lovely day it was. We went to church in the morning, the first time we have heard the morning service since leaving Sydney (here the service is always in the afternoon), and after dinner we rambled about the garden of an old deserted house in a wilderness of roses, honeysuckle, bignonia, jessamine, with acacias, willows and oranges overhead.

It was so quiet that an inquisitive cow came rambling up the garden path and stood and looked at us as we sat on the grass in front of the veranda. The house belonged to the A.A. Co., and as they asked such a rent for it that no one would take it, it was falling down.

Then we climbed a steep green hill above Stroud and sat down there in the shade till sundown, admiring the lovely view. Stroud buried in its gardens and the beautiful wooded ranges rising all round it—and talking of past, present and future.

Sometimes I am half afraid of this change, though we have so often looked forward to having a home of our own, but we have been so very happy here that I sometimes fancy any change may make us less so. Of course there will be more cares in a place of our own, and we shall not be well off for some time. We hope to fence in part of our land the second half of this year, but we cannot reckon on being able to get any sheep till next year, if then, and till we do there will be nothing coming in beyond income.

I heard from Biddulph just before he left Sydney. I was sorry not to be able to see him during his visit, but I could not go down then nor could he come here.

The garden is beautiful since the autumn rains. I am quite sorry to leave it, but I hope soon to have one of our own. Mr Taylor is entreating me to "look at the clock", as it is just ten.

My kindest love to yourself, Mr Boyce and the children. Ever, my dearest Etta,

Your very affectionate sister,

RACHEL TAYLOR

"THE PEACH TREES,"
MARCH 18TH 1870

My Dearest Etta,

Thank you for your nice long letter of December last, with all its home news. You need not tell me "not to mind" your writing about the children. I like so much to hear about them, what they learn, how they amuse themselves, even what they wear is pleasant to hear and about yourself also. I was quite interested to hear that you had a new black silk made with short sleeves and ruffles, like our grandmother's (and very pretty they must be).

Did you ever take to wearing your hair on the top of your head like our mother's picture? I did as soon as the fashion came in, only not so high up quite, and I liked it, but I am sorry to hear it is going out again now, probably is never seen in England; only we are usually about three months behind you, and in the bush about a year behind, as we get hold of a fashion when we go to Sydney, and wear it till we go down there again.

I sent your letter on to Annie, and, by reason of the floods, I have not got it back again, so I haven't it to answer.

You are thinking about spring in England, and I dare say the children are making early expeditions to the Leigh Woods and rejoicing in wildflowers. I remember now the pleasure of the first spring days, when the sun came out warm, and we found the first primroses and violets in sheltered nooks.

Here we are rejoicing at the departure of summer, though it has made its exit in a very unpleasant manner this year. We have had almost incessant rain for nearly three weeks, and it is still "hard at it". A rain of such duration is almost unprecedented in this dry country, where in the heaviest floods it seldom lasts for more than a week. I have no doubt we shall hear of terrible floods in the low-lying districts, but as the mails are all stopped we do not know what is going on in the world outside. There has been no mail to Stroud for ten days, and we have not been in there for more than a month. The man has continued to go in once or twice for meat, when the rain has been a little less. The creeks are all swollen and impassable on the usual road, but

238

there is a very bad one over a range, by which it is possible to get to the town without passing the creeks.

There is a stream flowing right through Stroud which has only a footbridge across it, and this being generally covered in a high flood and the stream itself being, of course, impracticable for horses, half the town is thus cut off from the other half, to the great inconvenience of the inhabitants. One unfortunate old gentleman, who is a magistrate, went in to attend the courthouse on Tuesday, the creek being then fordable, but by the time the sitting was over it had risen so that he could not get back, and was "bailed up" in Stroud for two days before he could return to the bosom of his family.

There are very few bridges as yet in the country parts, and when the creeks and rivers are flooded it is a great inconvenience to the inhabitants. A man died last week at some distance from Dungog, and his coffin had to be floated over a river, as it was where there were no boats to be had.

The floods never do us any harm, beyond general dampness and mouldiness, as we live on a hill at the foot of which the creek runs and roars, but it never gets over the steep banks. The gardens look dilapidated, the flowers are washed out of all colour and Mr Taylor's beautiful crop of corn is growing in the stalks. Of course all outdoor work is at a standstill. Mr Taylor carpenters in the shed, and the man cleans the mould off the saddles and bridles, rubs up the bits and gets periodically wet in fetching up the cows morning and evening, and I put the house neat and practise and work and walk disconsolately on the veranda (which is three feet from the ground and floored and always dry), and survey the soaked lawn below, and make sorties when the rain ceases for a minute to tie up some favourite plant that has been blown over.

You would not think much of a month of wet weather in England, but here such a break in our outdoor life is quite an event. The whole summer has been wet, and though a wet summer is far pleasanter than a drought, and we have been rejoicing in flowers and green grass, yet it is not so healthy in this climate. There has been a great deal of fever about, and two or three weeks ago I got one of my old feverish attacks and, for the first time since I was married, actually breakfasted in bed!

Mr Taylor, who had never seen me ill before, was quite frightened, and insisted on riding into Stroud to get me some medicine. I would not let him bring the doctor out, as I thought the guineas which he would have charged were too much for a cold. We had two doctors in Stroud, and he did not doubt that he should get something nasty from one of them, if the other was tipsy, but when he got there he found that one doctor had drunk himself to death the week before and was buried, while the other, after drinking himself mad for four days, and parading Stroud in an airy costume, to the great scandal of the inhabitants, had finally been taken into custody, and was then in the lock-up, an abode where he spends a good part of his time.

I got well without their aid—all the sooner perhaps—and with Mr Taylor's nursing it is almost a pleasure to be ill, he is so kind. But it is fortunate we are blessed with such good health, seeing what our medical attendance is.

Do you remember, years ago, a doctor who used to come to Taunton, and hold meetings and preach for the "Channel mission"? The Stroud doctor is his son. He is very clever in his profession, when he is sober, and a gentleman, but when he drinks he becomes quite mad. He says his father is insane now, and he shall become so likewise. He has a wife and two little children, and is very fond of them, when he is sober, but when he comes home tipsy she has to hide the children and fly for her life, as he always threatens to kill them.

Sometimes he parades Stroud with a revolver, to the great terror of the inhabitants. There is scarcely a court day that he is not fined for something or other, and about a year ago he was summoned for causing the death of the wife of one of the innkeepers here. He shook the old woman violently one day when he was tipsy, and she had a fit and never recovered. He got off, as she was proved to be subject to fits, but you see it is as well not to be ill if you can help it!

Thank you for sending on Aunt's letter. We are always interested in the Taunton news. I am very glad that both she and Uncle are tolerably well this winter. I hope to write to Aunt soon, but I never seem to have much time for letters, and when the mail-day comes have never done half of what I intended. You said in your letter that Laura was expecting another baby. It always seems to me rather a miserable life when people go on, year after year, constantly having children, like Laura, and never knowing what health is, but I suppose they get used to it, like the eels.

We have been taking a course of poetry lately. I borrowed Robert Browning's poems a short time ago, and on first reading did not much like them, and on second reading liked them greatly. I never met with them before, curiously enough. Do you know them? Then Mr Taylor rummaged out Southey's

NORMAN LINDSAY

"... parading Stroud in an airy costume."

poems from the bookcase the other day, and was so pleased with *Thalaba* and *Kehama* that I read them again also, and was quite surprised to find how much I liked them. It is years since I read them. Do you remember you and I copying a great lot of *Thalaba* once? I remember Uncle William reading us *Madoc* in the evenings that winter we spent at Taunton. I mean to read that again also. Mr Taylor is now deep in it. I saw some long extracts from Tennyson's new poem in the *Home News* and liked them, though I wish he had a better subject.

Unless the rain stops soon this epistle will not reach Sydney in time for the March mail; the rivers must be half over the country.

Kind love to Mr Boyce and the children, and with much to yourself.

Believe me, dearest Etta, ever your affectionate sister,

RACHEL TAYLOR

"THE PEACH TREES,"
JULY 1ST 1870

My Dearest Etta,

It was pleasant to hear from you of the English spring. How I used to love it when the first fine mild days came, and primroses and violets and cowslips were out! Just now we are enjoying just the same kind of weather here, only we do not have such cold winds; this is a lovely winter day, warm and bright in the sun, though rather cold where you get in the way of the west wind.

Mr Taylor is busy in the orchard that is to be, and I have been busy ever since breakfast making a cake and afterwards making up some butter, which I churned yesterday, to say nothing of watering geraniums and feeding dogs; and now, when it is nearly dinner-time, I have to begin English letters. It is a mystery to me where the time goes, but the days always seem past before there is half the day's work done.

We have only just come home from a visit to Stroud. We went in on Saturday afternoon, stayed over Sunday and Monday, and returned on Tuesday morning. We both rather enjoyed our visit, and while there we rode over with Mr and Mrs Shaw to Booral, a place about five miles from Stroud, to call upon some people who have a nice garden which we wanted to see.

I rather pity Mrs Shaw today, for the Governor, Lord Belmore, with his brother and his aide-de-camp, are coming to Stroud, and Mr Shaw asked them to lodge at the Parsonage instead of at the inn, which is a very indifferent one. It is only for one night, but still it entails a dinner and breakfast and great turning out of rooms for their accommodation. The Shaws asked no one to meet them, as to do so would have necessitated asking a great many, and it does not do for the clergyman to offend people under the voluntary system. The Governor is making a tour up the country to Gloucester, Dungog, Maitland, etc.

We are looking forward to our visit to Sydney in August next. We always enjoy staying with Biddulph and Annie, and we always take the opportunity of supplying ourselves with stores, clothes, etc., for the year. Mr Taylor wants some things, but I shall not get much in the way of garments this time as I got Annie to send me up some mourning when the news came of Mrs Taylor's death. This reminds me to thank you for the notice from the *Athenaeum* which you sent in your last letter.

I am writing a most stupid letter, but I have nothing new to tell you. We are remarkably jolly, but it is in a quiet way that gives nothing to write about, and though the garden and the new orchard and the trees that are coming up from Sydney for it, and the dairy and how the butter grieved my soul by taking an hour and a half to "come" this morning, and how the calves got out of the calf paddock last night and so we had no milk today, etc., are all highly interesting events to me and my "old man", as he is generally called in private life, I cannot expect such items to be amusing when they are filtered through fifteen thousand miles.

Annie and Amy and Biddulph tell their own histories, I suppose; the first and last are capital correspondents. Amy does not write to me so often.

I am going out to garden now. Mr Taylor and I are planting a new bed of flowering shrubs, and it is such a lovely afternoon, though it is midwinter, and there are still lots of white roses in the garden.

Ever, dearest Etta, your most affectionate sister,

RACHEL TAYLOR

"THE PEACH TREES,"
NOVEMBER 1ST 1870

My Dearest Etta,

Now we are at home again, and you will be surprised to hear that we persuaded Annie to bring Teddy and come up with us for a month. Biddulph was away at Bathurst and Mr Hedgeland away all the day, only coming home in the evening, and there are good trustworthy servants at "Green Mount", so she could not have a better opportunity for leaving home.

The weather was so bad the week we had fixed for going home that Annie was afraid to venture with Teddy, so Mr Taylor went up before us and I remained to escort the "infant". We got up about four o'clock last Monday morning to finish packing and get breakfast, and started by the steamer at seven o'clock. We had a tolerably calm passage up, but Annie was sick and Teddy rather so, but he went to sleep and was not much trouble. We reached Raymond Terrace at five. Mr Taylor had taken rooms for us at the inn, and we were very comfortable there. The next morning at ten we set off by the mail buggy for Stroud, a distance of thirty-two miles. Teddy was very good and went to sleep part of the way. It was a beautiful day when we started, only rather hot, but it clouded over afterwards.

Mr Taylor came on horseback as far as the river, to meet us and see us safely over. The water was rather deep owing to the recent rains. It was very nearly over the buggy floor, but not quite. Just as we reached the other side, about six miles from Stroud, a tremendous thunderstorm came on. Annie wrapped Teddy up in a waterproof and managed to keep him dry, but all the rest of us got rather wet. Mr Taylor, who was on horseback, was nearly wet through.

We reached the Parsonage at last, where Mrs Shaw very kindly took us all in for the night, and we were soon dry and comfortable.

The next morning David, our present factotum, came in with quite a drove of horses, and after breakfast we started in procession for The Peach Trees, to the great edification of the Stroudites. Mr Taylor rode old Charley, who is the quietest horse we have and warranted to carry double, and on a small pillow in front of the saddle he carried Teddy, who was quite delighted with his ride and laughed and chattered the whole way. Annie and I rode by him, and David brought up the rear, leading a packhorse, with such of our property as we immediately wanted.

We had quite a pleasant ride, and reached The Peach Trees in time for dinner. Charlotte, the servant we had left behind in care of the house, had everything ready for us, the house beautifully clean, and everything taken care of.

In the afternoon we unpacked and took a survey of the premises. The plants had grown wonderfully and the garden is very gay, but I am sorry to say the weeds have grown as fast as the flowers, and it is a perfect jungle. All the animals were well taken care of; the dogs are in good order, the horses ditto, and two pretty calves have been added to the herd of cattle.

It was fortunate we came up when we did, or we should not have got here yet, as it has rained ever since we came home. I do not think there ever was such a season for wet, and the worst of it is that the damp has given Teddy a cold, and one night he had a slight attack of croup, to our great terror. Neither Annie nor I had ever seen the croup before, and we were eight miles from a doctor, but Charlotte, who was summoned to the rescue, said that one of her little brothers often had it and did not seem to think much of it. Mr Taylor lighted a great fire in the sitting-room, and we soon had a hot bath into which we put Teddy and dosed him with honey and vinegar; and in a short time he got better. It was not a severe attack, but we were much frightened at first. I never saw anyone so quiet and self-possessed as Annie, considering it was her only child who was at stake, and that we were all alone in the bush.

The next day Mr Taylor went into Stroud and got some medicine and directions from the doctor, and Teddy is pretty well again, though we keep him indoors and out of the damp as much as possible. He is a very pretty child, with golden curls all round his head, and for an only child who has hardly ever been contradicted he is really very good. I could not believe he would be so little trouble as he was on the journey.

It is very pleasant to have Annie here. I hardly hoped we should ever get her to come so far, for it is a formidable journey to take with a little child. I hope she will stay a month or more; it is not worth while to come so far for a shorter time.

Kindest love to yourself and to the children,

Your affectionate sister,

RACHEL TAYLOR

"GREEN MOUNT,"
NOVEMBER 30TH 1870

My Dearest Etta,

I wrote to you last on November 1st, shortly after we had returned to The Peach Trees, taking Annie and Teddy with us. It was very pleasant having them, but their visit was not such a prosperous one as we hoped it would be, owing to the dreadful weather. Such a season as the past autumn, winter and spring has not been known in Australia in the memory of the oldest inhabitant, and while Annie was at The Peach Trees the rain was almost incessant, so that we could not get any nice rides and walks, such as we had calculated upon.

Then I stayed out too late gardening one evening and caught cold. Annie and Mr Taylor were the very kindest of nurses, but I was so vexed that her visit should be taken up in that way. However, thanks to their care, I got better in about a week, and then as it was time for Annie to go home, and I had still a very bad cough, Mr Taylor insisted on my returning to Sydney with her for a change of air, and also to get some advice. I was exceedingly unwilling to come, as I did not like leaving home again, and it was so dreadfully dull for Mr Taylor to be left alone in the bush. However, I was overruled and had to come, so here I am.

It was fortunate, in one way, for we had a very rough passage down, and Annie was dreadfully ill, so if I had not been there there would have been no one to look after poor little Teddy, who was ill also. We arrived at Sydney last Saturday, and I hope to get home again next week if all goes well. I think I have written enough about Number One.

Although she had such bad weather for her visit, everyone says that Annie looks better for the change, and Teddy is the picture of health. Biddulph is still away. You know he went on a country tour before Annie left Sydney for The Peach Trees. He is expected home at the end of this week, so I shall just see him for a few days before I return again to the bush.

Green Mount is looking as pretty as ever. It certainly is a lovely place. The garden is full of flowers, but rather wild with the wet weather. It is a most extraordinary season, although it is less than a month to Christmas, the mornings and evenings are so cold that we are glad of a fire, and this in Australia. If it would only get really warm I know I should soon be quite well.

I have not yet thanked you for your letter of September 1st. It did not arrive till after I had written my last letter to you. Thank you also for Aunt's and Rose's letters enclosed. The latter writes nicely and kindly of poor Rachel; I am so very sorry for her. She must be living so miserably.

I was very much interested by your account of Walton and all our old haunts about Clevedon. I do not think that being happy in the present makes one care less about the old times and places. It would be a great pleasure to me to visit all the old scenes, and I always look back on the Backwell era as the happiest part of my unmarried life.

As you conjecture we were rather relieved when Thunderbolt was removed from the scenes of his depredations. He was not hung. One of the mounted police got on his tracks and gallantly followed him alone for miles, till Thunderbolt's horse knocked up, and he dismounted and stood at bay in a creek. He refused to surrender, and after a desperate hand-to-hand fight with revolvers, the trooper shot him dead.

About the same time, another noted bushranger was tracked to his lair and shot by another party of police, and at present New South Wales is relieved from their presence. Walker, the man who shot Thunderbolt, was promoted and a subscription made for him, which he deserved, for a more dangerous service than he performed could hardly be.

It is no use to write about this dreadful war, as your news is so much later than ours. The last account that reached us was that Paris was surrounded and the bombardment to begin in two days. You know the results long ere this, and we have to wait another three weeks for further news. I hope it may be peace. The suffering and loss of life must be frightful. One is rather sorry for the French now, but there is no forgetting that they began the war.

My kindest love to Mr Boyce, yourself and the children.

Ever your affectionate sister,

RACHEL TAYLOR

"THE PEACH TREES,"
JANUARY 16TH 1871

My Dearest Etta,

We have had what the Sydney newspapers call an unusual quantity of the "pluvial element". In plain English, it has done nothing but rain for the last nine months, and the oldest inhabitant never remembers such weather. The rivers and creeks have been up and the mails have been stopped about every other week, and this catastrophe happened just when I ought to have written to you last.

I wrote to you last from Sydney during my second visit there. I was very unwilling to go, both on account of the expense and of leaving my husband. I stayed only a fortnight, and then came home.

Whilst in Sydney staying at Green Mount Biddulph told me what Biddulph Pinchard had told him about the Shrapnel Ghost in Taunton, Somerset. It is interesting, so I will write it as our brother Biddulph told me. He said Biddulph Pinchard disliked speaking of it, and he said he had failed to even account for the disturbances.

247

The worst time they had was a little before Christmas. For three days and nights then the hammering and rapping was almost incessant and so loud that sometimes you could hardly hear yourself speak. He had four policemen in the house at the time, to try to discover if anyone was playing tricks, but they could make nothing of it. You might open the door of a room where the knocking seemed to come from and there was nothing to be seen inside. I believe the policemen were awfully alarmed, as was no wonder.

He also told me that locked doors were always being opened. This was constantly happening. Directly after the three days' uproar Biddulph had to take his wife and two boys away, as they were all ill with fright, and I think, excepting a day or two, they have never slept in the house since.

Another thing Biddulph told me was that after they had all left, and the house was closed up, one of the Miss Alfreds, happening to pass the house, heard music. As she knew they were all away, she went into the garden and went all round the house. Every door and window was fastened and the music still went on. She described the music as wonderfully sweet; quite heavenly. Another lady heard the music at another time.

Biddulph Pinchard himself is not the least nervous and would have remained in the house if his wife and boys could have lived there. He says he did his utmost to discover the cause of the disturbance and completely failed. He is sure the servants had nothing to do with it; he had only two women servants in the house, and they were as much frightened as the others. The housemaid is still with them.

The present tenants, a doctor and his wife, have not been disturbed, excepting that they find the doors opened unaccountably, and this they do not seem to mind. The doctor's wife has had a baby born since she has been in the house. They must certainly be brave ever to have gone there.

That is Biddulph's account.

I came home by the morning boat, and when I arrived at Newcastle (which is the termination of the sea voyage, before going up the river to Raymond Terrace) you may fancy how delighted I was to see Mr Taylor come on board. I did not the least expect him, as I had written to beg him not to come down for me, but he had, and I am sorry to say, had been waiting two days while I was detained in Sydney by the everlasting rain.

I had quite a pleasant journey after that. We reached Raymond Terrace that evening, slept there at a very comfortable inn, and the next day went on to Stroud, I by the mail buggy and

Deighton rode. We got to Stroud that day, slept at the Parsonage, and the next morning rode home to The Peach Trees, which I hope I shall have no occasion to leave again till next spring, when we look forward to our usual visit to Sydney—that is, if the Russians and Yankees have not battered it down in the meantime.

David came home yesterday aghast with the news that Paris was destroyed and England had gone to war with Russia and America, and that an army of two hundred men had enlisted at Newcastle to defend Australia, and that he supposed he should be wanted.

I do not know of any way in which the real news could have come yet, so I suppose somebody invented it, but I am afraid there is probability in some of it. I do not know what will become of Sydney in case of war; the town is defenceless, except a few ill-placed batteries. They have never been able to agree upon the best means of defence and meantime have none. Melbourne is better off, as she has just got an iron-clad sent out.

I found everything in good order at home, and Charlotte had done her best to make Mr Taylor comfortable while I was away. The garden was looking beautiful. I had not seen so many flowers since I left, though they have a pretty garden at Green Mount, too. We had some hot weather for a few days, and then down came the rain again.

Christmas Day was the climax. It blew a gale of wind with very heavy rain and was so cold we were glad of a good fire, by which we sat all day. We were to have gone into Stroud to spend the day with the Shaws, but, of course, the weather prevented anyone going out, and I think we enjoyed ourselves at home just as much. The Shaws were to have come here on Boxing Day to spend it with us, but all visiting was put an end to.

It is fine again now, and we are just in the middle of a great mess, as the sitting-room is being boarded and whitewashed, preparatory to being repapered. It was formerly papered over canvas, which did not answer, as in damp weather it all "bagged" out. So now that whole room has been lined with sawn boards, which will look well when papered over.

The ceiling requires a great many coats of whitewash, and this causes the present state of mess. The piano and sofa are covered with old canvas wrappers, the floor is a mass of whitewash, in the midst of which I am sitting like Captain Cuttle on his island.

I hope the last coat of whitewash will go on this evening, and tomorrow Mr Taylor and I will be able to paper. We shall look

"The ceilings require a great many coats of whitewash."

quite respectable again then, for it is a very pretty room when the paper is clean.

There are two long French windows opening on the east veranda and two casement windows, one on each side the fireplace, opening on the north veranda, and when these are hung with green moreen curtains and you see a vision of flowers and trees and wooded hills from every one of them, you do not mind the floor being carpetless and some of the furniture being of home manufacture. It is not that we could not afford a piece of India matting or a cheap carpet, but they are such a dreadful harbour for insects in the bush that we prefer having the floors scrubbed every week and contenting ourselves with a hearth-rug. But this is enough of home matters, you will think.

We have quite a farm now. We are milking three cows and make all the butter we use, besides having plenty of milk. I have been churning this morning. I always do that myself; I do not like the butter handled, and Charlotte has plenty to do besides. She is washing today; washing-day has been a movable feast lately, owing to the constant rain, and sometimes the clothes have hung on the line for days before they would dry.

They are dried in the little paddock at the back of the kitchen out of sight of the house. Sometimes the calves eat a few socks, but that is a trifle. Mr Taylor is at work in the kitchen garden with David, ploughing up a piece of ground for potatoes; he is exceedingly fond of his kitchen garden, and with reason; it supplies us with abundance of vegetables all the year, and we give away a great many besides.

I must say good-bye now. Give my love to Mr Boyce and the children, and all good wishes for a very happy New Year to all of you, with much love to yourself,

Your very affectionate sister,

RACHEL TAYLOR

"THE PEACH TREES,"
OCTOBER 3RD 1871

My Dearest Etta,

I was so sorry I could not write to you by the September mail to thank you for the very pretty song you sent me, but I was just starting for Sydney when it came, and really had not a moment to write.

You will probably hear from Biddulph by this mail, and will read in his own hand of the great event that is at present the talk of the family. Namely, that he has at last chosen himself a wife! We are all very much pleased at his choice, too. Annie and I always used to say we wished he would marry Emily Tucker. However, when I went down to stay at Canterbury House at the beginning of this month, Annie invited Emily out there at the same time, and Biddulph used to take us drives before breakfast, and rides in the evening after he came home from business.

"We are all very pleased at his choice."

We played croquet on the lawn, and walks in the grounds, and so it all ended in an engagement.

She is the eldest daughter of Mr William Tucker. Her father has a beautiful place called Clifton[2] on the North Shore, and is very well off. Emily was educated in England, and very well,

2 In Carabella Street, Kirribilli.

too. She is a fine, stylish-looking girl, with a splendid figure, and dresses exceedingly well, having abundant means thereunto. I think there is every prospect of their being very happy.

But I must tell you about my visit to Sydney. I went down by myself this time, as no persuasions could induce Mr Taylor to accompany me. It has been a very dry spring and we are surrounded by long grass and dead timber, and he was afraid of bushfires, and of finding the little homestead burnt on our return. So, as I wanted to see them all at Sydney, and to do some shopping, I actually made up my mind to go down for three weeks alone. Deighton rode down to Raymond Terrace with me, and saw me on board the steamer, and the same evening I reached Canterbury House.

It is about the most charming country house I ever saw even in England. About half a mile from the Ashfield station you come to a white gate which brings you into a drive through what would be called an open wood in England, and is called open bush here. The drive is planted with firs at the sides, and well gravelled and kept, in half a mile more there is an iron gate, and the road goes on through beautiful flowering shrubs, turns round a bed of perfectly dazzling azaleas and camellias, and there is the house.

A very pretty house it is, raised on a slope of green turf, with a double row of white steps leading to the balcony and door. Inside it is very comfortable—a dining-room, drawing-room, and billiard-room and another little room, and, upstairs, five large bedrooms. The kitchen, servants' hall and servants' rooms are all at the back. There are also a laundry, dairy, etc., in a stone court, then up some steps you come to a back paddock, round which are built the coachhouse, stables, cow-houses, milking bail, pigsties and fowlhouses, these last covered in with wire-netting.

There is a large kitchen garden, vineyard, etc., and any amount of lawn and flower garden. I never saw such quantities of flowers anywhere. Just in front of the house the drive goes round an immense bed of azaleas, camellias and rhododendrons. There are, besides, roses and camellias and geraniums everywhere. The azaleas were in full bloom when I left. A mass of white, purple and red. As you will easily believe, I enjoyed my visit exceedingly, and if Mr Taylor could only have come, too, I should have liked to spend six weeks there instead of three, but I did not like being away from him longer.

We got through a good deal of shopping and visiting, though both were rather under difficulties, as, besides the walk or drive to Ashfield station, there were five miles of railroad to be travelled to get to Sydney.

I went to the opera twice, and then we had to sleep in Sydney. There is a very good Italian company performing there now. I saw *Lucia di Lammermoor* and *Norma*, and should have liked to go oftener, but it is an expensive amusement.

Before I left we were all invited to a dinner at Clifton to celebrate Biddulph and Emily's engagement, which all parties seem delighted at. It was prettily arranged, *à la russe*, a style which suits this land of flowers and sunshine.

Mr Tucker makes a good "heavy father". Mrs Tucker is very handsome still. None of her daughters has such good features. Alice, the second of them, is married to a Dr Dansey. Fanny, the youngest, is a pretty little bright girl. Emily has great depth of character, and energy and home qualities. I got to know Emily well while we were both at Canterbury House, and the more I knew of her the more I liked her.

I left Sydney on Thursday last. Harry Hirst saw me on board the steamer, which sails at 11 at night. I reached Raymond Terrace at 8 next morning, and found my dear husband waiting for me.

Ever your affectionate sister,

RACHEL TAYLOR

"THE PEACH TREES",
NOVEMBER 23RD 1871

My Dearest Etta,

I was amused at your account of Miss West. Fancy an old lady of sixty going in for costumes and short dresses! The latter have never "taken" in Australia except for quite young girls. You seldom see married or middle-aged ladies in them. Neither Annie nor I have ever worn them shorter than touching the ground, and the same with most of our contemporaries. Emily Tucker, Biddulph's intended, who is one of the best-dressed girls in Sydney, never wears them.

I told you in my last letter about my visit to Sydney (for Mr Taylor did not go) and Biddulph's engagement. I do not know yet when the wedding is to be. We are expecting Biddulph up here for a few days before Christmas. It will be such a pleasure to see him; he has only been here once before. Annie says that he and Emily are very much in love with one another, and never happy when apart, which is all as it should be. I believe in "love matches", as they are called, as much as any young girl of eighteen!

I hope by this time they have sent you a photograph of Emily. She is a very fine-looking girl and has a magnificent figure. We all like her, and think Biddulph very fortunate, and I am sure she is fortunate also.

I wish you could see The Peach Trees now. The garden is lovely, such a glow of flowers of all kinds and colours, to say nothing of the stands of pelagoniums in the veranda, which are my especial pride. We have had a beautiful summer hitherto after all the prophecies of a drought. There has been rain once a fortnight at least, and everything is green and luxuriant.

I am busy rearing poultry now, and have two families of chickens to attend to. I have also just cut out and begun another pair of trousers for Mr Taylor, and have completed a bolster for the spare bed, while Charlotte is taking feathers off our own defunct fowls for a pillow. A good deal of home manufacture goes on in the bush, and it saves a great deal of money.

Our piano wears very well, and I must again thank you for sending me "The Kelpie's Bride". It is a charming song, and Mr Taylor is never tired of hearing it. I cannot think how you know so well what suits me, when it is so many years since you have heard me sing.

A piece of Stroud news is that one of our neighbours (who lives by the way in one of the best houses in the district), having been put in the lock-up by the constable for drunkenness, took to parading Stroud on horseback with a loaded revolver in his hand, threatening to shoot the said constable if he again interfered with him. Said constable, not liking the revolver, sat quietly on the veranda of his house and surveyed the horseman, who paraded for several days and nearly frightened old Mr Larman, the magistrate's clerk, into fits by riding after him with the weapon pointed at his head. After keeping Stroud in a mild state of alarm for some days the man got tired and left off, to the relief of the inhabitants, for though he probably did not mean to shoot anybody, a loaded revolver may go off when in the hands of a half-tipsy man.

Next Monday we expect to come out and spend a week with us friends who are so very kind in accommodating us at all times that one cannot but be glad to see them. Otherwise I do not cotton very much to visitors beyond our own family. When you have only one servant who is an indifferent cook it is rather a trouble to entertain people.

Ever your affectionate sister,

RACHEL TAYLOR

255

"... *riding after him with the weapon pointed at his head.*"

My Dearest Etta,

I am sorry to say that I missed writing to you by the January mail, partly through not knowing when it left Sydney, and partly through having had my thoughts very full of our own concerns just then, for we are contemplating a remove from The Peach Trees, a great event in our quiet lives.

I wish I could send you a sketch of our house, but I am afraid now it will have to be a view of the next house we live in, for we have made up our minds to leave this as soon as we can sell it. It is not that we are tired of the place, for it grows prettier every year and we shall both be very sorry to give it up; but we have both come to the conclusion that it is too lonely a place to grow old in!

We are nearly three miles from the nearest farm, eight from Stroud, and almost three days' journey from Sydney. The ride to Stroud and the journey to Sydney we think little of now, but some years hence it may be different, and in case of illness (and we cannot reckon on having always our present good health) we are from help of any kind, medical or otherwise. Besides these reasons, Mr Taylor would like a place where he is near a market and can get better sale for his pigs and cattle, so we are only waiting to sell this farm to move. We can let it easily, but we want to sell it and have no more trouble about it.

We have advertised for a farm "within thirty miles of Sydney and five of a railyway-station", and have had numbers of answers. Some of them seem eligible, but one cannot decide on anything till we can sell this and go down and look at some places. Biddulph is very kind in making inquiries for us also; he was up here for a flying visit shortly before Christmas, and he strongly advised our moving. Next time I write I hope to be able to tell you something definite, and in the meantime do not direct here any more but to the care of Messrs Tucker and Co.

Deighton has just called me out to look at a "death-adder" which he killed among the cucumber-vines. Some of the snakes are very pretty, but this is a horrid-looking thing about two feet long and as thick as your wrist, with a flat, wicked-looking head and the tail tapering suddenly, not gradually, like most snakes: a dirty brown colour. It is one of the most poisonous of all, and there is no antidote known for its bite. I have been remonstrating with the "old man" about meddling with the cucumbers any more, for fear there should be another adder there; it is not often you hear of accidents, but such possibilities make one uneasy.

You must excuse me if my letter is a little unconnected, as the Irishman said of Johnson's dictionary, as I have a new servant just caught from the bush, and have to make sallies into the kitchen to tell her into what saucepan to put the potatoes, etc., as otherwise I might possibly find them in the tea-kettle. She had never seen a pair of bellows when she came, and asked me why we kept a bottle of water on the washstand. She is exceedingly willing and industrious, however; we give her 8s. a week.

Although you would not think there was much to do in the bush, it is astonishing how many things there are to see after. We generally get up about six, and yet the day is always gone too soon. We are having a very hot summer, though not a dry one. We have had a great deal of rain, and that and the hot sun has made everything grow quite wild; the garden, though it is full of flowers, looks like a wilderness, and now that we are going away I do not care to take much trouble about it. I shall be very sorry to leave the garden; both that and the house are so pretty, but wherever we are we shall soon make a garden.

It will be very pleasant to be within easy reach of Sydney now that Annie and Biddulph are both settled there; a thirty-mile journey by railway is nothing, and we could often run up and see them and they could come and see us as well as other of our friends.

Biddulph's house on the North Shore is in progress. I know the situation, and it will have a most lovely view. Old Mr Tucker declines to give his daughters any money during his life, but he builds them a good house when they marry, and as those North Shore houses let for £150 a year it is not to be despised.

But I suppose Annie keeps you informed of all Sydney news. Do you remember Mr Aylward, Biddulph's tutor at Exmouth? I saw his death in the *Home News* this month. He was vicar of Chesharn in Buckinghamshire. How many of that Exmouth party are gone now, and how old the rest are getting!

And yet I don't think one feels much older. Life seems just as pleasant, perhaps pleasanter.

It is time to conclude when one begins to cut shorter the way with moral reflections. I must go and make some melted butter for the vegetable marrow and cut up a cucumber. Deighton brought down a bucketful this morning.

With very much love, believe me, my dearest Etta,

Your affectionate sister,

RACHEL TAYLOR

MOUNT VERNON,[3]
AUGUST 9TH 1872

My Dearest Etta,

Annie and Mr Hedgeland are both gone to bed very tired, and my husband has taken the carriage to fetch Biddulph back from a friend's where he has been spending the evening.

We have, I think, at last found an abode that will suit us. About a fortnight ago Mr Taylor and I made an excursion to Wollongong to look at some farms that we had heard of there. We went down by the steamer, which only takes about five hours going from Sydney, took up our residence at the Queen's Hotel (a very comfortable place), and spent the next day in driving

[3] The Sydney suburban home of the Hedgelands.

out to see the farms in question. There were two by Lake Illawarra that we did not like, but one on what they call American Creek we were delighted with.

The land is very good. There is a tolerable house which we can inhabit while we build another, a creek (as they call a brook here) running right through the farm, and a site for a new house[4] where there is a most lovely view of the whole Bulli Range. We heard today that the owner will accept the sum we offered for it, so if the title, etc., prove satisfactory, we shall probably complete the purchase.

We shall be very glad to be settled again, as you may imagine. If we do go to Wollongong we shall be within easy reach of Sydney and all our friends here, as besides the steamer there is a coach road over the mountains. We returned that way, and a very good road it is. It was made, I believe, chiefly in consequence of Biddulph's representations when he lived there.

Of course it is steep in parts, and passengers with any humanity in them generally walk to the top, but you can hardly imagine anything more beautiful than the scenery. Sometimes at a turn of the road you look down upon green depths of tropical vegetation, cabbage palms and tree-ferns and magnificent trees, etc., all bound together by festoons of flowering creepers. The whole valley of Illawarra lying below, and the sea and the "Five Islands" beyond all. The beauty ceases at the top of the mountain, and a dull road leads to Campbelltown, where you take train for Sydney.

Our farm is not near the Bulli Mountain, but three miles on the other side of Wollongong, where, however, the scenery is also very beautiful. Having once seen the Illawarra district quite spoils you for any other part of Australia. If no unexpected hitch occurs I hope we shall soon have a home of our own there.

They are all prospering here. Mr Hedgeland has as much work surveying as he can get through, and must be making a great deal of money. Biddulph ditto, as well by copper, gold and tin mines as by his regular business. He is looking so well and full of spirits. This morning he made me a most welcome present of a very nice horse that I have long been in love with but did not dream of possessing. Biddulph bought him for his own riding some time ago, when, by the way, I was the first lady

[4] Springfield, on American Creek, near Fig Tree, two or three miles out of Wollongong, was the new house, and it was built for Rachel and Deighton during 1873 and 1874. They lived there until 1896 and it was only Deighton's ill health that caused them to leave. The house subsequently disappeared but the property continued to be known as Springfield.

who ventured on his back, for he is very spirited. Then Biddulph strained him in galloping over rocks, and he was sent up to The Peach Trees for rest. He recovered there, and we brought him down with us, and now Biddulph, having several other horses, has given him to me to take down to Wollongong.

He is the kindest of brothers. A week or two ago he gave Annie a set of real sables, magnificent to behold. This has been a very cold winter, and fur is universally worn.

I suppose your children were looking forward to the holidays when you wrote, and I hope you had better weather than that you describe. The season here has been exactly the reverse. We have had a drought for nearly four months, and although it is beautiful weather, the matter is getting serious, as very soon there will be nothing for the cattle to eat in districts where the land is poor.

We have been down here more than two months now, and I have never taken out an umbrella since we came. The dust is as bad as in the height of summer, and winter clothes show it so much that we are always brushing. We have had a great deal of cold wind. Nevertheless, the days have been bright and beautiful, and the flowers are coming out in the bush. I often take Teddy for a walk on the wild hills that lie between Randwick and Botany. They are low hills of white sand, and are covered with low-growing shrubs and flowers of all descriptions. There are also a great many flowers in the garden—geraniums and petunias and hyacinths and jonquils. Annie, however, does not take any great interest in the garden as the Hedgelands do not mean to continue in this house after Biddulph is married, which will be shortly now. They will move to some place that will be more convenient to Mr Hedgeland's work than this is.

I sat down intending only to write a short letter, and it has lengthened itself out into two sheets. Annie sends kind love. Good night and good-bye, with best love to Mr Boyce and yourself. Believe me, dearest Etta,

Ever your affectionate sister,

RACHEL TAYLOR

MOUNT VERNON,
DECEMBER 1ST 1872

My Dearest Etta,

Now I suppose you will like to hear about the wedding, that great event having come off on the 26th of November. I came up from Wollongong, and Amy from Bathurst to be present at the ceremony. Neither Mr Taylor nor Mr Sloman could come. The 26th turned out a beautiful day contrary to our fears and expectations, for it had been cloudy and rainy for some time before.

We were very busy all the morning packing Biddulph's things and getting all ready, and at last he drove us into Sydney in the buggy—that is, Annie, Mr Hedgeland, "Little Teddy" and myself. Biddulph went off to join his "best man", and we proceeded to Amy's lodgings, where we found her ready dressed and "Little Annie" also waiting for us. She had some views of taking the nurse and baby to the wedding, but this we providentially overruled.

Mr Hedgeland had ordered a close carriage, and we all—that is, Annie, Amy, "Little Annie", Mr Hedgeland and I—drove down to the Circular Quay and crossed, carriage and all, in the *Transit*, a large steamer that takes vehicles over to the North Shore. Biddulph was in the same boat in a carriage with a pair of grey horses.

We drove straight to the church[5] where the James Tuckers, Hirsts,[6] Thorntons,[7] etc., were also assembled. It was the first wedding at the new church, and the building was dressed with flowers for the occasion, the altar with white lilies alone, and very pretty it looked.

The church was quite full of spectators, but the choristers' stalls were reserved for the guests, so we were close to the communion rails. The bridesmaids were ranged by the door waiting for the bride, and I never saw a handsomer set of girls. There was not one who was not above the average in appearance, while four at least are extremely handsome.

There were eight of them. Fanny Tucker (Emily's sister), three James Tuckers, three Hirsts and Constance Sloman. They were dressed in clouds of tarlatan, with ribbons of the new sea-green, and tulle veils in their hair and bouquets of double scarlet pomegranate and white jessamine.

Biddulph came up to the rails soon after we took our places with Mr Walker, who was his best man. He looked so well and was not at all nervous. Then the bride came in with her father. She was magnificently dressed in white satin trimmed with Maltese lace and wreaths of clematis, a wreath of clematis and orange-blossom and a tulle veil. She is a tall, stately-looking girl and looked extremely well.

[5] Christ Church, Lavender Bay.
[6] Mrs Hirst was formerly Caroline Tucker.
[7] George Thornton was twice Mayor of Sydney, and became an M.L.C. in 1877.

"She was magnificently dressed."

There were two clergymen, who gave us the benefit of the whole service. Everybody behaved very well. There was no crying, and the responses were distinctly audible. When we went into the vestry afterwards the clergyman of the new church presented Biddulph and Emily with a Bible and prayer-book, theirs being the first wedding there. Then we all drove down to Clifton, Mr W. Tucker's place, where we found Mr and Mrs Henning standing in the large drawing-room and looking very happy and comfortable.

There was no sitting-down breakfast, but sandwiches, ices, etc., handed round, and unlimited champagne. They had invited no one beyond the respective families, but these made a very large party, and very well dressed.

Mrs W. Tucker, Emily's mother, wore a beautiful violet moire and violet and white bonnet. Aunt Emily a sort of pearl-grey silk with white bonnet and pink roses. Annie wore a white and mauve dress trimmed with mauve silk ruchings and a white bonnet with feathers tipped with mauve. Amy a stone-coloured silk trimmed with fringe of another shade and a white bonnet with pink flowers. I a sort of thin mohair of the lightest grey all but white, trimmed with green satin and a white bonnet trimmed with green and white.

Curiously enough, there was no blue costume in the whole party except Teddy's dress, which was blue poplin with one of the new broad sailor's hats with a blue ribbon.

Annie Sloman went with us to the wedding, but was not one of the bridesmaids. She looked very nice in white book-muslin with any amount of frills and pink ribbons in her hair; but perhaps you have had enough of millinery! About four o'clock Emily went up to change her dress, and came down in a grey Japanese silk trimmed with satin of a darker shade and a hat trimmed with blue. The carriage came to the door, and off they went amid a shower of white shoes and cheers from the gentlemen.

They drove to the station and took the train for Bowral, a place among the hills near Picton. We heard from Biddulph yesterday. He said they were very well and very happy.

We left soon after the bride and bridegroom, drove back to Amy's lodgings, where we left her, and then Mr Hedgeland, Annie, Teddy and myself returned in the buggy to Mount Vernon, all very tired and glad to go to bed early.

There was a dance at Clifton for the young people, and Annie and Constance Sloman stayed for it under the care of Aunt Emily; she is a sort of general aunt to all the rising generation out here. She went over to Clifton the first thing in the morning to dress the bridesmaids, and very well she did it, too.

I only came up for a fortnight, as Mr Taylor could not accompany me, and we neither of us like being apart. I go home on Wednesday by the steamer, and as soon as I get back I expect we shall begin building. The new house ought to be up in about three months, and I hope it will be a very pretty and comfortable one.

I wish you could come out and see us all in our new habitations. I suppose you and your children are all looking forward to the Christmas holidays now. It seems quite strange to us now to associate Christmas with cold and frost and snow. Here it brings the idea of intense heat, and we are always glad when it is over.

Believe me, my dearest Etta, your very affectionate sister,

RACHEL TAYLOR

P.S. I forgot to say that Biddulph bought a very handsome family Bible partly with the money you so kindly sent him. He was well off for presents. A dinner service, three plated salvers of three sizes, a silver kettle, teapot, two plated butter-dishes, egg-stand, pair of small breakfast cruet-stands, silver napkin-rings, fish-rings, were among the principal. He gave brooches or earrings to all the bridesmaids and a magnificent brooch to Emily as a wedding present.

SPRINGFIELD,
WOLLONGONG, N.S.W.
JUNE 11TH 1873

My Dearest Etta,

Now I must tell you about our visit to Sydney. Biddulph and Annie both asked us to stay with them, so we went to Linton[8] first and paid our first visit to Biddulph and Emily in their new home. Biddulph seems exceedingly happy and fond of his wife, and, though he had a bad cold when we were there, and was generally obliged to go indoors as soon as he returned from the town instead of taking a drive, or gardening (as he likes to do), he was always cheerful and full of fun. He reminds me more and more of what I remember of our father in his home ways.

Emily certainly has drawn a prize, and I think she knows it, for she is wrapt up in her husband. She is a most kind and pleasant hostess, and has everything in her house in such beautiful order. You seldom find in Australia or even England a house so thoroughly furnished and appointed as Linton is. They have two good indoor servants and a man who gardens and looks after the horse and carriage. The garden is new-looking at present, but both Emily and Biddulph are so fond of gardening that they will soon improve it.

While we were there we drove out to Baptist's nursery and ordered a quantity of pines and cypresses and other shelter trees. Biddulph also has bought about half an acre of land adjoining to enlarge his garden, and a most picturesque bit it is, with masses of grey rock and groups of gum-trees. When it is planted and laid out it will be beautiful. I envy them the rocks. We have none here.

We spent a pleasant week at Linton, and then Mr Taylor left me and went to Milleewah for one night and thence home, as he did not like to leave his beloved farm any longer. I remained a few days longer at Linton, and then went on to stay with Annie

8 In Pitt Street, Kirribilli.

and Mr Hedgeland. I went by train to Ashfield, which is about twenty minutes' journey from Sydney. Annie and Teddy met me at the station, and a quarter of an hour's easy walk brought us to Milleewah, which, in spite of its outlandish name, is a charming place. It took my fancy exceedingly.

It is a large old-fashioned house with large lofty rooms, windows down to the ground and a wide veranda on three sides, and it stands in about forty acres of bushland, surrounded by fine old trees, so that though it is so near Sydney it is as much in the country as we are. There are fields all round, or, as we call them here, "paddocks". There is a flower garden in front of the house and stabling, etc., at the back. The house is so large that they do not occupy more than half the rooms, and Teddy makes railways and builds Exhibition Buildings in the empty ones. It is altogether the most delightful place for a child with such abundant space out of doors and in. The rooms they use are very comfortably furnished, though not exactly in the style of Linton (where the drawing-room is in walnut and satin damask), but they have good dark carpets and respectable cedar, so that Teddy can rampage without fear of much damage.

They are very comfortably off, for the Government are paying Mr Hedgeland at the rate of two guineas per day. He has the "alignment" of all Petersham and Ashfield, which sort of surveying requires most accurate work and calculation, and all surveyors cannot do it, so that he is well paid.[9] He is looking very well. Annie, I thought, was looking thin, but that she always does. She seemed well when I was there, and we used to take pleasant walks together.

On May 6th I put myself on board the steamer and came home, leaving dear Annie, who insisted on coming to see me off, apparently quite well, and it was that very day a few hours afterwards that she was taken ill. I was very glad to be at home again, for it is lonely for Mr Taylor when I am away, and I do not half enjoy myself without him.

I found all well at home; the servants had managed very fairly in my absence, and "Springfield" looked prettier than ever. The timber for the house is nearly all come and lying in piles upon the site. The garden has been fenced round, and now we are only waiting for fine weather to begin the house and to plant the garden. I do not suppose the dwelling will be finished before the end of the year, as while we are about it we think it is best to

9 The old records disclose that George Caleb Hedgeland was appointed as a licensed surveyor in the Department of Lands on 14th July 1871 and was engaged in that year in the survey of Bligh Street, Newtown.

build a comfortably large house, for we hope to spend the rest of our lives there.

We hope to make the garden very pretty by and by. There is every advantage of soil and situation and the best climate in Australia, but it will take time, of course, and patience. Mr Taylor thoroughly likes farming, and I think the farm will in time pay us very well.

Ever your affectionate sister,

RACHEL TAYLOR

SPRINGFIELD,
APRIL 8TH 1874

My Dearest Etta,

As I told Mr Boyce, I was very much surprised to hear of any fresh emolument coming to me from Aunt Vizard's property. Whatever it is it will be very acceptable, for the expenses of a new farm are considerable, to say nothing of the house, which has cost nearly £300.

So much for business. As for pleasure, we are having lovely weather now—after three months of such rainy skies as would not have disgraced England. However, though it was unpleasant at the time, it has made the country look beautiful. The grass so green and the garden so full of flowers. When fine, the Australian autumn is the perfection of weather; cool and bright, and with a clear atmosphere that makes the distant hills and woods and farms stand out nearly as clear as if you saw them through a glass.

Our house is very comfortable. We have just had the sitting-room papered and the ceiling whitewashed, and yesterday it was cleaned out preparatory to the furniture being moved in. It is a large, pleasant room with three French windows and a lovely view therefrom. We are at present using the spare bedroom as a sitting-room, but now that we are going to move out of it we have written to ask Biddulph and Emily to come down and pay us their promised visit before the cold weather comes on. The bedrooms are rather rough yet, being unpapered, but they will not mind that.

Biddulph is very fond of Illawarra, and will enjoy the rides and drives here. Emily has never seen the district yet. They talk of driving down in their own buggy, as neither of them likes the steamers, and the coach is often so crowded. I am expecting to hear every day when they will come.

I have the house all to myself this morning, with the exception

266

of a few cats and a couple of dogs! Mr Taylor is down in the lucerne paddock, turning over some hay. I can see him from the window, a white spot in the distance. Both the servants are gone to a school feast and picnic up the mountain, which they preferred by way of an Easter holiday. You are obliged to give your servants a great many holidays here, to keep them at all, and I do not think they are any the worse for them, nor are we. I have dinner cooked the day before, and it is not much trouble to boil the potatoes and lay the table and to get the tea.

The "upper ten" (leaving out the thousands) of Wollongong never think of going out on any of the people's holidays; they generally have to take care of their houses and take their own pleasure at other times. It is curious that in these republican countries where "Jack is as good as his master", and much better in his own estimation, there is a much wider gap between class and class than there is in England. There, at least in the old times, you would go and see your poorer neighbours and rather enjoy a talk with them, especially in the country. Here if you did anything of the kind they would return your call and bring their children to tea. The consequence is that, though we are surrounded by little farms, I do not know one of the farmers' wives, even by sight, except an old lady, whose milking-yard borders the road to the post-office, so that I have seen her in passing.

Mr Taylor knows most of the men, so far as saying good day to them, but any further intimacy would lead to their borrowing every tool and instrument on the farm, to say nothing of horses and oxen.

The Hedgelands are still looking out for a house, and have not much time to find one, as they leave Milleewah at the end of this month. Houses are very difficult to get near Sydney now, especially one with land attached to it, which Mr Hedgeland wants for his horses. He is making a great deal of money by his profession, but the drawback to it is the frequent moving it entails, unless he took a permanent residence and "camped out" for weeks together, as some surveyors do, and this neither he nor Annie likes, and I am sure I do not wonder at it. I should go and camp out, too. Annie is better, but not very strong. I think she does too much. She is one of those active people who are always moving about, and will not sit down till she is thoroughly tired out and is obliged to. I am about quite as much or perhaps more, but then I am stronger. I think I have gained strength as I have got older, while both Annie and Amy have done the reverse. I hope you have followed my example, not theirs.

I often hear from Biddulph, and Mr Taylor was staying with them about a fortnight ago, when he went to Sydney on some business. Biddulph and Emily seem very happy and flourishing. Mr Taylor says Linton is looking beautiful. It is the prettiest and best-kept place on the North Shore. I wish we could emulate it, but a farm to look after does not admit of the lawn being mown every day. Biddulph's man has nothing to do but garden and look after the horse and carriage.

I am busy making some curtains for the sitting-room. We had some green moreen curtains at The Peach Trees, and I have had them dyed and am putting some new binding on them which will make them look quite respectable again. We have also invested in a new tablecloth and hearth-rug, but just yet we can not afford a great deal in the way of furniture: the cottage has cost so much. However, I think Mr Taylor was wise to build it of a good size, because we could never have enlarged the rooms, and all accessories can be added hereafter, when we are better off. The farm is so good it only requires time to pay well, but the great drawback is the difficulty of getting labour.

Since I have been writing, a ragged and barelegged apparition invaded the lawn and threw "Jip" into paroxysms of barking, and this proved to be a small boy come to be engaged. Mr Taylor had been inquiring for one for the last six months. This urchin is not eleven years old and does not know how to drive bullocks, but Deighton was only too glad to engage him at 4s. a week, to be increased to 5s. when he has learned the above-mentioned art. He will run away before that. David, our factotum, has 14s. a week, and Maggie, the general servant, 8s. Wages are getting enormous out here. In Sydney a thoroughly good cook and laundress gets 20s. a week. Annie is giving a very indifferent one 12s.

Now I must end this long letter. Give my love to Aunt and Uncle when you write to Taunton, and with much to Mr Boyce, yourself and the "children".

Believe me, my dearest Etta, ever your affectionate sister,
RACHEL TAYLOR

PARRAMATTA,
FEBRUARY 17TH 1875

My Dearest Etta,

It seems to be some time since I have written to you, but I have had a very busy summer, and not much leisure for anything.

I am staying now at Parramatta with Annie. I came here

". . . a ragged and barelegged apparition invaded the lawn."

about ten days ago, and intend going on to Linton on Friday for a week and then home. I do not like being away from home very long. It is so lonely for Mr Taylor without me, and now that we have two men, besides the girl in the kitchen, we do not like both to leave the farm at once, so that a visit to Sydney is not half the pleasure it used to be, when we could go together.

I did not expect to like the Parramatta house very much, after Milleewah, but, although the rooms are not so large, it is a much more cheerful place, and, I should think, healthier, not being so buried in trees. The house stands by itself on a hill, with a grove of trees behind it, and in front a wide prospect; and in clear weather you can see the lighthouse on Sydney Heads.

It is quite out of the town, not even in sight of it, Parramatta lying low behind a hill. They have a nice little garden and a buggy and a dog-cart (in which Mr Hedgeland goes on his surveying expeditions) and two horses. Also two maidservants and a man, and everything very comfortable.

I have not had very nice weather since I came. It has been either intensely hot or rainy, so that we have not been out very often. We walked one evening to the "Domain", a very pretty sort of park on the banks of the river, where I saw the finest oaks I ever beheld out of England, and where there are some deer and some emus, which it is Teddy's great delight to feed with acorns.

We also made expeditions into Sydney and paid a visit to Farmer's, where I fitted out myself with some new garments, which I badly wanted, not having been in Sydney for a year before. The said Farmer's is a most convenient place. It is an immense establishment divided into departments for everything; you can choose a dress, have the material sent to the dressmaking department, where it is made for you in the best fashion; go to another for a mantle, another for a bonnet, another for underclothes; another large room is for carpets and upholstery, and all the very best that can be had in Sydney. It is a wonderful save of time and trouble.

I have only seen Biddulph for about half an hour at his office, during the before-mentioned expeditions to Sydney. He was looking well and said that Emily has quite recovered again. I shall be able to tell you more about them in my next letter after I have paid my visit to Linton. They have Upcott and Amy Sloman staying with them now. Emily very kindly asked them down for a change after the measles. When they are considered quite purified they are to come on here, but Annie is afraid of Teddy taking the complaint, as he has never had it. It has been very fatal in Sydney this summer. So many children have died from it, or rather from the after-effect.

Since I have been here I have been reading Mama's letters, those which Aunt Henrietta sent to Annie. I was very much interested in them; they so brought back old times. We all say, however, that we remember our dear mother as a much more cheerful person than anyone would think her to be from reading those letters, but perhaps we were too young to know all her troubles and anxieties about us. What a comfort it would have been to her if she could have foreseen how happily we are all provided for now!

I have not told you anything about my own home. I am quite ashamed to think how long ago it was that I last wrote to you. I am afraid it was just after Biddulph and Emily's last visit, and soon after they were gone our troubles began.

The servant I had had for two years took it into her head to be married. She behaved very well, and gave me a month's notice, and Bella engaged a servant for me at Shoalhaven, so I thought I was all right, but this last girl failed me at the last minute (I think her mother was ill), and it was then too near Christmas to get anyone else, for servants here never will take a place at Christmas, and often leave their situations for a few weeks at that season, knowing that they can easily get another whenever they like.

The result was that for six weeks I had no servant at all—a boy whom we employed on the farm helped a little at the rough work, such as washing up and sweeping the kitchen, but most of the work fell on me, and very glad I was when, the Christmas gaieties being over, I contrived to get a domestic again. These sort of interregnums are frequently happening in the best-regulated families, especially in the country. I like the girl I have now very much; if she will stay as long as the last—nearly two years—I shall be very fortunate.

We keep two farming men now; one has been with us for five years, and the other we engaged in place of the boy above-mentioned, as a great deal too much hard work fell on Mr Taylor when there was only one man on the place.

We have just got through a serious drought; beyond a few showers we had no rain for five months, and we are more than satisfied with the way our farm stood the trial. We had always abundance of water in the creek and plenty of grass, though it was dry. The cattle and horses also kept as fat as possible on the dry grass. The drought also raised hay to a great price; and hay is our staple product.

People used to come almost praying Mr Taylor for a bale of lucerne hay. Now, I am thankful to say, the weather has changed, and we have had abundant rains. The whole country is green, like spring, and when I get home I expect there will be a fine show of autumn flowers in the garden.

I have a great horror of droughts. They cause such suffering among cattle; though our animals looked so well, the cattle were dying on some of the overstocked farms, even in Illawarra, and it was worse in Queensland, where in many places there was a dearth of water as well as grass.

Ever your affectionate sister,

RACHEL TAYLOR

My Dearest Etta,

Thank you very much for your Christmas letter and for the very pretty Christmas card that accompanied it.

It is very difficult to write you anything that will interest you from Wollongong. Though it is a pleasant, peaceful life we lead here, there is nothing to write about. None of the adventure and newness of station life, and at the same time you know none of our acquaintances or surroundings, so that you cannot be interested in them as I am in any news about Bristol.

There is only one family down here that we are at all intimate with, and they are the Jenkinses, of Berkeley. Mrs Jenkins died about a year ago, but old Mr Jenkins and the sons and daughters are great allies of Mr Taylor's and mine. We exchange visits about once a week, and sometimes go for rides and excursions on the lake with them. I do not know if I ever told you about Lake Illawarra. It is about four miles from us and is a beautiful sheet of water, about the size of Windermere. There are two wooded islands upon it, and the banks are very pretty, though rather flat on one side. Mr Jenkins has a boat upon it. We went for a picnic with them a week or two ago, dined on one of the islands under the shade of an enormous fig-tree, and spent most of the day rowing about and fishing. I caught several fish myself, and, among others a large eel, which rather alarmed us by wriggling all over the boat and refusing to be quiet.

Another day we made a party and ascended Mount Keira. We rode up as high as the horses could go, and then tied them to trees and climbed the rest of the way. There is a magnificent view from the top. Our farm lies in a sort of horse-shoe between Mount Keira and Mount Kembla. I have often wished to get up Mount Kembla. Mr Taylor went up last summer with a party of gentlemen, but he said it was an awful climb. The last part up a nearly sheer precipice which ladies could never get up.

I should like you to see Illawarra now. After a very dry summer we have had some heavy rain, and the effect was like magic. The whole country is the most lovely green, and flowers have come out everywhere. I think the autumn is the pleasantest season in this country. The spring is very beautiful, but is often too dry. The less said about Australian summers the better, and, though there are some lovely days in the winter, when there is still weather, we get too many cold westerly winds for it to be a very pleasant season.

272

Annie Hedgeland has had quite a large party staying with her this Easter—Biddulph and his wife, with the nurse and baby, and Aunt Emily and Fanny Tucker. I am now trying to persuade Annie to come down here for a fortnight before winter. I am sure the change would do her good.

We miss dear old Biddulph's visits very much, but now that Captain Tucker is in England[10] he cannot leave home for long enough to come here. Of course the whole of the business devolves upon him, and from Parramatta he can go by train to Sydney every day.

I suppose he has told you that they have taken Canterbury House again and go there this month. They are going to let Linton. They think that both Biddulph and Emily will be better for the change inland away from the sea air, and Biddulph has always had a hankering after Canterbury. He lived there with Annie and Mr Hedgeland before he married. It is a very pretty place. I think they sent you some photographs of it.

Next week the Sydney Exhibition[11] opens, but neither of us cares to go and see it. When it is an annual thing, as it is here, there is a great sameness in it. The best part is the show of cattle, dogs and horses. The Jenkinses exhibited Hereford cattle, and got the second prize last year for an enormous bull.

How I wish we could have an hour's talk instead of letter-writing. How much more we should know of each other's ways and habits and belongings!

I have just been reading Grantley Berkeley's *Life and Recollections*; and a most amusing book it is. Did you ever read it? There are many mentions of places we know; Berkeley Castle, of course, and Dursley.

The Jenkinses came from Gloucester originally, and Mr Jenkins's father named his house and estate after Berkeley. All the present family are Australians. Old Mr Jenkins is a great reader and has a fine library, as he gets all the new travels, etc., and lends us any books we like, a great advantage in a country where "Mudie" is not. Have you seen Tennyson's *Harold*? The reviews do not seem to admire it. I read his *Queen Mary* last year and thought it great rubbish.

Mr Taylor is gone into town this morning, and I am writing before dinner. The windows and doors all open to the brilliant sunshine and slight breeze. Kembla, the black Newfoundland, lying panting on the door-mat, and my little terrier, Jip, stretched just outside the window. The lawn is so green after the rain and

10 Biddulph had become manager of Tucker and Company.
11 The Sydney Show.

the flower-beds brilliant with autumn flowers. A sort of autumn haze over Mount Keira, and the wooded hill in front of it standing out bright in the sunshine. I am writing at the desk Mr Boyce gave me, and which is still in excellent preservation, and using the ink out of Mama's silver inkstand. The table is round and the cloth is green and old (we have a better one for afternoons), and I am arrayed in a blue hair-striped print dress with white "facings", also the worse for wear.

I had got this far when Mary Ann came in to lay the cloth, so I had dinner, fondly imagining that Mr Taylor was also dining with a friend in Wollongong, and went out to water the plants in the veranda, when I heard the whistle by which he always announces his return as he goes along the road above the house, and presently he came in very hungry, and Mary Ann has just been frying chops for him.

He brought me your letter of February 15th, and I have been reading it while he has been eating the said chops, and am much interested in all its news.

The mission week must have been very interesting, and I hope productive of good. We had a mission here some time ago and enjoyed the mission services greatly. It was more to us than it would be to Clifton people, for we have such a wretched clergyman here; half the parish dislike him and the other half laugh at him.

I know that lovely early spring weather in England. How pleasant the few fine days are, but, if I remember right, they are rather treacherous, and frost and snow sometimes come after, but your present winter is what I should like if I were in England. Here it is never very cold, and we have already flowers. Last June (our midwinter month) all the roses were in full bloom, summer roses and all. They had been checked by the drought and came out late.

I cannot half answer your long interesting letter, as this must be posted today to catch the mail. The post is half a mile from us,[12] and Mr Taylor is waiting to send one of the boys with it. If you have your likeness taken again for Annie, I hope you will have it done without your bonnet this time. The one you sent me was very good, but it gives you a better idea of a person to see the hair also.

Kind love to Mr Boyce and with much to yourself and Mr Taylor's kind regards,

I remain, my dearest Etta, ever your affectionate sister,

RACHEL TAYLOR

12 At Fig Tree.

274

My Dearest Etta,

The months fly by so quickly that I almost lose count of them sometimes. It seems only yesterday that it was hot summer, and now we are in the middle of winter—but such a winter! We have had about six weeks of the most glorious weather, cold mornings and evenings with sometimes a slight frost, and still bright sunny days that make you feel it is a pleasure only to be alive!

You have heard of Biddulph's removal to Canterbury House, where as you may remember Annie and Mr Hedgeland lived with him before he was married. It is a beautiful place, and both he and Emily seem to be the better for the change from the sea air. Biddulph was always very fond of the place. There is such a nice garden full of camellias, azaleas and all sorts of flowering shrubs. I have not been there yet since they moved, but I hope to go up in the spring to visit both Biddulph and Annie.

Annie has not been very strong this winter, but seems to be better now. She has just been staying at Canterbury for a fortnight with Teddy, while Mr Hedgeland was away surveying, and enjoyed it very much.

We have two side-saddles now, as Biddulph gave me Emily's when she left off riding, and it makes us very independent when any friend is staying here. Mr Taylor is a great deal too busy to go out, and a Miss Ebsworth, who has been staying with me, and I used to ride about everywhere together. One day, in company with two other ladies, we made an expedition up Mount Keira. We rode as far as we could up a very steep road, and, when it came to climbing, we tied up our horses under some trees and scrambled up the rocks to the top of the mountain. We got to the edge of what is called the Victoria Rock, with a sheer descent in front of us for some hundred feet, and such a glorious view there was of the whole valley of Illawarra at our feet and an illimitable sea view beyond.

I was the leader and promoter of the expedition, and I confess I felt rather uneasy lest during our absence anything should have frightened our horses and they should have all broken their bridles and gone home leaving us in the lurch. However, we found them all right when we came down again, and then we rode to a place where there was a beautiful little clear spring coming out of the rocks, where we had lunch, after which we dug up ferns for the gardens and then rode home after a very pleasant day.

"We got to the edge of what is called the Victoria Rock."

Miss Ebsworth and I also used to take long walks and explore the mountains about here. She is a great walker and does so thoroughly admire the scenery, and there is nothing like the Illawarra scenery in Australia.

She brought down with her some books on the Anglo-Israel theory, which she used to read to me on all convenient occasions. She firmly believed every word of one childish book, even the account of the arrival of the prophet Jeremiah and the Jewish princess in Ireland in company with the Scone coronation stone. Also that the American people are the tribe of Manasseh, and that the Irish are the evil-doing Hirites and Hittites! No doubt it is an interesting speculation where the lost tribes are, and it is easy to imagine that in the general migration from eastward to westward some of the Israelites found their way into Europe and may be among the Teutonic nations. This one can believe; but it requires great faith to swallow the prophet Jeremiah and the holy stone.

I think it must be since I last wrote to you that we have taken to dairying instead of exclusively depending upon hay-farming. I persuaded Mr Taylor into it, as I thought he was working too hard, and that butter-making would pay as well and be easier work, as the two lads we have on the farm can do the milking, etc. We got a few good cows besides those we had before, and I think the new speculation will pay very well. We make now about thirty pounds of butter a week and get 1s. 6d. per pound for it in the keg or wholesale.

We shall soon be milking more cows, and of course shall get more butter. In the summer the butter is much cheaper, but then you get more of it.

I have been very busy gardening since Miss Ebsworth left. The garden is always rather neglected when there are visitors here, as I have to go out every afternoon. It is getting a pretty place now. I should like to show it to you. The trees and shrubs are growing up, the veranda pillars are covered with flowering creepers, and the beds are always full of flowers.

Last year we made a drive with a circle for carriages to drive round, and the trees and shrubs are planted round it and growing wonderfully. Now Mr Taylor is just beginning to make a new approach to the house. The old way follows the road and comes in through the barns and stockyard, etc., at the back of the house. The new way will avoid all the outbuildings, cross a very pretty creek by a bridge, and come up to the front of the house; but I could not make you understand the difference without a map of the farm.

The bridge is just begun, but I do not suppose the road will be made for another year, as there is a great deal of work in it and we cannot afford to put on a number of men and get the work done at once, but perhaps there is more pleasure in making improvements when you have to wait for them and do them bit by bit. There is great pleasure in having a place of your own and seeing it gradually grow into beauty.

Now I must say good night, as it is ten o'clock, and we keep early farmhouse hours. Mr Taylor, having finished his book, says it is time to have prayers and go to bed.

My kindest love to you all. Ask Mr Boyce what he thinks about the Anglo-Israel theory.

Your most affectionate sister,

RACHEL TAYLOR

My Dearest Etta,

I generally write to you when I am away from home, as I have more time when I am on a visit than when I have the house, etc., on my hands. I came up from Springfield to Parramatta on August 15th to spend a month between Annie and Biddulph. It is nearly two years since I have been up before; somehow I find it very difficult to get away from home. There is so much to do and see after on a farm.

I found everything pretty much as I had left it at Parramatta —the bright little house and garden and the beautiful view from the hill on which it stands

Mr Hedgeland is looking very well. He is now a Government staff surveyor and keeps two men to help him in his work. They are often at home for days together while Mr Hedgeland is mapping out his surveys, etc., so Annie is able to have her garden kept in nice order. However, they are thinking of leaving Parramatta as it is rather a lonely place for Annie when Mr Hedgeland is out all day.

Teddy is very much grown since I saw him last year; he is a nice little boy, and very clever, I think. Annie still teaches him, and he is getting on very well with her. He is learning Latin now. Annie says he ought to go to school, but there is no good school at Parramatta for little boys.

I spent a fortnight with Annie and came here on Tuesday last. As you know, Biddulph is now again living in that pretty house he had before he was married. It looks much the same except that the shrubs and trees have grown a good deal in five years. I was quite glad to see it all again. Biddulph is looking well, but rather thin. I think that during Captain Tucker's absence it was rather a worry to him to have the whole business of Tucker and Co. on his hands.

Emily is looking very well, though she is expecting another baby in January. *The* baby is a darling little fellow; that likeness Biddulph sent you home does not the least do him justice. I had no idea he was such a pretty child. The photo gives you the idea of small eyes, but he has beautiful eyes, very large and soft and blue. We all think they are like Annie's. He has also very pretty soft curly hair · just the colour that Biddulph's was when he was a little boy. This is a pleasant place to stay at, such a lovely garden and grounds. There are real *trees* of camellias here, and, as you may fancy, there are any quantity to gather, and the house is full of camellias and azaleas.

278

I have had a good deal of shopping to do as I have not left Wollongong for nearly two years. It is not quite so convenient to shop from here as it is from the North Shore.

Mr Taylor is very good about writing and sends me the home news every other day. It is rather lonely for him while I am away, but he is busy about the farm all day.

Captain Tucker arrived about a week ago; you will have seen by the papers what a wonderful passage the *Lusitania* made, forty days—the fastest trip on record. Captain Tucker looks all the better for his year in England.

Upcott Sloman came down last Saturday, and I think he is the nicest boy I ever knew. He is not seventeen yet, but he is nearly six feet high and very handsome. He is very gentlemanly, but at the same time thoroughly simple and boyish in all his ways, and with none of the colonial coolness and assurance that we English all hate so. Amy says that it is a great trial to her to part with him, and I do not wonder at it. I do hope he will get on well. I think they were right in choosing surveying as a profession for him; it pays well out here, and Mr Hedgeland will be able to help him so much.

With very much love to yourself, believe me, dearest Etta, ever your affectionate sister,

RACHEL TAYLOR

SPRINGFIELD,
MARCH 25TH 1878

My Dearest Etta,

I am afraid I have two letters of yours unanswered, but I rather delayed replying to the last, in order to make some inquiries about the old King's friendship with Grandpapa. From Hannah Dashwood's note, which you forwarded to me, however, I suppose you no longer want the information you asked for.

However, for our own satisfaction, I ascertained beyond a doubt that the intimacy was during our grandmother's life and not after Grandpapa had married Mrs Buxton. I think it was the Princess Sophia, not Amelia, who was thrown from her horse near Poxwell, and lay ill there for some days, and it was on this occasion, I suppose, that she presented the silver tea and coffee service to Mrs Henning.

Amy has the teapot, and I think the Edmund Buxtons have the coffee-pot. The inscription on the former I got Amy to copy for me; and it is as follows:

The gift of her Royal Highness the Princess Sophia to Elizabeth Henning, September 21st 1799.

279

Grandpapa did not marry Mrs Buxton till 1808 (see *Life of Sir Fowell Buxton*), so this inscription settles the question at once.

In 1811 the King was pronounced insane and the Prince of Wales appointed Regent, so I suppose his trips to Weymouth were over by that time, or a year or two earlier.

The illness of the Princess Sophia was most likely the beginning of the acquaintance, and it must have continued some time after our grandmother's death, for I remember a story of Aunt Harriet's—she kept house at Poxwell after Mrs Henning's death —and she said that on one occasion the Royal party were lunching there, and she was handing a tray of something to one of the royal dukes (I think the Duke of Sussex), and, seeing her standing, he got up and insisted on her sitting down and waited on her himself.

Then there was a story of the old King taking up our father in his arms, when he was a very small boy, and asking if he knew who he was, and being very much delighted when the child replied "Grandpapa King!" And you must remember Grandpapa's pet story about his meeting the King out riding shortly after our grandmother's death, when he was in great sorrow, and how the King desired his train to fall back, as "he wanted to speak to Henning alone", and then, riding on with him, "he talked to him like a father" and advised him to marry again, for the sake of his young family: "But mark my words! Mark my words! Mark my words, Henning! If you ever expect to find another such woman as your first wife, you will be disappointed." I remember exactly how Grandpapa used to move back his plate and tell that story.

Another of Grandpapa's stories was that one day the King came from Weymouth and inquired for Mrs Henning, and was informed by the servant that she was washing lace. The King had a way of repeating his words: "Washing lace, washing lace, is she? Then I'll go and help her." A comic-paper published in Weymouth produced an illustration of the King and Mrs Henning over a wash-tub, washing lace together.

I am certain it was at Poxwell, not at Weymouth, that the King used to visit, because while at Poxwell Grandpapa was farming the estate himself, but when he went to Weymouth he was a banker (and, if you recollect, it was the run on that bank that ruined him), and another of his stories was that one day he was complaining to the King of the difficulty of getting sufficient men to make the hay, and the next morning he found a small detachment of soldiers drawn up before the door, they having

"Mark my words! Mark my words, Henning!"

been sent by the King with orders to make Mr Henning's hay.
I believe they performed more in the way of consuming bread
and cheese and beer than in haymaking.

I have been able to get the inscription on the gold cup, which
Biddulph keeps at his bankers' and I dare say he will get it out
at the new baby's christening and fill it with claret cup to drink
his health. The inscription is as follows:

First of all there is the Royal coat-of-arms on the gold cup,
then:

Honi soit qui mal y pense.
Dieu et Mon Droit.

Given September 26th 1800, to Edmund Henning, of Poxwell, in the county of Dorset, esquire, by his Majesty King George III.

In some of your summer trips you ought to go to Weymouth and visit the old places. It is a pretty drive of about four miles to Poxwell. It must have been a fine old place once, built in a square round a court and with stone-mullioned windows and a large low hall with oak rafters and a great oak table where, very likely, "sacred Majesty took his déjeuner", and a fine old brick gateway, or, rather, gatehouse, with a small chamber over it, where there is a legend that some heiress of the Henning family was shut up for contumacy, and betimely escaped therefrom with her lover.[13]

I used to hear a great deal of family history from Uncle and Aunt John Henning, but I have forgotten it now. There was an old place called "Henning's Crookston" where our great-grand-papa lived, and where all his family were brought up. Then there is a most picturesque old manor house, called Radypoll, close to Weymouth, which also belonged to Grandpapa and afterwards to Uncle John.

Wolverton was a very fine old place with an ivy-covered gatehouse as large as a modern cottage and the house a sort of castellated building. Biddulph was the rightful heir to these properties.

I do not think you have read this poem of mine, so I will inflict it on you:

THE DAYS OF CHILDHOOD

The happy days of childhood, how swift they fleet away;
How soon beneath the world's cold breath its feelings must decay,
Its fervent warm affections, its confidence and truth,
With all its bright imaginings and cherished hopes of youth.

The gladsomings and gaiety its sunny light that throws
O'er every time and scene till all in its own bright sunshine glows.
Alas! That life's dark clouds should e'er that fairy dream destroy
And overcast that rosy dawn of innocence and joy.

There is no spot so lovely as our early childhood's home,
And thither still the heart returns, wherever we may roam;
The tangled brakes where wildflowers grew its overshadowing grove,
Its streamlets and its valleys claim our first and latest love.

[13] Poxwell House was built by John Henning, an ancestor of Rachel's, during the reign of Queen Elizabeth I.

There is no joy like that we felt when in the springtide hours
We bounded o'er the wild, free hills, and plucked the mountain flowers
Where tall fern waves and harebell blue with purple heather blend
Such gay, unfettered happenings with the years of childhood end.

There are no friends like those who for our infancy have cared,
And no companions dear as those who all its pleasures shared.
Oh, what is like a mother's love, or who her place can fill
When her cheering smile has passed away and her gentle voice is still!

And none can e'er such sympathy in weal or woe impart
As a sister gives who aye hath shared each feeling of the heart;
And where shall we such shelter find, in trouble or in harm,
As in the sure protection of a brother's' shielding arm?

We may form new ties of friendship and other bonds of love,
But they are not like the flowery links that our happy childhood wove
For the world its chilling influence upon our hearts has thrown,
And though the chain may sparkle still, its first bright glow is gone.

How often when around the earth the shades of twilight close
And evening's gentle hand hath hushed all nature to repose
The visions of the past arise, and many a vanished scene
To memory appears, as though no change had ever been.

And mid the stillings of that hour we seem to hear a sound
Like whispers from the spirit-land breathed in the air around;
Voices of those whose pilgrimage has long been ended here,
O'er whom the quiet grave has closed since many a weary year.

And for a while as once we were again we seem to be;
Again we feel the gaiety of a soul unworn and free.
But the dream decays, and life once more assumes a dreary hue,
And all its sad realities again stand forth to view.

There are hours of happiness on earth, but their sunshine may not last,
And the joyous days of childhood must be soon for ever past.
They are like the gleams of treacherous light that on the storm-cloud
    play
Then fade away, and deeper gloom succeeds the short-liv'd ray.

I must conclude. Fond love to Mr Boyce and the children and
to yourself.

Believe me, dearest Etta, your most affectionate sister,

RACHEL TAYLOR

My Dearest Etta,

I was going to write to you by this mail, and now I have to thank you for two copies of the *Graphic*, which we have received lately. The last arrived only a few days ago. Thank you very much for sending them; it is a great pleasure to us to see them, as we do not take in any illustrated paper. The war pictures are very good.

We all rejoiced greatly at the English victories in Egypt, and generally think that it is a pity we cannot manage to "annex" Egypt. The Anglo-Israelites in particular appear to think that the Great Pyramid belongs especially to us. I was reading Piozzi Smith's book about the Great Pyramid lately—I forgot whether I spoke of it before—it is rather interesting, some of it, but I do not the least believe in the conclusions he draws from his elaborate measurements and calculations. I think our distance from the sun is more likely to be made out (within a million or two of miles) by some of the expeditions now looking out for the transit of Venus than by measuring the base of the Great Pyramid, and I do not think that coming events are likely to be foretold by counting the stones in its dark passages.

Since I wrote to you last we have had a visit from Biddulph. He came down in October and stayed a week with us. It is always so pleasant to have him, but we were most unfortunate in the weather. After a drought that had lasted for months the weather broke up the very day after his arrival, and it rained during nearly the whole of his visit, so that he could hardly go out at all. We were thankful enough for the rain, for after a dry autumn, winter and spring everything was burnt up and there was no grass for the cattle, but it was unfortunate that it should have come during his visit, as his great pleasure is to ride and drive about the country. We took a few rides, but generally got caught in the rain.

When we do get rain, the effect is like magic in this country; in a few days the hills and paddocks are of a brilliant green, and the garden full of flowers.

Mr Taylor wanted some fencing put up the other day on the farm and one man refused to do it because, he said, he could not make 9s. a day at the work, the ground being hard; 6s. to 7s. per day is the regular wages of a labourer, and the difficulty is in general to find men to do any work that may be wanted.

The railways employ a great many now. The Illawarra railway

284

is making great progress, and will, it is said, be finished in two years, as far as Wollongong. I do not think it will be by any means an unmitigated gain to the district. It will be very convenient when we want to go to Sydney, but it will bring down, on holidays and so forth, all the rag-tag and bobtail of Sydney, to invade our beautiful hills and valleys.

It will make land more valuable, though. Already Sydney speculators are buying land for villa sites, etc. Mr Taylor was offered £30 an acre, lately, for what we call the "hill paddock". It is a hill containing about thirty acres, partly covered with trees and bush. We keep all our horses and cattle there, so, of course, we should not think of selling it, or, indeed, any of the farm, but it shows how land is going up, as, nine years ago, we gave £11 per acre for the whole farm.

I do not suppose we should ever like to sell it, whatever its value, for we should never find a place we liked so well, or in the midst of such lovely scenery as Illawarra. And when you have made a place entirely, as we have this, built the house and planted every tree and shrub, you get fond of it. It is wonderful how the trees have grown in nine years. The house was built on a bare paddock, and now, at a little distance, it looks as if it stood in a grove of trees: pines, cypresses, mimosas, etc., although there are none very near the building.

Just now everyone is talking of the accident to the *Austral*, lamenting that the finest passenger ship in the world should have been allowed to sink at her moorings in calm water from sheer carelessness. The captain, chief officer and chief engineer asleep in their cabins, with all the coaling ports open on one side and no water in her ballast tanks. I suppose they will get her up again, but it will cost an immense sum.

The other disaster of the year, the burning of the Garden Palace, was also caused in a great measure by Government carelessness, only one watchman to look after that immense building. Quantities of Government papers were destroyed, and, among others, most of the railway plans. The Illawarra line is being resurveyed for one.

I heard from Amy a little while ago. They seem all well and very gay at Bathurst. The girls go out a good deal, and I think it is a very good thing for them. Having no servant, I shall not be able to ask any of them down here this Christmas, but I always fancy this is rather a dull house for young people (girls, I mean; Teddy delights in it). There is not much in visiting in Wollongong.

Mr Taylor, now and then, goes out. But I never do, as with

only one servant we cannot return people's hospitality without an enormous deal of trouble; besides, I cannot afford evening dresses! However, as you know, I never liked parties even when I was young, and should think them the greatest bore now I am old. Mr Taylor's gentlemen friends sometimes drop in to tea, and that is the extent of our entertaining.

Biddulph and his family were to go up to Bowral this week to spend a month among the mountains. He will only be able to stay part of the time. Annie seems to be very comfortable in her new house; but you will have heard all their news at first hand.

This will reach you about Christmas, or a little later. We shall think of each other then.

Kind love to Mr Boyce, the girls, Leighton and yourself.

Ever, dearest Etta, your most affectionate sister,

RACHEL TAYLOR

EPILOGUE

AND so end, nearly thirty years after she wrote, from England, her first letter to Biddulph and Annie in Australia, the letters of Rachel Henning that have been retained and preserved by her family. But though, in her last letter of the collection, she mentions that "I never liked parties even when I was young, and should think them the greatest bore now I am old"—she was then fifty-six—Rachel was, in fact, very little past the middle of what was to be the span of her adult life. She was to live long enough to see the outbreak of the first world war, to ride in a motor-car and see an aeroplane in flight. She died on 28th August 1914 at the age of eighty-eight.

Her lifetime, in effect, linked the end of the period Jane Austen portrayed in *Pride and Prejudice* with the beginning of the present age. It also linked the culture of genteel mid-Victorian England with pioneering Australia and the fever of the gold-rushes. When Rachel arrived in Australia there was no railway yet in service. When she died there were 22,000 miles of railroads throughout the Commonwealth.

All the youthful Hennings who came to Australia, with the exception of Amy, lived to a great age. All except Amy outlived their spouses. Biddulph—Rachel's "darling Biddulph"—though he came to Australia in the first instance because he was considered delicate, lived to be ninety-four; he died on 8th June 1928. Annie—charming, gracious Annie, who was Biddulph's almost constant companion in his early adventures in "the bush", though she appreciated the gaieties of the cities more than her sisters did—died in between Rachel and Biddulph. Amy Sloman, first of the sisters to marry in Australia, though the youngest of them, died in Bathurst on 6th June 1891. She had nine children.

Biddulph had three children, Annie Hedgeland one. Rachel had none. Etta—"My dearest Etta"—had three. Etta's eldest daughter, Constance, mentioned by Rachel in her letters, in 1883 married Edwin Lester Arnold, son of Sir Edwin Arnold—the "Mr Arnold" of Rachel's early letters from England. Rachel was never to see Etta or England again after she came to Australia the second time in 1861. Etta's husband, the Reverend

287

T. W. Boyce, died in June 1890, while Biddulph, his wife and three children were visiting England. Etta herself lived on for another thirty years—until five years after Rachel's death.

Rachel's husband, Deighton Taylor, became a chronic sufferer with asthma, and it was decided to sell their home, Springfield, near Fig Tree (the nearest railway station being Unanderra), on the New South Wales south coast. They left it, with the beautiful garden Rachel created there, in 1896, and joined the Hedgelands in renting a house called Lynwood, in Terry Road (on the corner of Commissioner's Road), Ryde, near where Biddulph had his home (Ermington, at Ermington Park, on a site now occupied by the Ryde-Parramatta Golf Club). Both husbands died at Lynwood. The widowed sisters then took a house—called Huaba —at Hunter's Hill.

Ermington Park was a fine old home, somewhat inaccessible but lending itself to entertaining. Guests usually stayed the week-end. There was a large ballroom, a tennis court, and boats on the river. On Sundays guests and family drove to St Anne's Church at Ryde.

Biddulph and his family afterwards moved to Hunter's Hill, and it was at his home there—Euthella—that his wife Emily died in September 1902. He then bought Passy, in the same suburb, from the Garrick estate. Passy had previously been rented by Sir George Dibbs, a Premier of New South Wales. This historic house was built by Italian labour, and each stone in it had to be handled by two men. A handsome circular cast-iron staircase rose from the centre of the large reception hall. Passy was occupied or owned by the Henning family from 1904 until December 1937.

The Hennings in Australia always sought a place of naturally beautiful surroundings in which to live. This is obvious to any-one who has visited their old homes. And it is especially true of Rachel, who often sacrificed convenience for a pretty outlook.

When Biddulph's three children married, his two sisters came to live with him. It was at Passy that they spent the remainder of their lives. It was perhaps strange, but very appropriate, that the surviving Henning children who started life together in Australia should end it together as brother and sisters. As they were together at Exmoor, in Queensland, so, forty years later, they were togther at Passy.

Rachel—as may be imagined from her writings as a younger woman—as an old lady was a distinctive character, keenly obser-vant and critical but undemonstrative, of strong opinions but rarely letting her personal feelings appear on the surface, reserved

288

except when among her relations and intimate friends of long standing, a dry wit at all times, and often a very baffling person to strangers. Her little nephews and nieces, who themselves are now grandparents, regarded her sometimes with awe.

The outstanding features of her life were her affection for Biddulph, for her younger husband Deighton Taylor, her appreciation of the natural beauty of rural England and (in time) of Australia, her fondness for poetry, and her love of flowers and pet animals. Horses and horse-riding she adored.

One of those delightful sidelights on the different interests and natures of the Henning family is given by Rachel in her letter of 9th August 1872, when she says:

"This morning he [Biddulph] made me a most welcome present of a very nice horse that I have long been in love with but did not dream of possessing. Biddulph bought him for his own riding some time ago, when, by the way, I was the first lady who ventured on his back, for he is very spirited. Then Biddulph strained him in galloping over rocks, and he was sent up to The Peach Trees for rest. He recovered there, and we brought him down with us, and now Biddulph, having several other horses, has given him to me to take down to Wollongong.

"He is the kindest of brothers. A week or two ago he gave Annie a set of real sables, magnificent to behold. This has been a very cold winter, and fur is universally worn."

Rachel was an intellectual and an individualist to the end, slow to make friends but just in her dealings, and always more at home in the library or the garden than in the kitchen. The most active hours of her later life were spent in the garden of Passy, in Passy Avenue, Hunter's Hill, where she ignored Fashion's changes and frivolities but remained constant to the affections and sentiments—and maybe many of the prejudices— of her youth.

THESE arms were granted in 1612 to John Henning, whose father, also John Henning, built Poxwell House, and was Mayor of Dorchester in 1570. The arms are described as "barry wavy of six argent and azure on a chief gules three plates". The crest: "A seahorse naiant argent, holding in paws a plate."

According to Henning family records, "There are MSS. which distinctly assert that the Hennings of Henning's Crookston, County Dorset, are derived from the royal and naval hero referred to by Florence of Worcester, Speed and Hasted [a chronicler monk who died in 1118]. The word Henning in the Danish language—like that of Hengist and Horsa—signifies a horse; and the Henning crest is a seahorse, signifying that they were formerly sea-kings or Vikings; and the Danes called their ships steeds of the ocean, or seahorses."

Some members of the Henning family adopt the motto *Tutus per undas*; others, *Saepe caveto saepe*; while another branch uses what is believed to be the oldest and original motto, *Undis undique ditant*. The last-named is on a hatchment bearing the family arms, and date 1658, in Folke Church, near Sherborne.

John Henning the second, besides owning Poxwell House and Nash Court, Marnhull, also had estates at Sturminster, Newton Castle, Todber, Winterbourn St Martin, Dorchester, Watercombe, Warmwell, Maiden Newton, Weymouth and Melcombe Regis. He was born in 1531 and died in 1617. He was High Sheriff of Dorset in 1609. His grandson and heir, Edmond Henning, fought for Charles I and was imprisoned in Corfe Castle by the Roundheads; he died in the castle at the age of twenty-six. Edmond's son Henry became heir to the Henning estates.

Rachel Henning's line comes through Robert Henning (1590-1660) of Henning's Crookston, Dorset, uncle of Edmond Henning the Cavalier and Royalist.

FOR THE BEST IN PAPERBACKS, LOOK FOR THE

PENGUIN

THE PENGUIN AUSTRALIAN WOMEN'S LIBRARY

Series Editor: Dale Spender

The Penguin Australian Women's Library will make available to readers a wealth of information through the work of women writers of our past. It will include the classic to the freshly re-discovered, individual reprints to new anthologies, as well as up-to-date critical re-appraisals of their work and lives as writers.

The Penguin Anthology of Australian Women's Writing
edited by Dale Spender

'Only when all the women writers of Australia are brought together is it possible to identify . . . a distinctive female literary tradition.'

Australia has a rich tradition of women writers. In 1790 Elizabeth Macarthur wrote letters home while she travelled to Australia; in 1970 Germaine Greer published *The Female Eunuch.* Thirty-seven writers – working in every genre – are included in this landmark anthology.

Margaret Catchpole	Mary Grant Bruce
Elizabeth Macarthur	Miles Franklin
Georgiana McCrae	Dymphna Cusack
Louisa Ann Meredith	Katharine Susannah Prichard
Catherine Helen Spence	Nettie Palmer
Ellen Clacy	Marjorie Barnard
Mary Fortune (Waif Wander)	Eleanor Dark
Ada Cambridge	Dorothy Cottrell
Louisa Lawson	Christina Stead
Jessie Couvreur (Tasma)	Sarah Campion
Rosa Praed	Kylie Tennant
Catherine Langloh Parker	Nancy Cato
Barbara Baynton	Faith Bandler
Mary Gaunt	Nene Gare
Mary Gilmour	Olga Masters
Henry Handel Richardson	Oriel Gray
Ethel Turner	Antigone Kefala
G. B. Lancaster	Germaine Greer
Mollie Skinner	

Mr Hogarth's Will   by Catherine Helen Spence

Jane and Alice Melville have been disinherited by their uncle, who believes that a 'boys' education will serve them better than an inheritance.

The sisters struggle for independence and fulfilment takes them from Scotland to Australia and a new vision of their lives.

First published in 1867.

Kirkham's Find   by Mary Gaunt

Phoebe Marsden wants a place of her own. At twenty-four she refuses to compromise her ideals and marry for expediency. Her younger sister Nancy does not share her ideals. Against everyone's advice Phoebe decides to set up on her own and keep bees.

Phoebe is one of the first Australian heroines to choose between marriage and a career. Her choice has unexpected ramifications for another sister, Lydia.

First published in 1897.

The Peaceful Army   edited by Flora Eldershaw

In 1938, at the time of Australia's 150th Anniversary, this collection was published in honour of women's contribution. The list of contributors is a veritable 'who's who' of women in Australian cultural life. They include: Margaret Preston, Marjorie Barnard, Miles Franklin, Dymphna Cusack and a young Kylie Tennant. They write about Elizabeth Macarthur, Caroline Chisholm, Rose Scott and early women writers and artists.

In 1938 Kylie Tennant concludes the volume. Just before her death in 1988 she reflected on the intervening fifty years.

FOR THE BEST IN PAPERBACKS, LOOK FOR THE

PENGUIN

Her Selection:
Writings by Nineteenth Century Australian Women edited by
Lynne Spender

Ninteenth-century Australian women writers were published widely in
magazines, newspapers and books in Australia and abroad. Their writings provide an insight into the lives of women, the opportunities and
obstacles, the hardships and the successes. This lively collection brings
together works that have been unavailable for many years.

Included are works by Georgiana Molloy, Louisa Lawson, Annabella
Boswell, Mary Fortune and 'Tasma'.

A Bright and Fiery Troop:
Australian Women Writers of the Ninteenth Century edited by
Debra Adelaide

Who was the most popular detective story writer of the nineteenth
century? A woman, Mary Fortune.

Who was the internationally famous botanist and artist who also wrote
novels? A woman, Louisa Atkinson.

Who wrote the first convict novel? A woman, Caroline Leakey.

Who wrote the first novel with an Aboriginal protagonist? A woman,
Catherine Martin.

This book opens up the hidden history of Australian literature and is the
first critical appraisal of the major Australian women writers of the
nineteenth century.

The book includes photographs.

FOR THE BEST IN PAPERBACKS, LOOK FOR THE

PENGUIN

Rooms of Their Own
Interviews by Jennifer Ellison with:

Blanche d'Alpuget	Jessica Anderson
Thea Astley	Jean Bedford
Sara Dowse	Beverley Farmer
Helen Garner	Kate Grenville
Elizabeth Jolley	Gabrielle Lord
Olga Masters	Georgia Savage

Rooms of their Own is a collection of interviews with twelve authors of contemporary Australian fiction.

Jennifer Ellison's rapport with the writers and their writing has elicited surprisingly frank views on the relationship between authors and publishers; the place of writers in society; the role of gender in writing; and many other issues. Together, the interviews form a dynamic account of the creative, professional and personal motiviations of some of Australia's most important living writers.

The Penguin Book of Australian Women Poets
edited by Susan Hampton and Kate Llewellyn

This anthology represents eighty-nine Australian women poets, from tribal Aboriginal singers through to the present.

The range of subjects and styles is as wide as the differences in the lives of the poets. There are poems about the selector's wife and daughter, factory work, prostitutes, social conventions, feminism, lovers, Japan, old age, happy marriage, the conflict between love and independence, and the Sydney Harbour Bridge. There are poems that do not exist in official histories, as well as poems that have come to be regarded as classics.

The Penguin Book of Australian Women Poets presents for the first time an overview of the traditions, the voices and the range of women's poetry in Australia.

FOR THE BEST IN PAPERBACKS, LOOK FOR THE

PENGUIN

BOOKS BY JESSICA ANDERSON IN PENGUIN

Tirra Lirra by the River

A beautifully written novel of a woman's seventy-year search to find a place where she truly belongs.

For Nora Porteous, life is a series of escapes. To escape her tightly knit small-town family, she marries, only to find herself confined again, this time in a stifling Sydney suburb with a selfish, sanctimonious husband. With a courage born of desperation and sustained by a spirited sense of humor, Nora travels to London, and it is there that she becomes the woman she wants to be. Or does she?

Winner of the Miles Franklin Award.

Stories From the Warm Zone and Sydney Stories

Jessica Anderson's evocative stories recreate, through the eyes of a child, the atmosphere of Australia between the wars. A stammer becomes a blessing in disguise; the prospect of a middle name converts a reluctant child to baptism. These autobiographical stories of a Brisbane childhood glow with the warmth of memory.

The formless sprawl of Sydney in the 1980s is a very different world. Here the lives of other characters are changed by the uncertainties of divorce, chance meetings and the disintegration and generation of relationships.

Winner of The Age Book of the Year Award.

Last Man's Head

Detective Alec Probyn has his enemies too. His recent stand on police violence has led to his being suspended from duty. He has a growing suspicion that a vicious crime is about to be committed. All the more disturbing as the suspect and the victim are both members of his own family.

How can Probyn prevent this crime and its shattering consequences? In the savage resolution he discovers that his anti-violent stand has not magically cancelled out the violence in himself.

An Ordinary Lunacy

When David Byfield sees Isobel for the first time at a party, he decides that he has fallen in love with her. An attractive and successful lawyer, David is being groomed for a political career; his experience with love and intimacy, however, is limited.

Months after the party, Isobel's alcoholic husband is found dead in their shabby apartment, an apparent suicide. Then Isobel is accused of his murder and David steps up to defend her both as lawyer and friend. But Isobel's case is more than he bargained for . . .

Set in contemporary Sydney, Jessica Anderson's first novel is a perceptive and witty portrait of men and women caught between their desires and their obligations, and the choices we all make for – or in spite of – love.

The Commandant

In the 1830s the penal settlement of Moreton Bay on the Brisbane River is under the command of Patrick Logan, a fanatical disciplinarian. In his charge are convicts whom no flogging can break. But in spite of his precautions some still escape to the bush and take refuge with the Aborigines. Logan's administration has been denounced by the liberal press in Sydney, but he scorns such criticism. How can it harm him when he has governed according to the rules?

He cannot continue to ignore the growing opposition to his harsh discipline after the arrival of his wife's younger sister, Frances O'Beirne, a girl imbued with radical ideals. She cannot accept the brutality of chained and toiling men, punishment parades and the lash, and it is she who precipitates the crisis from which the final drama springs.

BOOKS BY THEA ASTLEY IN PENGUIN

Hunting the Wild Pineapple

Leverson the narrator, at the centre of these stories, calls himself a 'people freak'. Seduced by north Queensland's sultry beauty and unique strangeness, he is as fascinated by the invading hordes of misfits from the south as by the old-established Queenslanders.

Leverson's ironical yet compassionate view makes every story, every incident, a pointed example of human weakness – or strength.

Beachmasters

The central government in Trinitas can't control the outer island. But then neither can the British and French masters.

The natives of Kristi, supported and abetted by some of the *hapkas* and *colons* of two nationalities, make a grab for independence from the rest of their Pacific island group. On their tiny island, where blood and tradition are as mixed as loyalties and interests, their revolution is short-lived. Yet it swallows the lives of a number of inhabitants – from the old-time planters Salway and Duchard, to the opportunist Bonser, and the once mighty *yeremanu,* Tommy Narota himself.

Salway's grandson Gavi unwittingly gets caught up in Bonser's plans and, in a test of identity too risky for one so young, forfeits his own peace.

An Item From the Late News

Wafer, who saw his father blown apart by a bomb in the second world war, and who grew up under the shadow of the nuclear bomb, seeks to spend his middle years in a place of solitude where he can prepare for the inevitable . . .

Allbut, scarecely a dot on the map in the vast Queensland outback, seems to be the perfect place.

But Wafer's peace-loving ways are not understood by the clean and decent locals and when it comes, the final blast is not the one he expected.

It's Raining in Mango

Sometimes history repeats itself.

One family traced from 1860s to the 1980s: from Cornelius to Connie to Reever, who was last seen heading north.

Cornelius Laffey, and Irish born journalist, wrests his family from the easy living of nineteenth-century Sydney and takes them to Cooktown in northern Queensland where thousands of diggers are searching for gold in the mud. The family confront the horror of Aborginal dispossession – Cornelius is sacked for reporting the slaughter. His daughter, Nadine, joins the singing whore on the barge and goes upstream, only to be washed out to sea.

The cycles of generations turn, one over the other. Only some things change. That world and this world both have their Catholic priests, their bigots, their radicals. Full of powerful and independent characters, this is an unforgettable tale of the other side of Australia's heritage.

Blood in the Rain   Margaret Barbalet

Jessie's life, is in many ways, ordinary – a young girl growing up and reaching for maturity in the Australia of the Great War and the Depression, as she moves from country town to country town and eventually to Adelaide. But Margaret Barbalet's evocative novel follows Jessie's odyssey to self-acceptance with a perception and compassion that reveals a person who is quite extraordinary.

'She writes with a delicate power of the elusive joys and the tangible pains of childhood until finally they become the shape of an adult.'
Helen Daniel

FOR THE BEST IN PAPERBACKS, LOOK FOR THE

PENGUIN

BOOKS BY SARA DOWSE IN PENGUIN

West Block

Canberra's attendant lords look like settling down after a crisis that has rocked Australia.

In West Block, the flawed human world behind the headlines, George Harland consummates his career as a public servant; Henry Beeker prepares to fight for a policy; Catherine Duffy confronts the consequences of Australia's Vietnam policy; Jonathan Roe stumbles on happiness; and Cassie Armstrong's ironic intelligence leads her to despair.

But the whispers of a different past move through the rumbling hulk of a building which embodies the history of a capital city and has a future as uncertain as the nation it symbolizes.

Silver City

From the turbulence of war-torn Europe to the Australian bush: the story of one woman's attempt to bridge the two worlds. Nina, a young Polish refugee, struggles to forge a new life for herself, but the man she loves is reluctant to let go of the past.

The past is not easy to escape. Silver City, a transit camp in the Australian countryside, is too much like the refugee camps they have left behind, except that the rows of curved iron huts dazzle in the hot Australian sun. Yet Nina's triumph is to survive in the face of disillusion and loss.

FOR THE BEST IN PAPERBACKS, LOOK FOR THE

PENGUIN

No Place for a Nervous Lady   Lucy Frost
Voices from the Australian Bush

A fascinating collection of previously unpublished, intimate letters and diary entries by thirteen women in nineteenth century Australia. It captures the fearful isolation of life in the bush and the marvellous friendships that developed between correspondents.
A McPhee Gribble/Penguin Book

Autobiography of My Mother   Meg Stewart

An unusual biography of Australian artist Margaret Coen, written by her daughter, that provides a portrait of an independent woman determined to be a painter in difficult times. It is set in the lively artistic and literary worlds of Australia in the 30s and 40s.

Solid Bluestone Foundations   Kathleen Fitzpatrick
Memories of an Australian Girlhood

This 'magnificent book of memories', as Manning Clark has called it, represents the life of Melbourne historian Kathleen Fitzpatrick. Growing up in Australia in the 1920s, in a world fragmented by religion and class differences, Kathleen came to associate the bluestone foundations of her grandparents home with the security and abundance she needed. Later Melbourne University with its bluestone foundations became her source of 'constant enrichment'. Kathleen Fitzpatrick's delightful autobiography is itself a rich source of wisdom and wit.

Accidental Chords   Patricia Thompson

In a style both earthy and urbane, Patricia Thompson tells a simple story: her childhood in staid Auckland: her youth in 'jazz age' Sydney; the adventures of young womanhood in brilliant London; the grey world of maddeningly complacent Perth and, finally, her discovery of Paddington, Sydney, which she and her poet husband John set about rescuing from the urban dumps. Through the book runs a vein of outrageous fun, especially in the figure of her zany mother Grace, and her four husbands. But there is a darker side to Patricia's life, the shadow cast by her dominating mother, the shadow she never quite managed to overcome.

FOR THE BEST IN PAPERBACKS, LOOK FOR THE

PENGUIN

The Penguin Book of Australian Autobiography
John and Dorothy Colmer

A lively and stimulating introduction to more than forty Australians who write of their own lives. They include Kylie Tennant, Patrick White, Joan Lindsay, David Malouf, Miles Franklin, Henry Lawson, Judah Waten, Henry Handel Richardson, Charles Perkins, Stella Bowen, Donald Horne, Oriel Gray, Albert Facey, Clive James, Robin Eakin, George Johnston and Mary Gilmore.

A Foreign Wife   Gillian Bouras

In 1980 Australian-born Gillian Bouras set off with her Greek husband to live in Greece. Her fellow-villagers fondly regarded her, a migrant in their midst, as something of a curiosity. They in turn were the source of admiration and curiosity to her. This is to her account of her experience in a 'small quiet world' which caused her so much perplexity and pleasure. McPhee Gribble/Penguin

Don't Take Your Love to Town   Ruby Langford

Ruby Langford is a remarkable woman whose sense of humour has endured through all the hardships she has experienced. Her autobiography is a book which cannot fail to move you.

'I felt like I was living tribal, but with no tribe around me, no close-knit family. The food gathering, the laws and songs were broken up, and my generation at this time wandered around as if we were tribal but in fact living worse than the poorest of poor whites, and in the case of women, living hard because it seemed like the men loved you for a while and then more kids came along and the men drank and gambled and disappeared. One day they'd had enough and they just didn't come back . . . my women friends all have similar stories.'

Born at Box Ridge Mission, Coraki, in the 30s, Ruby Langford's story is one of courage in the face of poverty and tragedy. She writes about the changing ways of life in Aboriginal communities – rural and urban; the disintegration of traditional lifestyles and the sustaining energy that has come from the renewal of Aboriginal culture in recent years.

FOR THE BEST IN PAPERBACKS, LOOK FOR THE

PENGUIN

Women of the Sun   Hyllus Maris and Sonia Borg

Though they lived in different eras they shared the same resilience and spirit – these Women of the Sun.

ALINTA – she is one of the first to see the men with faces of clay, and one of the few to survive their invasion of the land of the Ancestors.

MAYDINA – she must submit to a new Law, which preaches love while it takes her daughter away.

NERIDA – she seeks the strength to defy tyranny and give her people hope.

LO-ARNA – she discovers the secret of her origin and must come to terms with all that it means.

This quartet of stories speaks with the simplicity and power of the Aboriginal voice, illuminating from their perspective the experience of two centuries of white domination.

Inside Black Australia   edited by Kevin Gilbert

From the campfires and 'reserves' of the desert, from riverbanks and prison cells, from universities and urban ghettoes come the inside voices of Australia.

These are tough poems that resist the silence of genocide and the destruction of culture. The collection is an angry call for justice and the restoration of the land and the Dreaming. The Aboriginal lives glimpsed give white Australians a hint of the deep possibilities of belonging in this land.

Forty voices are heard in this first anthology of Aboriginal poetry.